WORLD DEBT CRISIS

WORLD DEBT CRISIS
International Lending on Trial

Edited by
MICHAEL P. CLAUDON

BALLINGER PUBLISHING COMPANY
Cambridge, Massachusetts
A Subsidiary of Harper & Row, Publishers, Inc.

International Standard Book Number: 0-88730-052-9

Library of Congress Catalog Card Number: 85-15781

Printed in the United States of America

Library of Congress Cataloging in Publication Data

Main entry under title:

World debt crisis.

"Collection of essays that grew out of the 1984 Middlebury College Conference on Economic Issues, 1983"—Pref.
 Bibliography: p.
 Includes index.
 1. Loans, Foreign—Developing countries—Congresses.
 2. Debts, External—Developing countries—Congresses.
 3. Financial institutions—Developing countries—Congresses.
 4. United States—Economic policy—1981-   —Congresses.
 I. Claudon Michael P.   II. Middlebury College Conference on Economic Issues (7th : 1984)
 HG 3891.5.W67 1985   336.3'435   85-15781
 ISBN 0-88730-052-9

Dedicated to
The Institute of Economic and Monetary Affairs
whose generosity made possible
the conference upon which this volume is based.

CONTENTS

vii

LIST OF FIGURES

xi

LIST OF TABLES

ACKNOWLEDGMENTS

The papers in the volume were originally presented at the Seventh Annual Middlebury Conference on Economic Issues, which convened in September 1984, at the Breadloaf Mountain Campus of Middlebury College in Vermont. That the conference produced two and a half days of what can only be characterized as energetic, if not impassioned, dialogue and debate is due in no small part my senior seminar students' significant preparation and commitment to intellectual growth, and to the substantial contributions made by the conference participants one and all. Therefore special thanks must be extended to all of them. Ranking high on the list of those deserving thanks is the Institute of Economic and Monetary Affairs. Its sponsorship makes the conference series possible, thereby offering the Middlebury College community an unparalleled opportunity to set aside one three-day period each year to closely examine currently topical economic issues and events. Middlebury College, as well as those who attend and support each year's conference, is deeply indebted to the Institute.

I would be remiss if I did not single out two people who made the difficult task of running a conference ever so much easier. Kim Davis, a member of the Middlebury Class of 1985, deserves special thanks. Her professionalism, careful attention to detail, prodigious organizational skills, and positive, can-do attitude made the conference infinitely more enjoyable for all of us. And it was Sheila Cassin, the

Economics Department secretary, who once again produced order where there would probably have been mass confusion.

Finally, I would like to recognize the members of my senior seminar, whose careful and painstaking dissection of each paper greatly assisted my job as editor. They offered important insights and allowed me to see relationships among the papers that I may have otherwise missed.

Middlebury, Vermont   **Michael P. Claudon**
June 1985

FOREWORD

Middlebury College has the agreeable practice of using the munificent donation of The Institute of Economic and Monetary Affairs in part to fund a conference each year on a problem in economic policy. The year I taught there, the conference was on the multinational corporation, the following year on "rent-seeking activities" in business activities that produce no goods or services but divert wealth from one set of actors to others. In 1984 the conference dealt with Third World debt. I was originally set to go but was prevented at the last minute by a conflict. The next best thing is to read the papers early, as Michael Claudon has asked me to do.

There have been and no doubt will be many conferences and conference books on Third World debt, but this one seems to me extraordinarily well planned, innovative, rounded, and complete. Kristin Hallberg has produced a wealth of empirical material. Lance Taylor and Larry Sjaastad contribute penetrating contributions to the theory of bank syndicated loans to sovereign developing countries. There are separate papers by experts writing from the perspective of the World Bank (Barend de Vries), the International Monetary Fund, (Margaret Garritsen de Vries) and the Federal Reserve Bank (Robert McCauley), although each writes in a personal capacity. McCauley's is particularly interesting as it focuses on the role of the IMF in pressuring banks to keep on lending when each would love to stop if it could do so without penalty. Leonard Santow offers a Wall Street perspective that might have been expected to be detailed and explicit steps for banks, but takes the form primarily of admonitions to governments for stricter policies.

In a brief introduction, I cannot provide one-sentence descriptions of all the attributes of this book, but attention should be drawn to three chapters focusing on the behavior of banks: those of William Darity, Jr., who suggests that the banks forced the loans on pliable borrowing countries, and Philip Wellons, who writes of the public-good problem in rescheduling and the free-rider principles that would unravel projected solutions in the absence of strong governmental leadership, and the paper of Stephen Magee and William Brock that extends their analysis of rent-seeking in tariffs presented at the 1983 Middlebury Conference to free-and-easy bank lending by institutions and borrowing by countries that took excessive rises in the knowledge that they would be bailed out by taxpayers somewhere.

The conference was dismissed with a benediction from Frank Morris, President of the Federal Reserve Bank of Boston, consisting of a brief personal statement linking the debt crisis to U.S. inflation.

All in all, a conference and a book that stand out above the pack, on an engrossing subject.

May 23, 1985   **Charles P. Kindleberger**
Lincoln Center, Massachusetts

INTRODUCTION

The International Monetary Fund (IMF) was about to convene its annual meeting in Toronto, Canada, when, in August 1982, Mexico shocked the financial community by declaring itself unable to meet its debt service obligations. Brazil and a host of other major borrowers quickly followed suit. Those declarations pushed the world banking system to the brink of financial chaos. Foreign lending was on trial.

That the 1982–85 acute phase of the global debt crisis was grave is hardly debatable. Only fifteen countries were in arrears on payment of external debt in 1975. By the end of 1981, fully thirty-two countries were experiencing difficulties servicing their external debt. The twenty-four major borrowers among the less developed countries (LDCs) experienced a net funds outflow of $37 billion in 1982, followed by $10 billion more in the first six months of 1983. When the crisis erupted, U.S. bank claims on LDCs that are not members of the Organization of Petroleum Exporting Countries (OPEC) totaled $98.6 billion, or 149 percent of total bank capital. Over half of this debt was held by just three countries, Argentina, Brazil, and Mexico. These three alone owed U.S. banks $52.4 billion, or 84 percent of the lending banks' total capital. Worse yet, the vast majority of these claims were owned by the nine largest U.S. money-center banks. This group had lent $60.3 billion, 222 percent of its total capital, to all non-OPEC LDCs, but $30.5 billion of that total was lent to only three countries, Argentina, Brazil, and Mexico. On paper at least, these nine banks were bankrupt after the fateful declarations of August 1982.

What followed the Latin American pronouncements can only be described as frantic episodes of crisis management. The result was a precarious system of eleventh-hour "bridge" loans, controlled debt-service moratoriums that fell just short of technical default, and hastily arranged debt payment rescheduling agreements. However makeshift the arrangements might have been, though, quick reaction to the crises by the IMF, the World Bank, and the U.S. government has prevented outright default or debt repudiation.

Abatement of the crisis was also aided by a fortuitous combination of stronger commodity prices, renewed international economic growth, lower interest and inflation rates, and a strong U.S. dollar, which expanded Latin American export revenues. LDC defaults, debt repudiation, and the potential for failure of one or more U.S. money-center banks, has been averted, at least in the near term. The consensus in this book is that we can be guardedly optimistic, but that the time bomb of global debt has not been completely defused. It is still armed, and it still has the potential of exploding into a new acute crisis. The current situation is extremely fragile, and our prospects for successfully dealing with global debt problems over the long term are not good in the absence of major structural and institutional changes. The sixteen largest LDC debtors are still saddled with the reality of a $520 billion external debt and interest payments totaling $55 billion annually. They also face the necessity of sustaining high growth rates and adhering to politically expensive austerity programs dictated by the IMF. Simultaneously, servicing their debt requires continuation of very high rates of real growth. A major economic downturn or spike in interest rates in the United States, a softening of commodity prices, or another energy price shock would almost certainly trigger the resurgence of severe problems in debt servicing and repayment.

Herein lies the goal of this book, a collection of essays that grew out of the 1984 Middlebury College Conference on Economic Issues. That the crisis was severe is not much debated, but there is much less understanding of its root causes, of the relative efficacy of the actions taken to date, of the implications of these actions for domestic economic policy in the United States, of who the winners and losers were, and most important, perhaps, the medium-term and long-term workout prospects.

The book is divided into four parts. The opening part provides an historical touchstone for the rest of the book. Here is a detailed dissection of the crisis's historical antecedents, of the crisis management period, and a glimpse of what the future portends for the debt problem. Part II offers three refreshing perspectives on the crisis. How the Federal Reserve System viewed the crisis and played a role in management of the crisis as well as the influences of the crisis on U.S. monetary policy are discussed. Wall Street's reaction to the handling of the debt crisis and to the debt problem's future prospect is also discussed.

Part III examines the international financial institutions' (especially the IMF's) view of the crisis and how it was dealt with. The global debt crisis is assessed from the IMF's perspective. An upbeat IMF view of the prospects for debt management over the medium term is followed by a pessimistic assessment of the IMF's decision to alter its previous arm's length relation with commercial banks. Part III closes with an intriguing look at multinational institutions' performance as international lenders of last resort during the debt crisis.

Different facets of the question, "Why is the debt crisis concentrated in Latin America?" are examined in Part IV. The answers, each drawn from a formal model, are as varied as are the perspectives from which they are drawn, but they all agree on one central point, that the set of underlying forces and institutions that contributed to the 1982–85 crisis remain largely intact. The time bomb, though it may be temporarily defused, is still ticking. The patchwork quilt that saw us through the acute phase of the crisis will most certainly be put to the test anew when the world dips into the next major recession.

THE DEBT CRISIS
Origins, Lessons and Future Prospects

How did it happen, what can we learn from it, and what are the future prospects of managing the debt crisis? Kristin Hallberg provides an extensive overview answer to these questions in Chapter 1. After establishing that the current crisis has antecendents in history, Hallberg argues that the current crisis resulted from three causes: external economic shocks, internal economic policy of the less developed countries, and the loan policies of Western banks. Her discussion of the medium-term future sets the tone of guarded optimism that is shared by her fellow contributors.

Richard Mattione's contribution, in Chapter 2, is to assess the relative contribution that each of the factors identified by Hallberg made to the debt crisis, and to draw lessons from that evaluation for possible future crises. His chapter foreshadows those in Part IV somewhat by exploring the implicit question of why the crisis was concentrated in Latin America.

Barend de Vries's chapter seeks ways to reverse the same forces that precipitated the crisis. He argues that, in addition to reversing the contributing factors, a lasting solution to the debt crisis requires a restructuring of debt due later in this decade. Failure to restructure the debt, he argues, greatly increases the probability that the decade will close with a crisis of nightmare proportion similar to the crisis we experienced as the decade began.

1

1 INTERNATIONAL DEBT, 1985
Origins and Issues for the Future

Kristin Hallberg

The relation between sovereign borrowers and their creditors is like that of partners in a three-legged race: they can run, limp, or fall together, but they cannot part company.

—World Bank, *World Debt Tables*, 1983–84

External debt servicing problems are not new. Direct investment and loans flowing from capital-abundant advanced countries to capital-scarce developing countries, have been an instrument of economic development throughout modern history. Creditors always assumed the risk that a debtor, because of internal or externally caused difficulties, might not be able to meet the original terms of debt service. What is new about the present situation is the severity and speed with which the crisis developed.

Developing countries' "current" debt problems most likely began in the early 1970s when the Organization of Petroleum Exporting Countries' first oil price increase in 1973 created an unprecedented need among oil-importing developing countries to finance large current account deficits. Between 1972 and 1979, developing countries' nominal external debt increased 400 percent. Unlike the previous capital flows, which were mainly direct investments and long-term loans on concessionary terms by multilateral institutions, this financing came mainly in the form of loans from private creditors. The growth and new form of the debt caused very few eyebrows to be raised, however.

Until 1980, high inflation rates and wide fluctuations in commodity prices kept the growth in the LDCs' real debt and debt service within seemingly manageable proportion. Real debt and debt service grew by 4.7 percent and 8.7 percent yearly between 1973 and 1979. Though it was recognized that the experiences of individual countries varied widely, the debt burden seemed to be manageable. Congratulations were given to the international financial system for its flexibility, and to the commercial banking community for its success in "recycling" OPEC surpluses.

Economic events in the early 1980s—events largely outside control of debtor countries—greatly worsened the debt picture. A second round of OPEC oil price increases in 1979–80 led to a sharp deterioration in oil importing countries' current account balances. The 1980–82 global recession made matters worse by reducing both prices and volumes of these countries' exports. Responding to tight monetary policy and large fiscal deficits in some industrial countries, rising nominal and real interest rates dramatically increased the cost of servicing new and existing debt.

Commercial bank lending to developing countries expanded considerably until 1982. At that time, however, the large size and the rapid rise of borrowing countries' external debt and current account deterioration in the maturity structure of their debt caused sharp reductions in private creditors' new loans. This credit contraction imposed extreme financing constraints on the nonoil developing countries, and led to the disruption of debt servicing by all three of the largest developing country debtors—Brazil, Argentina, and Mexico. By the end of 1982, thirty-four countries were in arrears on their debt, and a growing number sought to reschedule their external debt payments (Cline 1983: 10). During 1983, some thirty nations, owing more than half of the external debt of all developing countries, completed or were engaged in debt rescheduling with official or commercial bank creditors (IMF 1984c: 65–66). For early 1985, the outstanding external debt of developing countries was projected to be $812 billion (U.S. dollars) and annual debt service payments $122 billion (IMF 1984).

Can the debt situation be managed over the medium term? Are emergency lending facilities adequate to handle short-run liquidity crises? What amount of real resource transfer from debtor to creditor countries is desirable? Can the interest burden of debtor countries be lightened in a way that will maintain the willingness of banks to lend? Are present lending instruments, official and private, adequate and suitable to the needs of developing countries for external finance? Will the International Monetary Fund's present system of conditionality and negotiation of debt problems on a case-by-case basis succeed as strategy for the medium term? These questions are addressed in the remainder of this chapter.

ORIGINS OF THE DEBT CRISIS

The Current Debt Situation in Historical Perspective

Periods of rapid expansion of external capital flows and development loans have been followed by interruptions in debt service, partial or total debt repudiation, and waves of bank failures throughout the past two centuries. Post–1800 spurts of lending were typically set off by some displacement: an exogenous shock that drew attention to a new opportunity for profits. Following the initial displacement typically came a stage of euphoria, as investors attempted to get in on the ground floor. Bank expansion and "bond mania" during the 1870s provided funds to Russia, Spain, Turkey, Egypt, and numerous Latin American countries, as well as to the United States for railroad and canal construction. During the economic euphoria of the 1920s, floating one loan frequently came to be regarded as adequate justification for further issues to the same borrower or the same country without regard to the growing burden of indebtedness.

Widespread defaults by Latin American and East European nations followed the buildup of foreign lending in the 1920s. By 1932, defaults on a total of $2.6 billion had occurred, according to William Darity (see Chapter 11). Collapsing world trade, rapidly declining prices for developing countries' exports, accelerating debt service ratios, and a resulting unavailability of foreign currency to meet external debt payments were key elements in the defaults of the 1930s. During this final stage of the loan cycle, it became virtually impossible for developing countries to float new issues (see Chapter 11).

Between World War II and 1973, external capital flows financed postwar reconstruction in Europe and Japan, as well as development in Asia, Africa, and Latin America. Developing countries' external debt rose only slightly during the reconstruction period, but began to expand in the early 1950s with the tremendous growth in world trade and income, as well as the emergence of most of the developing world as nations. External debt increased faster than export earnings but did not generate defaults or debt servicing interruptions. By the early 1970s, growth in incomes, exports, and higher export prices were reducing the real burden of debt on developing nations.

Comparisons between past external debt crises and the current situation must be made with care. For example, although in the 1800s some then developing countries such as the United States and Canada carried ratios of debt to gross national product that were high even by today's standards, the capital-intensive development strategies that were common then appear not to be appropriate for today's developing world. External loans in the 1920s were predominantly bond issues rather than the mix of official development assistance and bank loans common today. Because of the large number of individual creditors and the lack of international financial organizations, negotiations to reschedule debt were difficult in the 1930s, so that debt servicing problems were likely to end in partial or total repudiation of debt.

Still, similarities to past crises remain. As in the past, much of the recent external capital flow to developing countries financed consumption rather than investment. Debt service must then come from curtailed consumption rather than increases in output. Darity believes that expansion of bank lending to developing countries until 1982 is uncomfortably similar to previous manias of overtrading and euphoric investing, in that overeager bankers pushed questionable loans on debtor nations. Finally, a review of history reveals many examples of default during recessions that cut debtors' export prices and volumes and made high levels of debt service impossible to maintain.

Trends in Debt and Debt Service

The rapid growth of international debt in the 1970s and early 1980s is shown in the appendix table 1A-1. In nominal terms, the outstanding debt of 142 nonoil developing countries rose from $130 billion in 1973 to an estimated $711 billion in 1984, an increase of approximately 5.5 times.[1] Adding the debt owed by the five OPEC countries that are not in capital surplus, the total outstanding debt of developing countries stands at an estimated $812 billion in 1984. Much of the developing countries' debt is owed by a relatively small number of countries. The twenty-five "major borrowers" accounted for 79 percent of the external debt of all developing countries in 1983.[2] The ten largest borrowers accounted for over 50 percent, and the five largest (Brazil, Mexico, Argentina, Korea, and Indonesia) accounted for more than 33 percent (IMF 1984c: 60).

The nominal value of nonoil developing countries' debt rose at an annual rate of 15.4 percent over the 1973–84 period. In real terms (deflating by an index of export prices), the debt increased by a more modest 8.3 percent per year. The growth rate of real debt exceeded both the growth rate of real gross domestic product of these countries (4.4 percent), and the expansion of export volume (7.1 percent). Thus, while high inflation rates during the 1970s moderated the burden of debt outstanding, the rise in real debt over the entire 1973–84 period still exceeded the growth of real resources.

More dramatic than the increase in the level of outstanding debt has been the rise in the burden of servicing that debt, particularly since the late 1970s. Interest and amortization payments paid by nonoil developing countries on medium- and long-term debt climbed from $18 billion in 1973 to $61 billion in 1979 and $108 billion in 1982 (Table 1A–2). The rapid increases in debt service during the 1979–82 period were caused not only by high debt levels and nominal interest rates, but also by the expiration of grace periods for loans contracted in the mid-1970s (IMF 1981: 13). Estimates of real debt service payments may be found by deflating interest plus amortization payments by either export or import unit values.[3] Over the 1973–84 period, since import prices rose faster than export prices for nonoil developing countries, debt service deflated by export unit values increased at an 8.8 percent annual rate, while debt service deflated by important unit values rose at a more moderate 6.4 percent per year. Thus both debt service burdens and the opportunity cost of debt were rising.

The debt service ratio, calculated as interest and amortization payments on medium- and long-term debt divided by exports of goods and services, remained fairly stable at about 15 percent for nonoil developing countries until 1978, then rose to almost 25 percent in 1982. Increases in the debt service ratio were greatest for the group of countries termed "major exporters of manufactures" and "other net oil importers" (mostly middle-income countries that export mainly primary commodities). Low-income countries, with greater reliance on fixed-interest loans on concessionary terms, had a debt service ratio in 1984 that was actually lower than in 1973. Interest payments absorbed 13 percent of the export earnings of nonoil developing countries in 1984, compared with 6 percent in 1973. Thus, the burden of external debt increased noticeably in real terms, by this measure as well. However, debt burdens of individual countries varied widely around the average. For example, the interest/export ratio in 1982 was about 6 percent for Nigeria (up from about 1 percent in 1979), 39 percent for Brazil (25 percent in 1979), over 20 percent for Peru (12 percent in 1979), and around 13 percent for Colombia and the Philippines (7 percent in 1979) (OECD 1984: 37).[4]

Though the debt service/export ratio is commonly used to estimate debt servicing capacity and to predict future debt servicing difficulties, it has limitations that could create misleading inferences. For example, it is strongly affected by inflation, tending to fall in the early phase of an inflationary period. In addition, its usefulness for comparisons of countries is limited, since these ratios do not measure differences in economic structures or political realities. Aggregate debt statistics mask the wide differences in terms and conditions of loans to individual countries, ranging from official development assistance loans at very low interest rates and medium repayment terms to floating interest rate syndicated credits. Accordingly, more careful attention needs to be paid to the composition of a country's debt stock, not just its level in nominal or real terms. Finally, the use of debt ratios to predict future debt servicing difficulties is limited, since global economic conditions change over time, and countries differ in their vulnerability to external shocks.[5]

Oil Shocks, Current-Account Deficits, and Patterns of Financing

Until the late 1960s, capital flows to developing countries were mostly in the form of direct investment, short-term trade-related credits, and long-term loans from official creditors. The last were frequently associated with project financing and were made on concessionary terms (IMF 1981: 4). Financing of temporary balance-of-payments deficits was largely accomplished by operations with the IMF. World payments patterns at this time were usually characterized by surpluses in the industrial countries and deficits in the non-oil developing countries, while oil-exporting countries were near balance.

Then came the first and second oil shocks, in 1973–74 and 1979–80, which resulted in dramatic shifts in the level and forms of financial flows to developing countries in the 1970s and early 1980s. Industrial countries' combined current-account surplus of $20.3 billion in 1973 became a deficit of $10.18 billion in 1974, while nonoil developing countries' combined deficit increased from $11.3 billion to $37.0 billion (Table 1A–3).

Part of the developing countries' current-account deficits were financed by reductions in reserves and by short-term capital movements. Nonoil developing countries' net external borrowing went from $15.2 billion in 1973 to $28 billion in 1974 and continued to increase throughout the 1970s, with the exception of a leveling in 1976 and 1977 (Table 1A–4).

After the sharp deterioration in 1974 and 1975, the current-account positions of oil importers gradually improved. Then the second OPEC oil price shock in 1979–80 threw the financial flows back into turmoil. Oil-exporting countries' current-account surpluses rose from $6 billion in 1978 to $63 billion in 1979 and $111 billion in 1980. Nonoil developing countries' combined current-account deficit doubled from $42 billion to $88 billion, and the industrial countries again moved from surplus to deficit (Table 1A–4). The renewed borrowing needs to finance the nonoil developing countries' deficits occurred in a sharply changed internal and external environment. There was little room left for further borrowing against debt capacity, and the cost of financing was increasing.

Though the sharp increases in oil prices of 1973–74 and 1979–80 have been called the single most important external cause of the debt problems of nonoil developing countries (for example, by Cline 1983: 20–22), a major part of the expansion of bank lending to developing countries was not coincident with these two periods of increased financing needs. In fact, bank lending to developing countries had already risen in the late 1960s and early 1970s, before the first oil shock (Tables 1A–5 and 1A–10). Official development assistance and official nonconcessional flows increased modestly in real terms between 1970 and 1973, but real private bank lending grew 144 percent during these years (Table 1A-10). Charles Kindleberger has noted that the expansion of bank lending coincided with the "cheap money" push of 1971, when bankers looked to developing countries for riskier investments to maintain their income.[6]

Bank financing again expanded between 1977 and 1978 on the heels of a strong improvement in developing countries' terms of trade, signs of balance-of-payments adjustment and continuing strong growth potential, and a healthy buildup of foreign exchange reserves (OECD 1984: 16). Hence it appears that the need for recycling oil revenues created twice by OPEC price increases occurred in the context of a general expansion in the financing role of international banks.

Domestic Policies in Debtor and Creditor Nations

The external economic environment that has been largely responsible for developing countries' debt problems was created to some extent by industrial countries' monetary, fiscal, trade, and regulatory policies. Industrial countries responded to the first oil shock by pursuing expansionary monetary policies, which combined with the oil price increase to cause a significant rise in inflation rates. Average annual inflation rates increased from 4.7 percent during the years 1963–72 to well over 10 percent in 1974–75. Real interest rates (measured as Eurodollar rates deflated by the increase in the U.S. producer price index) fell to –7.3 percent in 1974 and remained between 0 and –1.0 percent through 1980 (Heller 1983: table 3). Such inexpensive financing induced developing countries to borrow in order to avoid rapid real adjustment to external shocks that would have undermined development efforts.

The policy response of industrial countries to the second oil price shock was much different. Instead of using expansionary monetary policy to maintain real income levels, governments adopted tight monetary policy in order to combat inflation. Restrictive monetary policy together with persistently high inflationary expectations boosted real interest rates up to almost 10 percent in 1981 (Heller 1983: table 3). This flip-flop in industrial countries' monetary policy, particularly the United States', has been blamed for the recent series of debt servicing problems. Sharing the responsibility for recent high real interest rates are large fiscal deficits in the industrial countries, again in particular the United States.

Industrial countries' trade policies also contributed to the current debt problem (see, for example, Dornbusch 1984b). High unemployment rates in the industrial countries in the early 1980s led to protectionist pressures that made it more difficult for developing countries to export to these markets. In the United States protectionist commercial policies (quantitative restrictions and voluntary export restrictions on developing countries' exports), and criticism of the trade policies of debtor nations (such as export subsidies) hampered debt management through export growth.

Dornbusch (1984a) believes that U.S. regulatory policies have aggravated the international debt problem by failing to require banks to set aside appropriate loan loss reserves to meet the risk of debt service interruptions. Without such a requirement, debt write-downs create a threat to the international financial system, rather than affecting just the banks' stockholders. If U.S. banks held larger reserves against developing country loans, as do European banks, the international financial system would be less vulnerable.

Internal domestic demand pressures in the developing countries also contributed importantly to their payments problems. In nonoil developing countries, excess domestic demand in the 1970s and 1980s is usually attributed to expansionary government expenditure that led to fiscal deficits and overvalued real exchange rates (Khan and Knight 1983; Dornbusch 1984b). Partly as a result of these deficits, extremely high inflation rates became common in most nonoil developing countries, averaging about 29 percent per year during 1973–81 compared with about 12 percent for 1963–72 (Khan and Knight 1983: 4). More important for the current account was the tendency for exchange rates not to keep pace with the differences between domestic and foreign inflation, resulting in an appreciation of real effective exchange rates. In this way fiscal deficits, domestic demand pressures, inflation, and real effective exchange rates were closely linked, and tended to rise together. Not only were increases in real exchange rates a fundamental determinant of deteriorating current-account balances, they also have been blamed for the use of borrowed funds for consumption rather than investment, and to finance private capital outflows and private acquisition of foreign assets (Dornbusch 1984b).

Changes in Debt Structures, Maturity, and Interest Rates

At the end of 1972 the external debt of developing countries was almost evenly divided between official and private creditors. Following the first oil shock, developing countries turned more to private creditors (mostly banks) to finance their current-account deficits (Table 1A–4). As a result, the proportion of the total medium- and long-term debt owed by nonoil developing countries to private creditors increased from 54 percent in 1973 to an estimated 62 percent in 1984 (Table 1A–5). Funds from the syndicated loan market showed the strongest growth; loans from commercial banks greatly surpassed the more traditional private debt sources, such as bonds and suppliers' credits (Table 1A–8). By 1984 commercial banks' share of the total guaranteed medium- and long-term debt owed by nonoil developing countries to private creditors had risen to 86 percent.

Accompanying, and partly caused by, the growing reliance on private sources of credit has been a worsening in the average terms of developing countries' debt. The cost of loans to developing countries at fixed rates of interest (mainly at concessionary terms to official creditors) climbed steadily from 4.4 percent in 1972–73 to 6.7 percent in 1983; however, the cost of loans at floating rates, obtained mainly from private creditors, rose more sharply to about 17 percent in 1981–82, before market rates began to decline in 1983. Net interest payments were quickly affected by the change in interest rates, particularly for those countries with a large proportion of floating-rate debt—for example, Argentina, Brazil, South Korea, and Mexico, which in 1982 together accounted for 84 percent of the total floating-rate debt of developing countries (OECD 1982a: 12). Reductions in the London Interbank Offered Rate (LIBOR) since 1982 have had the reverse effect of lightening the debt service burden for those countries with a high proportion of floating-rate debt.

Also contributing to the deterioration in average debt terms was the rapid growth of short-term debt in absolute terms, which increased the pressure on borrowers to find lenders willing to roll over debt (Dale and Mattione 1983: 12). Mexico, for example, increased short-term debt from $8 billion in 1977 to $32 billion in mid–1982, or a change in the proportion of short-term debt from 41 percent to 50 percent over the period.

Bank Exposure and Risk Perception

Commercial bank exposure to developing countries expanded rapidly in the wake of the second oil shock. Claims by banks in the BIS reporting area on nonoil developing countries appproximately doubled during 1978 to 1980, from $155 billion to $306 billion (Table 1A–11). The exposure of banks to a few major borrowers increased more dramatically; the net external position to Argentina, Brazil, and Mexico more than tripled over this period, and accounted for over half of all external bank claims in 1982. The relative participation by U.S. banks in lending to developing countries, while remaining large at 37 percent in 1982, had declined from a 50 percent share in 1977 (IMF 1983c: 31).

Relative to capital, exposure of U.S. banks to East European and nonoil developing countries rose from 132 percent in 1977 to 155 in 1982 (Table 1A–10). Adding exposure to the five OPEC countries not in capital surplus (Algeria, Ecuador, Indonesia, Nigeria, and Venezuela), the ratio of claims to capital stood at 183 percent in 1982 (Cline 1983: 33). For the nine largest U.S. banks, these exposure ratios were even higher: 235 percent and 283 percent, respectively. Even though in recent years a greater number of small U.S. banks have been drawn into international lending, the nine largest U.S. banks accounted for 60 percent of lending to developing countries in 1982, and the next fifteen banks an additional 20 percent (Volcker 1983: 14).[7]

Following the escalation of commercial bank lending to developing countries in 1979–81, banks took a more cautious lending posture in 1981–82. They perceived the failure of borrowing countries to adjust to the deterioration in the global economy as reducing the quality of their international assets. In addition, banks became increasingly concerned about the uncertain prospects for sustained recovery in the industrial countries, about the high concentration of exposure in a few countries that were currently engaged in debt restructuring, about the behavior of smaller creditor banks, and about their ability to raise new capital in a weak bank equity market. Indeed, investor confidence in some heavily exposed banks was shaken in 1983 and 1984, as the public became more aware of heightened sovereign risk.

Commercial banks responded to higher perceived risk in 1981–82 by reducing the quantity of loans rather than to increase their price (by raising risk premiums). The choice of quantity adjustment over price adjustment may have been due to the bankers' worry that the largest debtors, who were already using a large part of export revenues to service debt, would simply fail to adhere to the terms of new loans contracted at higher interest rates. Bankers may also have chosen this response in order to ease the anxiety of their shareholders, who were becoming more nervous about heavy exposure to developing countries, particularly those in Latin America.

Debt Rescheduling

The marked reduction in new banks lending to developing countries in 1982, coincident with the rise in interest rates and declining export earnings, led to a significant increase in the number of countries experiencing debt servicing difficulties. Payments arrears, which had remained at about $6 billion over the preceding five years, rose to $18 billion by the end of 1982 (IMF 1983d: 4). Many countries, including some of the largest debtors, approached their creditors for a rescheduling of debt.

The international debt renegotiations that began in the summer of 1982 were without precedent in the number of countries involved, the frequency of the requests for debt relief, and the amount of debt rescheduled. Before 1982 most debt renegotiations were by low-income African and Central American countries, and the amounts restructured were small for the creditors. In 1982–83 more than thirty developing and East European countries began renegotiating the terms on which approximately $100 billion of public and private sector debt was originally incurred to foreign creditors, primarily commercial banks (World Bank 1984: xvii). Beginning in 1982 debt servicing problems increasingly affected large borrowers, and the amounts renegotiated were many times larger than those in previous years: the annual amount restructured averaged $2.7 billion during 1975–82; in 1983 over $67 billion in debt was restructured, including $23 billion with Mexico, $10 billion with Brazil, and $6 billion with Argentina (Table 1A–9).

Most agreements before 1983 covered debt owed by governments of developing countries to other governments, mainly those of Western industrial countries, and were renegotiated in the framework of creditor clubs (particularly the Paris Club). In 1982–83 this process was enlarged through multibillion dollar rescue packages, including official and private short-term bridging loans, International Monetary Fund agreements, long-term bank reschedulings, new bank loans, Paris Club reschedulings, and new export credits. American banks typically led the steering committees renegotiating Latin American debt, while European banks handled East European loans. The IMF took a primary role in this process, particularly in negotiating the required adjustment program.

ISSUES FOR THE FUTURE

Although the crisis has abated, concerns remain about the future of international financial flows, both in the next few years and over the longer term. The immediate debt management issue is whether certain large debtor countries will be able to meet their debt service obligations or continue to reschedule debt, and on what terms. Over the longer term, there is the need to restore growth in the developing countries while improving their position as debtors, and to maintain a system of international lending that is suitable to the needs of developing countries for external finance.

Several recent simulation models project an improvement in the debt servicing capacity of developing countries, in the aggregate, over the next three to six years. Prominent among these optimistic forecasts is the projection for nineteen large debtors made by William R. Cline, first published in 1983, and updated in 1984. Also included in this group would be the study of twenty-one large debtors by Morgan Guaranty Trust (1983); a Federal Reserve Bank of New York forecast for Latin America by Leven and Roberts (1983); the work of Dooley et al. (1983) at the board of governors of the Federal Reserve System, focusing on eight major borrowers; and the IMF projections for all nonoil developing countries in the 1984 *World Economic Outlook*.[8] The value of outstanding debt is projected to increase from $582 billion in 1984 to $676 billion in 1986 for the nineteen largest debtors (Cline 1983), and to $822 billion in 1990 for the twenty-one largest debtors (Morgan Guaranty). However, debt relative to exports of goods and services is expected to decline from 182 percent in 1984 to 123 percent in 1990 (Morgan Guaranty). For all nonoil developing countries, debt relative to exports is also expected to show an improving trend, falling from 145 percent in 1984 to 124 percent in 1990 (IMF).

The capacity to service debt, measured as debt service or interest payments relative to exports of goods and services, is expected to show improvement by the late 1980s after an initial rise in 1986–87, the latter arising from an increase in amortization as payments rescheduled in 1982–83 come due. In fact the Mexican rescheduling completed in 1984 will reduce this hump in amortization payments. The New York Federal Reserve Bank projects a return by 1990 to the debt service ratios in Latin America that were common in the late 1970s. For most of the eight major debtors covered in Dooley et al. (1983), the ratio of real interest payments to exports falls to roughly half its 1982 level by 1990, though remaining at levels that are high compared to the 1974–81 period.

Other simulation models, including those by the Brookings Institution (Enders and Mattione 1984), the Overseas Development Council (Fishlow 1984), and the Inter-American Development Bank (1984), come to less favorable conclusions. In some cases the authors make assumptions about international macroeconomic conditions similar to those made by Cline, but reach more pessimistic conclusions because different assumed response parameters—for example, lower elasticities for developing-country exports with respect to OECD income growth, or a lack of an impact of U.S. dollar depreciation on the dollar prices of traded goods. Enders and Mattione (1984) project that debt/export ratios for Latin American countries will decline by 1987, but by less than Cline predicts. Moreover, they come to much more pessimistic conclusions regarding Latin American growth rates, especially for Brazil and Mexico. Fishlow (1984) claims that past statistical evidence indicates a more modest response of developing countries' export prices and volumes to dollar depreciation and OECD recovery than Cline assumes. The result is that Fishlow (1984: 43) projects only a moderate decline in debt/export ratios by 1986 for twelve major debtors, to 154 percent, compared to Cline's (1983) 128 percent.

Given the projections of the developing countries' financing needs through the 1980s, much of the necessary accommodating financing from commercial banks is likely to be unspontaneous but will provide positive net benefits for creditor banks as a group. The IMF projects that, if the current real exposure of banks is maintained, more manageable current account and external debt situations for debtor countries will lead to an increase in the average "voluntariness" of new lending (IMF 1984c: 74). The important remaining issue will be whether the large, heavily exposed banks and the smaller regional banks will be able to negotiate a fair distribution of that exposure among themselves.

Even given accommodating lending by commercial banks, there remains the question of whether existing institutional arrangements, formal or informal, will be adequate to handle short-run liquidity crises. A paper by Nancy Teeters (1983) suggests that, in addition to a "reasonable" increase in the exposure of commercial banks and resources provided by the IMF, an adequate financing network should involve a source of funds that can be utilized on short notice when there are problems affecting major borrowers, or liquidity problems affecting bankers. She suggests that central banks, and in some cases treasuries or finance ministries, are institutionally in the best position to provide such funding. This sort of official funding would be provided on a very selective basis, where failure of the borrower to perform threatens the international financial system.

Pedro-Pablo Kuczynski (1983) and others argue that many debtor countries are currently in a crisis because of the heavy interest burden, and that some way must be found to reduce this burden during the present period of high interest rates. This raises the question of how the interest burden could be lightened in a way that will maintain the willingness of banks to lend. The way in which such interest rate reductions are reflected on banks' balance sheets is of course an important determinant of the banks' inclination to offer them, particularly in the case of U.S. creditor banks. Currently, banks must declare loans on which negotiated interest rate reductions take place as nonperforming, or substandard.

A plan to reduce interest burdens proposed by New York Federal Reserve Bank President Anthony Solomon has attracted recent attention. He has suggested that interest rates on loans to developing countries be capped, for example at 10 percent, with any excess charges being tacked onto principle.[9] This is essentially a proposal for "variable maturity" loans, in which interest is charged on accumulated deferred interest. Other methods of capping interest rates have been proposed by central bankers. These include (1) floating-rate loans with an interest rate cap, in which an interest deficit accumulates during periods when the market rate of interest rises above the cap rate, to be paid off when market rates move below the cap; (2) floating-rate loans with a maximum interest rate, whereby any shortfall from market rates are added into one final "balloon" payment at the end of the life of the loan; and (3) fixed-rate loans, funded in the bond market.[10]

While these interest rate capping schemes have support among some government officials, their attraction for commercial banks is less apparent. In addition to the problem of how the deferred interest would affect current earnings, there is the possibility that interest capping on a massive scale would cause a loss of confidence on the part of bank investors, who might believe that the risks of default or slow repayment were not adequately reflected in the banks' financial statements. Some bankers concede that a cap might work well enough to smooth out a temporary spike in interest rates, but wonder what would happen if interest rates climbed sharply and remained high ("Debate Likely . . ." 1984).

There are other, longer term, questions connected with caps. How should interest rate reductions be granted in conjunction with an IMF program? Would the imposition of a cap plan impair a debtor country's credit rating? Would such a scheme be politically acceptable in industrial countries, where a two-tiered interest rate system for foreign debt could bring demands for similar special treatment for domestic interest groups?

Medium-Term Strategies

Beyond the provision of emergency lending facilities for international payments crises, policymakers must consider strategies for the medium and long term. According to Dornbusch (1984a), U.S. policy in the debt question has favored the "muddling-through" strategy of rescheduling loans short term at considerable spreads. The argument has been that these spreads are required to maintain the flow of lending by banks. At the same time, the United States has endorsed stabilization programs under the IMF that Dornbusch believes have seriously harmed economic activity in several Latin American countries (Mexico being the exception), without promoting long-term improvement. Moreover, U.S. domestic trade policy has not been aimed at removing obstacles to exports from developing countries, frustrating export growth as the main engine of economic progress. This approach, Dornbusch claims, does not return the debtor countries to reasonably functioning market economies, and has spawned "siege economies" and resentment. He proposes the alternative of working on a double front: in the industrial countries, import barriers must be removed and banks must write down some debts (on interest or principal) in exchange for stabilization programs in debtor countries that have as performance criteria not budget cuts but real exchange rates and export growth. Creditor countries should not emphasize debt service too strongly and should take a more complacent view of debt write-down, since it is not in the national interest of creditor countries to seek full payments of bank debt at any cost to their own trade and to economic and social stability in the debtor countries. The choice of whether and how best to take delivery on the debt service will need to balance the claims of banks with other creditor countries' national interests, such as employment in those nations' export industries.[11]

AN INCREASINGLY POLITICAL PROBLEM

Recognition is growing that the international debt situation is not just a financial problem, but also a political one, jeopardizing social stability in the developing countries and undermining democratic governments. The austerity programs required as part of debt restructuring agreements helped thrust both Brazil and Mexico into recessions that may erode their capacity to meet future debt commitments. The newly elected governments of Argentina and Venezuela seem determined not to pay a similar price in order to meet their own debt service obligations. According to a recent report from the Latin American Debt Commission of the Americas Society, a New York based organization of U.S. corporations with operations in the region, "in virtually every Latin American and Caribbean country there are major pressures to turn inward, to reject cooperation with the IMF, to turn their backs on existing obligations and to look to solutions that stress a higher degree of protectionism and state control" ("The New Crisis for Latin Debt" 1984). Many fear that because existing governments have imposed austerity measures that reduce growth, employment, and social programs, extremist movements of the right and left are likely to take advantage of the resulting social unrest. Consequently, at least in Latin America, the debt crisis and ways of alleviating it are being viewed increasingly through a political prism. This has particularly been the case in recent months with Argentina, where the elected civilian government inherited a failing economy from an unpopular military regime and is now determined to consolidate the country's new democracy by reviving economic growth, even if this meets with the disapproval of foreign bankers and the IMF. In Peru, where real per capita incomes are 20 percent less than they were only four years ago, there is concern that economic problems might be great enough to cause the democratic government to falter ("Democracy in Peru Threatened by Terrorism and Debt" 1984).

Adding to the political tension of the debt situation is the feeling by creditors that some debtor countries could afford to meet more of their debt service obligations by drawing down foreign exchange reserves, but are unwilling to do so. Argentina, which at the end of the first quarter of 1984 was about $3 billion behind in interest payments, was estimated to have at least $1 billion in foreign exchange, and Venezuela was estimated to have reserves between $11 billion and $15 billion ("New Fears for Banks on Latin American Debt" 1984). Rather than depleting reserves to service foreign debt, both countries have indicated they will use the money to stimulate foreign investment. Some bankers fear that these policies could unravel recent progress in debt restructuring, during which cooperation among debtors, creditors, and the IMF have kept the international financial system intact.

Any judgment on the economic and political feasibility of the debtor countries transferring real resources to creditor countries depends also on another question: Can lending countries themselves deal with the problems of absorbing real resources on this scale? The required trade surplus of debtor countries, created by an expansion of their exports, may generate adjustment problems for the creditor countries. There is some concern that this transfer of goods to creditors would create difficulties reminiscent of those raised by the reparations that plagued the world's economy and politics after World War I (Lever 1984).

While many feel that the financial risk to banks of their loans to developing countries has been overestimated, the sums involved are now large enough not only to concern bankers and their stockholders, but also to risk the stability of normal trade flows and national monetary systems. Even those who place most of the blame on international bankers for the "hole" that developing countries have dug for themselves—for supplying the shovel, and then pushing them in—realize that a general write-off of debts would sacrifice far more than a few banks. Nevertheless, the governments of creditor countries governments and the IMF may have insisted too vigorously on timely, complete debt service, granting too high a priority to protecting the banks' current earnings (Dornbusch 1984). It is increasingly apparent that the economic and political costs of extreme austerity measures in developing countries will be borne by creditor as well as debtor nations. What is needed are more realistic policies by creditor governments and international organizations that avoid these extremes, balancing the need to support bankers' interests with economic growth and political stability in developing countries.

NOTES TO CHAPTER 1

1. Oil-exporting countries are defined by the IMF as those developing countries whose oil exports equal at least 100 million barrels per year. All other developing countries are called nonoil developing countries.

2. The International Monetary Fund so designates the twenty-five developing countries with the largest total external debt at the end of 1982, and which includes four major oil-exporting countries.

3. Scaling by export unit values again provides an indicator of a country's ability to service its foreign debt. Deflating debt service by import unit values gives a measure of the opportunity cost of debt: the imports that are foregone in order to meet debt service payments. Year to year the two measures generate different results, depending on the fluctuations in the terms of trade.

4. This criterion is frequently attributed to Somonsen (1983); see also Cline (1983, 1984b).

5. For a more detailed discussion of the conceptual and statistical aspects of debt ratios and debt service ratios, see IMF (1981: Appendix III; and OECD 1984): 31–33.

6. Charles P. Kindleberger, private correspondence, September 10, 1984.

7. Nevertheless, a withdrawal of regional banks from international lending could have serious consequences. A 1983 study estimates that, if the nine largest U.S. banks had to replace the small banks as lenders to non-OPEC developing countries, the exposure of the large banks would climb to 294 percent of capital, while their exposure to Argentina, Brazil, and Mexico would reach 155 percent of capital (Dale and Mattione 1983: 15).

8. The Morgan Guaranty (1983), Leven and Roberts (1983), and IMF (1984c) are studies reviewed in Cline (1984b), pp. 69–75. In their base-case scenarios, these models generally assume (1) moderate growth of real output in industrial countries, of about 3.0 to 3.5 percent per year; (2) gradual reductions in nominal interest rates, reaching 9 or 10 percent by the late 1980s; (3) a steady world price of oil in real terms; (4) no change in real exchange rates, or moderate devaluation of some debtor nation currencies; and (5) continued availability of commercial bank refinancing, so the banks maintain their current real exposure to developing countries.

9. *Business Week*, May 28, 1984, p. 28.

10. *Economist*, May 12, 1984, p. 97.

11. *Business Week*, March 19, 1984, p. 27.

APPENDIX
(Tables 1A-1 through 1A-11)

Table 1A-1.   External Debt of Nonoil Developing Countries, 1973–84 and of Eastern European and USSR, 1979–83 (*$ Billions*).[a]

	1973	1974	1975	1976
Nonoil Developing Countries				
Nominal debt	130.1	160.8	190.8	228.0
Long-term	111.8	138.1	163.5	194.9
Short-term	18.4	22.7	27.3	33.2
Real debt				
Deflated by export unit values, 1973 = 100	130.1	116.4	140.9	157.7
Deflated by import unit values, 1973 = 100	130.1	109.5	119.3	131.9
Nominal debt by analytical group				
Net oil exporters	20.4	26.0	34.1	42.4
Net oil importers	91.4	112.1	129.4	152.5
Major exporters of manufactures	40.8	51.7	60.9	73.1
Low-income countries[b]	25.4	29.7	33.2	38.3
Other net oil importers	25.2	30.6	35.3	41.1
Nominal debt by region				
Africa[c]	14.2	17.7	21.9	26.9
Asia	30.0	34.6	39.8	46.4
Europe	14.5	17.2	20.0	23.4
Middle East	8.7	10.3	13.3	16.1
Western Hemisphere	44.4	58.2	68.6	82.0
Eastern Europe and USSR				
Nominal Debt[d]				

a. Does not include debt owed to IMF. Figures for 1984 are IMF estimates.

b. Excludes China prior to 1977. "Low-income" countries are those with per capita GDP of less than $350 in 1984.

c. Excluding South Africa.

d. Gross debt in convertible currencies. Figure for 1983 is IMF estimate.

Sources: IMF *World Economic Outlook* 1983, 1984; and IMF *International Financial Statistics*, various issues.

Table 1A-1. continued

1977	1978	1979	1980	1981	1982	1983	1984	Average Rate of Change (%)
280.3	334.3	395.3	475.2	559.6	633.3	668.6	710.9	15.4
237.2	282.7	336.2	290.8	455.8	508.2	566.4	622.8	15.6
43.2	51.6	59.1	84.5	103.8	125.1	102.2	88.2	14.2
169.1	192.2	191.5	198.8	239.7	289.4	312.7	323.1	8.3
151.0	164.0	164.6	163.6	187.0	218.0	238.0	249.4	5.9
59.7	68.4	79.3	95.4	125.4	147.7	154.9	164.1	19.0
220.7	265.9	315.9	379.8	434.2	485.7	573.7	546.9	16.3
105.3	128.4	154.0	188.1	220.2	249.9	261.3	274.8	17.3
48.6	54.8	62.7	71.4	75.2	81.8	87.8	94.8	12.0
66.8	82.8	99.2	120.3	138.8	154.0	164.6	177.2	17.7
30.8	36.9	45.3	50.9	55.5	62.5	66.3	70.7	14.6
68.7	78.7	92.8	114.6	131.2	152.6	165.0	179.3	16.3
37.6	47.0	55.0	67.2	71.1	72.3	74.8	76.6	15.1
21.9	26.7	32.0	36.3	40.6	45.6	50.7	56.2	17.0
109.1	132.4	157.8	192.6	246.0	283.1	294.4	310.5	17.7
		76.5	82.0	86.5	82.5	79.5		

Table 1A-2. Nonoil Developing Countries: Debt Service and Debt Ratios, 1973-84 (*$ Billions; Ratios in %*).[a]

Nonoil Developing Countries	1973	1974	1975	1976
Debt service	17.9	22.1	25.1	27.8
Interest	6.9	9.3	10.5	10.9
Amortization[b]	11.9	12.8	14.6	16.8
Debt service deflated by				
Export unit values, 1973 = 100	17.9	16.0	18.5	19.2
Import unit values, 1973 = 100	17.9	15.1	15.7	16.1
Debt service/exports[c]	15.9	14.4	16.1	15.3
Interest/exports	6.1	6.1	6.7	6.0
Amortization/exports	9.8	8.3	9.4	9.3
By analytical group				
Net oil exporters				
Debt service/exports	29.0	21.1	24.2	24.4
Interest/exports	8.8	7.8	9.3	9.2
Amortization/exports	20.1	13.3	14.9	15.3
Major exporters of manufactures				
Debt service/exports	14.5	14.7	16.4	14.2
Interest/exports	5.6	6.1	6.9	5.5
Amortization/exports	8.9	8.5	9.5	8.7
Low-income countries				
Debt service/exports	14.6	13.7	14.5	12.8
Interest/exports	6.1	5.4	5.4	4.9
Amortization/exports	8.5	8.3	9.2	7.8
Other net oil importers				
Debt service/exports	12.7	10.6	11.8	12.9
Interest/exports	5.4	5.2	5.3	5.4
Amortization/exports	7.2	5.5	6.5	7.4
Debt/GDP	22.4	21.8	23.8	25.7
Debt/exports[d]	115.4	104.6	122.4	125.5
Reserves/imports[d]	31.4	21.6	19.1	23.6

a. Excludes data for the People's Republic of China prior to 1977. Figures for 1984 are IMF estimates.

b. Payments of principal on long-term debt only. Estimates for the period up to 1984 reflect actual amortization payments. Estimates for 1982 and 1983 reflect scheduled payments, but are modified to take account of the rescheduling agreements of 1982 and early 1983.

Table 1A-2. continued

1977	1978	1979	1980	1981	1982	1983	1984
32.8	47.5	61.0	73.4	97.2	107.7	96.6	103.4
12.7	18.1	25.9	39.0	54.7	63.0	59.2	63.7
20.2	29.4	35.1	34.3	42.5	44.6	37.4	39.7
19.8	27.3	29.6	30.7	41.6	49.2	45.2	47.0
17.7	23.3	25.4	25.3	32.5	37.1	34.4	36.3
14.8	18.1	18.1	17.2	21.3	24.5	21.6	21.1
5.7	6.9	7.7	9.1	12.0	14.3	13.2	13.0
9.1	11.2	10.4	8.0	9.3	10.2	8.4	8.1
26.4	30.5	31.4	22.6	28.3	31.1	31.0	30.6
8.7	9.8	9.9	11.3	15.8	19.9	20.7	20.0
17.7	20.7	21.4	11.3	12.5	11.1	10.4	10.6
12.2	15.6	15.2	16.2	20.8	25.0	19.4	19.1
5.1	6.2	7.3	9.0	11.8	14.5	12.5	12.0
7.1	9.3	7.9	7.2	9.0	10.4	6.9	7.1
12.1	12.1	10.5	10.3	12.6	14.6	13.3	12.8
4.7	5.1	4.5	4.4	5.1	5.4	5.4	6.0
7.4	7.0	6.0	6.0	7.5	9.2	8.0	6.8
13.9	18.7	18.7	18.6	21.6	23.8	24.0	22.6
5.6	7.3	8.7	10.3	13.2	14.5	13.8	13.5
8.3	11.4	10.0	8.3	8.4	9.3	10.2	9.1
23.7	24.1	23.3	23.9	27.1	32.5	36.7	37.5
126.1	127.7	117.2	111.2	122.5	144.1	149.5	144.7
25.7	26.4	22.6	17.8	16.4	16.9	18.9	20.0

c. Payments as a percentage of exports of goods and services.
d. Exports of goods and services.
Source: IMF World Economic Outlook, 1983, 1984.

Table 1A-3.   Current-Account Balances, 1973-84 (*$ Billions*).[a]

	1973	1974	1975	1976
Industrial Countries	20.3	-10.8	19.8	0.5
Seven largest[b]	14.8	-2.7	24.9	10.1
Other	5.5	-8.1	-5.1	-9.6
Developing Countries	-4.6	31.3	-10.9	7.7
Oil-exporting countries[c]	6.7	68.3	35.4	40.3
Nonoil developing countries[d]	-11.3	-37.0	-46.3	-32.6
By analytical group				
Net oil exporters	-2.6	-5.1	-9.9	-7.7
Net oil importers[d]	-8.8	-31.9	-36.4	-24.9
Major exporters of manufactures[e]	-3.6	-18.8	-19.1	-12.2
Low-income countries	-4.1	-7.5	-7.6	-4.3
Other net importers[f]	-1.1	-5.6	-9.7	-8.3
By area				
Africa[g]	-1.9	-3.2	-6.6	-6.1
Asia[d]	-2.6	-9.9	-8.9	-2.7
Europe	0.6	-4.4	-4.9	-4.7
Middle East	-2.6	-4.5	-6.9	-5.4
Western Hemisphere	-4.7	-13.5	-16.3	-11.8
Total[h]	15.7	20.5	8.9	8.2

a. On goods, services, and private transfers. Figures for 1984 are IMF estimates.

b. Canada, United States, Japan, France, West Germany, Italy, United Kingdom.

c. Algeria, Indonesia, Iran, Iraq, Kuwait, Libya, Nigeria, Oman, Qatar, Saudi Arabia, United Arab Emirates, Venezuela.

d. The People's Republic of China, which is classified as a low-income country but is also a net oil exporter, is included in the total (from 1977 onward) but not in the subgroups.

e. Argentina, Brazil, Greece, Hong Kong, Israel, Korea, Portugal, Singapore, Yugoslavia.

f. Middle-income countries that, in general, export mainly primary commodities.

g. Excluding South Africa.

h. Reflects errors, omissions, and asymmetries in reported balance of payments statistics on current account, plus balance of listed groups with other countries (mainly the USSR and other non-IMF-member countries of Eastern Europe).

Source: IMF, *World Economic Outlook*, 1983, 1984.

Table 1A-3. continued

1977	1978	1979	1980	1981	1982	1983	1984
-2.2	32.4	-5.4	-40.4	1.9	-1.4	-1.2	-22.5
10.0	35.9	6.9	-14.0	16.8	13.1	2.3	-23.0
-12.2	-3.5	-12.3	-26.4	-14.9	-14.5	-3.5	0.5
-1.0	-36.6	0.5	23.3	-55.7	-94.2	-72.6	-58.0
29.4	5.7	62.5	110.0	53.4	-12.0	-16.2	-8.0
-30.4	-42.3	-62.0	-87.7	-109.1	-82.2	-56.4	-50.0
-6.3	-7.4	-7.3	-10.2	-24.3	-14.4	-6.9	-9.5
-25.0	-34.2	-52.5	-74.2	-86.1	-73.5	-54.5	-43.5
-8.9	-10.8	-22.9	-32.5	-37.4	-34.6	-17.1	-12.0
-3.7	-8.2	-10.5	-14.1	-15.7	-15.1	-13.1	-12.5
-12.5	-15.2	-19.1	-27.6	-33.0	-23.8	-24.3	19.0
-6.6	-9.4	-9.9	-12.9	-14.0	-12.5	-10.8	-9.5
-1.5	-8.3	-16.9	-25.4	-23.2	-14.6	-10.7	-8.0
-9.1	-7.2	-10.1	-12.7	-10.4	-6.9	-5.5	-2.5
-5.1	-5.7	-7.2	-7.1	-11.5	-9.3	-12.0	-12.0
-8.5	-13.2	-21.4	-33.1	-45.5	-35.8	-18.5	-18.5
-3.2	-4.2	-4.9	-17.1	-53.8	-95.6	-73.8	-80.5

Table 1A-4. Current-Account Financing by Nonoil Developing Countries, 1973-84.[a]

	1973	1974	1975	1976
Current-Account Deficit[b] ($ Billions)	11.3	37.0	46.3	32.6
Use of reserves[c]	-10.4	-2.7	1.6	-13.0
Non-debt-creating flows[d]	10.3	14.6	11.8	12.6
Errors and omissions[e]	-3.8	-2.9	-5.6	-5.9
Net External Borrowing ($ Billions)	15.2	28.0	38.5	38.9
From private sources	10.1	19.6	24.4	23.7
Long-term capital	6.8	11.3	15.4	17.5
From banks[f]	6.5	10.3	14.2	15.3
Other	0.3	1.0	1.3	2.2
Short-term capital	3.3	8.3	9.0	6.2
From official sources	5.1	8.4	14.1	15.1
Long-term capital	4.9	6.8	11.7	10.5
Use of IMF credit and other[g] reserve-related credits	0.2	1.6	2.4	4.6
Accumulation of arrears	—	—	—	—
Net External Borrowing (percentage share)	100	100	100	100
From private sources	66	70	63	61
Long-term capital	45	40	40	45
From banks[f]	43	37	37	39
Other	2	3	3	6
Short-term capital	22	30	23	16
From official sources	34	30	37	39
Long-term capital	32	24	30	27
Use of IMF credit and other reserve related credits[g]	2	6	7	12
Accumulation of arrears	—	—	—	—

a. Figures for 1984 are IMF estimates. Excludes data for the People's Republic of China prior to 1977.

b. Balance on goods, services, and private transfers (with sign reversed).

c. Negative sign indicates accumulation of reserves.

d. Chiefly foreign direct investment, aid grants, and SDR allocations.

e. Presumed to reflect primarily unrecorded capital outflows.

f. Refers only to long-term lending by banks guaranteed by government of debtor country. Bank lending also accounts for large fractions of unguaranteed long-term flows (included in other long-term flows) and short-term flows.

Table 1A-4. continued

1977	1978	1979	1980	1981	1982	1983	1984
30.4	42.3	62.0	87.7	109.1	82.2	56.4	50.0
-11.5	-16.3	-11.8	-6.8	-5.4	3.8	-6.1	-13.3
14.1	17.0	23.7	24.1	27.2	23.9	21.3	23.0
-6.5	-6.9	-3.0	-15.4	-15.5	-18.8	-10.0	-5.0
34.4	48.6	53.0	85.9	102.9	73.2	51.2	45.3
18.4	32.8	36.5	60.6	70.5	36.2	20.2	21.2
10.9	22.8	31.5	38.4	50.9	22.3	43.1	35.2
6.8	22.0	23.3	27.8	28.8	15.7	40.2	35.6
4.1	0.8	8.1	10.7	22.1	6.6	2.9	-0.3
7.5	10.0	5.0	22.2	19.6	14.0	-22.9	-14.0
16.0	15.8	16.5	25.3	32.4	37.0	31.0	24.1
13.1	13.8	17.0	20.0	22.6	21.6	22.6	23.1
1.3	1.5	-0.9	3.9	7.2	8.3	10.2	5.0
1.6	0.5	0.4	1.4	2.6	7.1	-1.8	-4.0
100	100	100	100	100	100	100	100
53	67	69	71	69	49	39	47
32	47	59	45	49	30	84	78
20	45	44	32	28	21	79	79
12	2	15	12	21	9	6	-1
22	21	9	26	19	19	-48	-31
47	33	31	29	31	51	61	53
38	28	32	23	22	30	44	51
4	3	-2	5	7	11	20	11
5	1	1	2	3	10	-4	-9

g. Includes use of IMF credit and short-term borrowing by monetary authorities from other monetary authorities.

Source: IMF, *World Economic Outlook*, 1983, 1984.

Table 1A-5. Total Net Resource Receipts of 157 Developing Countries from All Sources, 1970-82—Current Prices (*$ Billions*).

	1970	*1971*	*1972*	*1973*
Official Development Assistance	8.23	9.14	9.84	12.68
Bilateral	7.16	7.84	8.46	10.72
DAC countries	5.66	6.31	6.61	7.08
OPEC countries	0.39	0.44	0.66	2.03
CMEA and other donors	1.11	1.09	1.19	1.61
Multilateral agencies	1.07	1.30	1.38	1.96
Grants by Private Voluntary Agencies	0.86	0.91	1.04	1.37
Nonconcessional Flows[a]	10.95	11.83	13.30	19.86
Official or officially supported	3.96	4.92	3.75	4.86
Private export credits (DAC)	2.09	2.71	1.44	1.16
Official export credits (DAC)	0.59	0.72	0.74	1.13
Multilateral	0.71	0.92	1.01	1.31
Other official and private flows (DAC)	0.25	0.28	0.45	1.02
Other donors[b]	0.32	0.29	0.11	0.24
Private	6.99	6.91	9.55	15.00
Direct investment	3.69	3.31	4.23	4.72
Bank sector[a]	3.00	3.30	4.80	9.70
Bond lending	0.30	0.30	0.52	0.58
Total Receipts	20.04	21.88	24.18	33.91
Memorandum Items				
Short-term bank lending	—	—	—	—
IMF purchases, net[c]	0.34	0.05	0.30	0.36

a. Excluding bond lending and export credits extended by banks which are included under private export credits. Including loans by branches of OECD banks located in offshore centers, and for 1980, 1981, and 1982 participations of non-OECD banks in international syndicates.

b. Other official flows from OPEC countries, Ireland, Luxembourg, Spain, Yugoslavia, India, Israel, and China.

c. All purchases minus repayments including reserve branches but excluding loans by the IMF Trust Fund included under multilateral official development assistance.

Table 1A-5. continued

1974	1975	1976	1977	1978	1979	1980	1981	1982
16.50	20.95	20.35	20.98	28.10	31.93	37.33	36.63	34.24
13.68	17.11	16.49	16.15	22.09	25.69	29.54	28.70	26.79
8.23	9.79	9.50	10.08	13.12	16.33	18.11	18.28	18.53
4.15	5.68	5.17	4.28	6.90	6.96	8.73	7.61	5.51
1.30	1.64	1.81	1.79	2.07	2.40	2.70	2.81	2.75
2.82	3.84	3.87	4.83	6.01	6.24	7.79	7.93	7.45
1.22	1.34	1.35	1.49	1.65	1.95	2.31	2.02	2.31
19.81	34.31	34.89	44.56	57.91	57.72	56.41	69.27	56.63
7.64	10.53	12.66	15.74	19.21	18.72	22.49	22.14	22.63
2.40	4.42	6.74	8.84	9.70	8.85	11.12	11.33	(9.00)
0.80	1.20	1.39	1.44	2.22	1.73	2.46	2.01	(2.45)
1.81	2.53	2.54	2.69	3.09	4.16	4.85	5.68	(6.68)
0.83	0.75	0.80	0.63	1.36	1.14	2.24	1.96	(3.00)
1.80	1.63	1.19	2.14	2.84	2.84	1.82	1.16	(1.50)
12.17	23.78	22.23	28.82	38.70	39.00	33.92	47.13	34.00
1.89	11.36	8.31	9.82	11.59	13.42	10.54	16.13	(11.00)
10.00	12.00	12.70	15.80	23.20	24.90	22.00	29.00	21.00
0.28	0.42	1.22	3.20	3.91	0.68	1.38	2.00	2.00
37.53	56.60	59.59	67.03	87.66	91.60	96.05	107.92	93.18
—	—	—	16.00	17.00	16.00	26.00	25.00	17.00
1.74	3.24	2.98	−0.43	−0.85	0.52	2.61	6.40	6.70

Table 1A-6. External Debt of Nonoil Developing Countries by Class of Creditor, 1973–84 (*$ Billions; Figure in Parentheses if Percentage Share*).[a]

	1973	1974	1975	1976
Total Outstanding Debt	130.0	160.8	190.8	228.0
	(100.0)	(100.0)	(100.0)	(100.0)
Short-term Debt	18.4	22.7	27.3	33.2
	(14.1)	(14.1)	(14.3)	(14.5)
Long-term Debt	100.8	138.1	163.5	194.9
	(85.9)	(85.9)	(85.7)	(85.5)
By type of creditor				
Official creditors	51.0	60.1	70.3	82.4
	(39.2)	(37.4)	(36.8)	(36.1)
Governments	37.3	43.4	50.3	57.9
	(28.7)	(27.0)	(26.2)	(25.3)
International institutions	13.7	16.6	20.3	24.8
	(10.5)	(10.3)	(10.6)	(10.9)
Private creditors	60.8	77.9	95.1	114.8
	(46.7)	(48.4)	(49.8)	(50.4)
Unguaranteed debt	29.3	36.0	40.8	45.9
	(22.5)	(22.4)	(21.4)	(20.1)
Guaranteed debt	31.5	42.0	52.4	66.6
	(24.2)	(26.1)	(27.5)	(29.2)
Financial institutions	17.3	25.6	36.7	49.0
	(13.3)	(15.9)	(19.2)	(21.5)
Other private creditors	14.2	16.3	17.6	19.8
	(10.9)	(10.1)	(9.2)	(8.7)

a. Figures for 1984 are IMF estimates. Does not include debt owed to the IMF.
b. Excludes data for the People's Republic of China prior to 1977.
Source: IMF, *World Economic Outlook*, 1983, 1984.

Table 1A-6. continued

1977	1978	1979	1980	1981	1982	1983	1984
280.3	334.3	395.3	475.2	559.6	633.3	668.6	710.9
(100.0)	(100.0)	(100.0)	(100.0)	(100.0)	(100.0)	(100.0)	(100.0)
43.2	51.6	59.1	84.5	103.8	125.1	102.2	88.2
(15.4)	(15.4)	(15.0)	(17.8)	(18.5)	(19.8)	(15.3)	(12.4)
237.2	282.7	336.2	390.8	455.8	508.2	566.4	622.8
(84.6)	(84.6)	(85.0)	(82.2)	(81.5)	(80.2)	(84.7)	(87.6)
97.6	116.3	133.4	153.2	170.2	189.3	211.9	235.0
(34.8)	(34.8)	(33.7)	(32.2)	(30.4)	(29.9)	(31.7)	(33.1)
68.3	80.5	90.1	101.8	111.5	123.2	138.3	153.3
(24.4)	(24.1)	(22.8)	(21.4)	(19.9)	(19.5)	(20.7)	(21.6)
29.3	35.8	43.2	51.4	58.6	66.1	73.7	81.7
(10.4)	(10.7)	(10.9)	(10.8)	(10.5)	(10.4)	(11.0)	(11.5)
139.6	166.4	202.8	237.6	285.6	318.9	354.5	387.8
(49.8)	(49.8)	(51.3)	(50.0)	(51.0)	(50.4)	(53.0)	(54.5)
50.4	51.7	62.4	75.2	94.2	102.0	104.2	103.4
(18.0)	(15.5)	(15.8)	(15.8)	(16.8)	(16.1)	(15.6)	(14.5)
89.2	114.7	140.4	162.4	191.4	216.9	250.2	284.4
(31.8)	(34.3)	(35.5)	(34.2)	(34.2)	(34.2)	(37.4)	(40.0)
63.1	83.7	108.0	128.9	154.7	176.4	209.6	243.2
(22.5)	(25.0)	(27.3)	(27.1)	(27.6)	(27.8)	(31.3)	(34.2)
26.1	31.0	32.4	33.5	36.7	40.5	40.6	41.2
(9.3)	(9.3)	(8.2)	(7.0)	(6.6)	(6.4)	(6.1)	(5.8)

Table 1A-7. External Debt of Nonoil Developing Countries by Creditor Source and Analytical Group, 1973–84 (%).[a]

	1973	1974	1975	1976
Net Oil Exporters				
Total outstanding debt	100.0	100.0	100.0	100.0
Long-term debt to official creditors	27.4	26.1	28.5	27.6
Long-term debt to private creditors	60.7	62.3	60.9	61.9
Short-term debt	11.8	11.5	10.6	10.4
Share in total debt of nonoil developing countries	15.7	16.2	17.9	18.6
Major Exporters of Manufactures				
Total outstanding debt	100.0	100.0	100.0	100.0
Long-term debt to official creditors	22.0	21.2	21.0	21.4
Long-term debt to private creditors	62.8	64.0	63.8	63.4
Short-term debt	15.2	14.9	15.1	15.3
Share in total debt of nonoil developing countries	31.3	32.2	31.9	32.1
Low-income Countries				
Total outstanding debt	100.0	100.0	100.0	100.0
Long-term debt to official creditors	84.5	83.6	83.4	83.2
Long-term debt to private creditors	13.3	14.1	14.0	14.1
Short-term debt	2.3	2.4	2.6	2.7
Share in total debt of nonoil developing countries	19.5	18.5	17.4	16.8
Other Net Oil Importers				
Total outstanding debt	100.0	100.0	100.0	100.0
Long-term debt to official creditors	36.8	35.0	34.0	33.0
Long-term debt to private creditors	39.7	41.1	41.3	41.7
Short-term debt	23.5	23.8	24.6	25.4
Share in total debt of nonoil developing countries	19.4	19.0	18.5	18.0

a. Does not include debt owed to the IMF.

Source: IMF, *World Economic Outlook*, 1983, 1984.

Table 1A-7. continued

1977	1978	1979	1980	1981	1982	1983	1984
100.0	100.0	100.0	100.0	100.0	100.0	100.0	100.0
30.2	32.0	30.5	28.5	24.1	22.3	24.7	25.7
59.4	56.3	58.0	54.8	54.1	53.4	62.2	62.2
10.4	11.7	11.5	16.7	21.8	24.3	13.1	12.1
21.3	20.4	20.1	20.1	22.4	23.3	23.2	23.1
100.0	100.0	100.0	100.0	100.0	100.0	100.0	100.0
19.5	19.3	18.5	16.4	14.7	14.1	14.9	16.4
62.6	64.4	64.6	61.6	63.8	63.0	64.5	69.1
17.9	16.3	16.9	21.9	21.5	22.9	20.6	14.5
37.6	38.4	39.0	39.6	39.3	39.5	39.1	38.7
100.0	100.0	100.0	100.0	100.0	100.0	100.0	100.0
75.4	76.1	75.3	76.0	79.0	81.1	82.3	82.9
20.0	20.2	18.4	18.1	16.7	15.6	15.0	14.9
4.5	3.6	6.2	5.9	4.3	3.3	2.6	2.3
17.3	16.4	15.9	15.0	13.4	12.9	13.1	13.3
100.0	100.0	100.0	100.0	100.0	100.0	100.0	100.0
33.5	33.8	33.7	33.9	34.7	35.6	37.9	39.0
42.8	41.2	46.1	46.9	46.6	45.3	46.6	46.0
23.8	25.0	20.2	19.2	18.7	19.0	15.6	14.9
23.8	24.8	25.1	25.3	24.8	24.3	24.6	24.9

Table 1A-8. Lending by Private Creditors to 102 Developing Countries, 1970–82 (*$ Billions*).[a]

	1970	1973	1976	1978	1979	1980	1981	1982
Debt outstanding to foreign private creditors (end year)	15.8	32.0	71.1	125.4	154.5	177.7	201.9	229.0
Financial institutions	5.0	16.4	48.5	89.6	118.2	140.0	164.4	190.3
At variable interest rates	0.5	9.3	33.7	64.3	89.2	107.4	131.9	152.8
At fixed interest rates	4.5	7.1	14.8	25.3	29.0	32.6	32.5	37.5
Bonds	3.1	4.5	6.3	13.5	14.1	15.5	16.6	17.1
Suppliers' credits	6.6	9.9	14.3	21.0	21.0	21.5	20.4	21.0
Other[b]	1.1	1.2	2.0	1.3	1.1	0.7	0.6	0.5
Disbursements by foreign private creditors	4.1	11.6	23.9	45.6	52.9	45.8	51.9	48.0
Financial institutions	1.8	7.7	17.7	35.3	45.9	38.6	44.8	39.2
At variable interest rates	0.4	5.7	11.6	27.7	38.1	30.7	37.3	32.0
At fixed interest rates	1.4	2.0	6.1	7.6	7.8	7.9	7.5	7.2
Bonds	0.1	1.0	1.5	3.9	1.9	2.2	2.3	3.0
Suppliers' credits	1.8	3.0	4.7	6.4	5.1	5.1	4.8	6.2
Other[b]	0.3	0.0	0.0	0.0	0.0	0.0	0.0	0.0

a. Data covers 102 countries reporting under the Debtor Reporting System.
b. Principally debt that stems from nationalization or compensation for expropriated foreign assets; this category also includes debt not otherwise allocated.

Source: World Bank, *World Debt Tables*, 1983–84.

Table 1A-9. Multilateral Debt Renegotiations, 1975–83 ($ Millions).[a]

Country	Number of Reschedulings 1975–83	1975–80 Paris Club	1975–80 Commercial Bank	1981 Paris Club	1981 Commercial Bank	1982 Paris Club	1982 Commercial Bank	1983[b] Paris Club	1983[b] Commercial Bank
Argentina	2		970						(6,000)
Bolivia	2				(444)				(536)
Brazil	2							(3,800)	(9,800)
Central African Republic	2			55					
Chile	2	216						(13)	(4,100)
Costa Rica	2							(107)	(1,259)
Dominican Republic	1								(660)
Equador	2							(200)	(2,150)
Gabon	1	105[b]							
Guyana	3		29				14		(24)
Honduras	1								(122)
India	3	436[d]	126		103				(166)
Jamaica	3	30		25					
Liberia	4			142			27	(25)	
Madagascar	3					103			(195)
Malawi	3					24		(30)	(57)
Mexico	2							2,000[e]	(22,550)
Morocco	1							(1,200)	
Nicaragua	3		582		190		(55)		
Niger	1							(29)	
Nigeria	1								(1,830)

(*Table 1A-9. continued overleaf*)

Table 1A-9. continued

Country	Number of Reschedulings 1975–83	1975–80 Paris Club	1975–80 Commercial Bank	1981 Paris Club	1981 Commercial Bank	1982 Paris Club	1982 Commercial Bank	1983[b] Paris Club	1983[b] Commercial Bank
Pakistan	1			263					
Peru	4	478	821					(450)	(2,320)
Romania	4					(234)	(1,544)	(195)	(572)
Senegal	4	66		77		84		(81)	(92)
Sierra Leone	2								
Sudan	4	373			638	174		550	
Togo	5	170	68	(92)				(300)	(84)
Turkey	5	4,696[d]	2,640		(3,100)				
Uganda	2			27		(10)			
Uruguay	1								(170)
Yugoslavia	1								(3,800)
Zaire	6	1,594	402	574				(1,600)	
Zambia	1							(320)	
Total	84	8,164	5,638	1,255	4,475	629	1,640	10,900	56,487

a. Arrangements concluded with commercial banks and official creditors in the same year are regarded as separate reschedulings. Figures indicate rescheduled amounts as reported by the countries or, if in parentheses, as estimated by IMF or World Bank Staff.

b. Covers arrangements signed, or agreed in principle, through December 1983. Cuba and Poland, which also renegotiated debt-service payments with commercial banks during 1983, are not members of the World Bank and, therefore, are excluded from this table. Panama's debt-restructuring agreement, signed with commercial-bank creditors in September 1983, was a refinancing, rather than a postponement or formal rescheduling of maturities, and also is omitted.

c. This was an agreement of a special task force.

d. Refers to Aid Consortia Agreements.

e. This was an agreement of a creditor-group meeting.

Table 1A-10. Exposure of U.S. Banks in Nonoil Developing Countries and Eastern Europe, Relative to Capital, 1977–82 (%, *End of Year*).

	1977	1978	1979	1980	1981	1982
All U.S. Banks						
Nonoil developing countries	114.9	114.4	124.2	132.3	148.3	146.1
Mexico	27.4	23.4	23.0	27.6	34.3	34.5
Brazil	29.4	28.6	27.3	25.4	26.9	28.9
Eastern Europe	16.7	15.8	16.1	13.9	12.9	8.9
Nine Largest U.S. Banks						
Nonoil developing countries	163.2	166.8	182.1	199.3	220.6	221.2
Mexico	32.9	30.4	29.6	37.8	44.4	44.4
Brazil	41.9	42.4	40.3	39.3	40.8	45.8
Eastern Europe	25.0	23.5	23.9	21.8	19.5	13.9

Source: Cline (1983), p. 32. From Federal Reserve Board of Governors, *Country Exposure Lending Survey.*

Table 1A–11. External Claims and Net External Position of Banks, 1978–82 ($ Billions).[a]

	Dec. 78	Dec. 79	Dec. 80	Dec. 81	Dec. 82
External Claims					
On nonoil developing countries	155.0	195.4	241.3	285.6	306.1
Argentina	6.7	13.1	18.9	22.9	22.7
Brazil	31.7	36.9	43.3	49.6	56.0
Mexico	23.2	30.7	41.0	55.5	58.9
Korea	6.9	10.3	14.0	16.9	18.8
On oil-exporting countries	53.0	60.0	65.3	66.7	73.2
On centrally planned economies[b]	40.9	47.0	49.3	50.3	44.3
Net External Position					
Nonoil developing countries	63.4	90.0	128.8	167.7	185.9
Argentina	2.0	5.3	12.3	16.3	16.4
Brazil	21.0	28.8	38.6	44.8	51.8
Mexico	16.8	22.5	31.6	43.4	48.5
Korea	4.4	7.2	10.7	13.7	15.1
Oil-exporting countries	-27.3	-57.6	-91.0	-87.0	-58.4
Centrally-planned economies[b]	30.8	32.6	35.0	36.0	28.6

a. Covers banks in BIS reporting area. A negative sign indicates that liabilities exceed claims.
b. Excludes IMF member countries.

Source: IMF, *International Capital Markets: Developments and Prospects, 1983* from BIS data.

2 MANAGING WORLD DEBT
Past Lessons and Future Prospects

Richard P. Mattione

When, in August 1982, Mexican officials suddenly announced their inability to meet maturing debt obligations, the free market in lending to developing countries was largely replaced by a system of rescheduled debt payments and coerced new lending. Restoration of a free market in developing country loans remains uncertain.

While developing countries have reduced their current-account deficits significantly since 1982, growth and internal balance have yet to be restored. Moreover, developing countries with debt problems will soon tire of satisfying the requests of external creditors if they cannot also satisfy the economic and political demands of domestic constituencies. Questions of growth and debt are and will continue to be linked, both structurally and politically.

CAUSES OF THE DEBT CRISIS

In the preceding chapter Kristin Hallberg identified the three contending causes of the debt problems of the less developed countries (LDCs): external economic shocks, internal LDC economic policy, and Western banks' loan policies. A consensus is emerging that all these factors played a role, though disputes still exist about the relative contribution of each.

43

External factors did matter a great deal. However, not all developing countries with debt problems were battered by an adverse external economic environment. Table 2-1 presents data on the shocks experienced by several of the larger debtors from 1979 to 1982, that is, roughly from the second oil shock to the beginning of the debt crisis.[1]

It is scarcely surprising to find that the country experiencing the biggest dollar shock was Brazil. What is remarkable is that Colombia, although it suffered the biggest shock in relation to GDP, had escaped rescheduling as of August 1985. Mexico, whose problems conveniently serve to date the start of the debt crisis, had a large favorable shock due to oil price movements. Nigeria and Venezuela also had large favorable shocks but still were forced into reschedulings. Furthermore, interest rate shocks had only a small direct role in precipitating the debt problems of developing countries. For the countries experiencing unfavorable shocks, interest rate shocks accounted for less than one-third of the total shock. Similar calculations show that this continued to hold true in 1983, largely because of continued slow growth in world trade.[2] For countries experiencing favorable shocks, the interest rate shock offset less than half the benefit derived from favorable terms of trade.

Table 2-2 classifies debtors even more clearly. Only Brazil and the Philippines actively adjusted, in the sense that the current account position deteriorated by less than the amount of the unfavorable shocks. Colombia was essentially neutral. In Chile and Argentina, on the other hand, domestic policies amplified the effects of unfavorable shocks. Mexico saw a large deterioration of its current account despite favorable shocks, and Nigeria used up almost all of its favorable shock. Investment fell as a share of GDP from 1978 to 1982 in six cases, the ratio held steady in two cases, and in Peru it actually increased.[3] Mexico did increase investment from 1978 to 1981, but this was more than undone in 1982. Table 2-2 also indicates that large-scale capital flight, driven by the expectation that higher returns could be earned abroad, helped to precipitate the problems of Argentina, Mexico, and Venezuela.

Domestic policies also contributed to the developing countries' woes. Real exchange rates appreciated sharply from 1978 to 1982 for most of them (see Table 2-2). In Argentina, Mexico, the Philippines, and Venezuela, where capital could move freely, exchange rate appreciation induced capital flight. In others such as Chile

Table 2-1. Sources and Magnitudes of External Shocks in Selected Developing Countries, 1979–82.

| Country | Billions of Dollars | | | | Percentage of GDP | Share of Trade[a] (%) |
	Total	Changes in Terms of Trade	High Real Interest Rates	Low Export Demand		
Argentina	-13.4	-6.2	-3.7	-3.6	-3.00	-21.9
Brazil	-48.5	-31.7	-8.9	-7.9	-4.56	-30.1
Chile	-4.8	-1.9	-1.5	-1.5	-4.61	-14.9
Colombia	-6.8	-4.3	-0.9	-1.6	-4.94	-22.7
Mexico	11.7	22.5	-8.4	-2.4	1.60	8.8
Nigeria	32.7[b]	34.1[b]	-0.9	-0.6	11.55	21.7
Peru	0.4	2.3	-0.8	-1.1	0.53	1.6
Philippines	-8.1	-4.3	-1.7	-2.1	-5.61	-13.0
Venezuela	19.1	24.0	-4.6	-0.3	7.79	16.6

a. Trade consists of exports and imports of goods only.
b. The terms of trade shock for Nigeria represents exports only, because no data were available on import prices.

Source: See Appendix 2A for methods of calculation and bibliographic references in the text for sources.

Table 2-2. Adjustment Efforts in Selected Developing Countries, 1979–82 (*$ Billions*).

Country	External Shock	Current Account Change[a]	Capital Flight[b]
Argentina	−13.4	−18.9	−14.3
Brazil	−48.5	−23.6	2.0
Chile	−4.8	−8.5	1.0
Colombia	−6.8	−6.6	0.7
Mexico	11.7	−18.7	−15.2
Nigeria	32.7	1.0	0.4
Peru	0.4	1.3	1.3
Philippines	−8.1	−4.4	−1.4
Venezuela	19.1	19.5	−13.0

a. Adjusted for inflation.

b. A minus sign denotes capital flight; that is, an unfavorable movement in the relevant items of the capital account.

Sources: See Appendix 2A for methods of calculation. International Monetary Fund (1983a, b; 1984a).

and Argentina, with relatively open trading regimes, a flight into goods resulted. Current-account positions deteriorated far more in these two countries than can be explained by external shocks (Table 2-2). Overvalued exchange rates helped to keep inflation down temporarily, but such policies could not be sustained without borrowing beyond what might have been appropriate in response to external shocks.

Soaring budget deficits (as a share of GDP) were also a problem in these countries. The deficits were funded largely by accelerating the growth in money supplies which helped fuel rapidly rising inflation in most of these countries. Argentina, Brazil, Mexico, and Peru all suffered from triple-digit inflation by 1983.[4]

Most countries seemed trapped by the spiraling inflation. Exchange rates became overvalued when nominal devaluations, intentionally or unintentionally, inadequately corrected for inflation, which in turn lowered the demand for real money balances by leading to expectations of future devaluations. Rising inflation also raised budget deficits when the real value of subsidies rose in response to inflation, and this led to an acceleration in domestic money creation, which fueled further inflation. Finally, inflation interacted with con-

Table 2-3. Real Exchange Rates in Selected Developing Countries, 1978-84 (*Constant Domestic Currency Units Per Constant Dollar*).

Country	1978	1979	1980	1981	1982	1983	1984[a]
Argentina	96.5	71.8	65.1	81.2	137.0	122.4	116.9
Brazil	99.6	107.3	115.9	107.3	110.0	133.5	132.2
Chile[b]	104.8	93.0	79.5	79.6	98.9	106.7	107.8
Colombia	94.3	90.3	92.2	93.4	89.3	91.5	99.4
Mexico	99.7	95.0	87.6	82.0	120.1	128.5	110.6
Nigeria[c]	89.8	86.3	80.2	81.3	84.6	76.8	62.3
Peru[c]	120.7	117.1	107.8	98.2	100.6	112.5	111.5
Philippines	101.0	95.7	93.9	95.2	95.0	110.1	104.4
Venezuela[b]	98.9	101.9	96.8	92.8	87.7	83.2[d]	105.2[d]

a. First half of 1984 only.
b. Home and imported goods price index used.
c. Consumer price index used.
d. The multiple-exchange-rate system introduced by Venezuela makes the calculation of real exchange rates for 1983 and 1984 problematic. If the normal rate of 7.5 bolivars per dollar is used instead of the essential goods rate of 4.3 bolivars per dollar, the index takes the values of 145.2 and 141.7 in 1983 and the first quarter of 1984, respectively.

Methods and Sources: Each country's real exchange rate was indexed to an average 1976-78 value of 100. The wholesale price deflator was used for the U.S. price index; the wholesale price index was also used for domestic prices in developing countries except as noted. Calculations are based on data in International Monetary Fund (1984a, b).

trolled domestic interest rates to lower real rates of return and thereby discourage domestic saving, which led countries to rely even more on foreign sources of credit.

Kristin Hallberg discussed the rapid expansion of bank lending during this period in Chapter 1 (Table 1A-8). But debt would not, indeed could not, grow this rapidly forever. Some adjustments would have to be made in the future. Moreover, expanded borrowing itself helped developing countries continue growing in spite of shocks, but sustaining the growth seemed dependent on rising real levels of debt.[5]

Bank debt was also an inappropriate form of lending for developing countries in many ways. Banks prefer to lend money for short periods because their own funding sources are short-term deposits. Developing countries preferred bank loans because they seemed cheaper than long-term bonds or foreign direct investment. But a gap still remained between the eight-year maturity that banks rarely allowed to be exceeded and the fifteen to thirty years necessary for developing countries to be able to repay. The notion that good borrowers would always be able to roll over maturing loans provided false comfort to both sides. Moreover, when countries saw their access to new loans reduced or simply disliked the terms available on longer term loans, they chose short-term bank loans. At the end of 1982, 49.5 percent of bank loans to developing countries had maturities of one year, or less, creating a continuous need to roll over large quantities of short-term loans. Combined with high debt/export ratios the rollover requirement forced one country after another into rescheduling (BIS July 1983; Dale and Mattione 1983: 15–16, 19–25).

RESCHEDULINGS AND ADJUSTMENT PROGRAMS

Table 2–4 provides details on the major reschedulings and new loans contracted between the debtors and the commercial banks of industrial nations. Looking at the deals made in 1983 for Brazil, Chile, Mexico, Peru, and Argentina, it can be seen that the basic terms on reschedulings were at first quite similar: maturities of seven to nine years, spreads of around $2\frac{1}{8}$ percent over LIBOR and 2 percent above the prime rate, and grace periods of three to five years. Mexico managed to extract the best deal; bankers have sometimes argued that those terms reflected Mexico's willingness to deal with the banks without delay and its rapid implementation of an IMF adjustment program. Terms have gradually eased for borrowers that behaved well—that is, for those countries that quickly rescheduled loans, reached IMF agreements, and fairly consistently hit IMF targets. Reschedulings of 1984 payments usually had longer maturities or slightly lower interest rate spreads.

Reschedulings have also routinely included provisions for new credits. In 1983 these were at slightly higher prices, because the fact that credits on the margin were more expensive helped preserve the fiction that the market was still functioning. During 1984, however, terms on new loans were at least as favorable as those on reschedulings or, as in Peru's case, the decision not to seek new loans led to a noticeable reduction in the spread applied to the rescheduling. If it is successfully completed, the new deal for Mexico covering payments due from 1985 to 1990 would represent a major concession to debtors.

The terms on Colombia's new loans reflect its ability to avoid calling on the Fund, and the seemingly favorable terms for Nigeria are due to the fact that mostly trade credits have been rescheduled so far. But the situations in Venezuela and Argentina demonstrate the limitations inherent in the bankers' strategy of better terms for better performances. Venezuela has reached tentative agreement with its creditors on a rescheduling with terms almost as favorable as Mexico's most recent rescheduling, despite two years of delays in rescheduling talks and the absence of an IMF program. Bankers may be able to rationalize favorable terms for Venezuela because the country has, to a certain extent, pursued a shadow IMF program of devaluations and spending cuts. Argentina talked and talked with the IMF but made little movement toward adjustment. Yet it was able to borrow $100 million from banks on very favorable terms in March 1984 as part of a package that reduced interest arrears at the banks because such a loan was in the bank's interest. Its next set of talks with the Fund yielded a stabilization program conditioned on a rescheduling from banks. Argentina was then able to reach a deal with banks that included terms almost as favorable as those granted Venezuela or Mexico. That deal probably reflects Argentina's ability to wait for such concessions by banks. Apparently the domestic economy did not benefit from such delays, for Argentina implemented a new austerity program in June 1985 after inflation reached 1000 percent at an annual rate.

For the last few years IMF adjustment programs and reschedulings have gone almost hand in hand; among major debtors, only South Korea has entered an IMF program without also entering into rescheduling negotiations with commercial creditors. In some cases, such as Peru and Turkey, IMF programs have become almost a permanent feature. Whatever the country, many recent programs have had to be reformulated, and both the IMF and borrowers have found room for compromise.

In three important cases banks slowed rescheduling negotiations pending the implementation of IMF-approved adjustment programs in the debtor countries. The Philippines had little choice but to accede to austerity, because its negotiating position was weak. Nigeria managed to reschedule some credits without an IMF program, and Argentina has used its leverage to pry new loans out of the banks even after its previous IMF package was suspended. All three coun-

Table 2-4. Major Commercial Reschedulings and New Loans for the Public Sector since 1983.

Country	Years Covered	Amount Rescheduled[a] ($ Millions)	Margin (%)		Maturity (Years)	New Loan ($ Millions)	Margin (%)		Maturity (Years)
			LIBOR+	Prime+			LIBOR+	Prime+	
Argentina[b]	1983	5,500	2.125	2.000	7.0	1,500	2.250	2.125	5.0
	1984	—	—	—	—	225[c]	0.125	—	0.5[c]
	1982–85	9,900	1.625	1.250	12.0	3,700	1.625	1.250	10.0
Brazil	1983	4,000	2.125	1.875	8.0	4,400	2.125	1.875	8.0
	1984	5,500	2.000	1.750	9.0	6,500	2.000	1.750	9.0
Chile	1983	1,100	2.125	2.000	8.0	1,300	2.250	2.125	7.0
	1984	1,000	2.125	2.000	8.0	780	1.750	1.500	9.0
Colombia	1983	—	—	—	—	210	1.625	1.500	6.0
	1984	—	—	—	—	370	1.625	1.250	8.0
Mexico	1982–84	23,000	1.875	1.750	8.0	n.a.	—	—	—
	1983	n.a.	—	—	—	5,000	2.250	2.125	6.0
	1984	n.a.	—	—	—	3,800	1.500	1.125	10.0
	1985–90	48,700	1.125	n.a.	14.0	—	—	—	—
Nigeria	1983[d]	1,351	1.500	1.375	3.0	—	—	—	—
	1984[d]	3,584	1.000	—	6.0	—	—	—	—
Peru	1983[e]	380	2.250	2.000	8.0	450	2.250	2.000	8.0
	1984[f]	1,555	1.750	1.500	9.0	—	—	—	—
Philippines	1983–86	5,770[g]	1.625	—	10.0	925	1.750	1.375	10.0
Venezuela	1983–88	20,750	1.125	n.a.	12.5	—	—	—	—

Notes to Table 2-4.

n.a. Not applicable.

a. Excludes agreements for the maintenance of trade credits and interbank lines.

b. Most of the 1983 rescheduling was unsigned, and drawings on that new loan were suspended. The 1982–85 agreement superseded many earlier agreements.

c. Backed by Argentinian deposits at the Federal Reserve Bank of New York. This actually consists of two loans; originally granted for three months, the first loan was eventually extended an extra forty-five days.

d. Rescheduling of short-term trade debt and letters-of-credit arrears.

e. Covers debt falling due until March 1984.

f. Covers debt falling due from March 1984 to July 1985.

g. Includes some private sector debts.

tries wanted the extra financing available after an adjustment program is approved, but were unwilling to bear the domestic political turmoil that might result from implementing such programs. Even so the Filipino and Argentinian packages required the implementation of certain policy changes and the construction and signing of financing packages from banks and official creditors before the programs were submitted to the approval of the IMF Board.

THE EFFICACY OF CURRENT PRACTICES

Many have questioned whether growth in the industrial countries combined with austerity programs in developing countries is sufficient to restore creditworthiness and growth in the debtor countries. Also much debated is the fairness and the appropriateness of austerity programs, usually as another manifestation of the debate on the appropriate degree of IMF conditionality. While it is theoretically possible that structural features prevent adjustment in developing countries, such an argument is not supported by the evidence. Accelerating money growth and appreciation of domestic currencies reflect conscious policy decisions that were common to developing countries that experienced debt problems. Moreover, the adjustment programs implemented by individual countries have usually included plans to reduce budget and current-account deficits as a share of GDP, to reduce inflation by slowing the rate of credit growth, and to devalue currencies. They were responding to large deficits, overvalued exchange rates, accelerating inflation, and sharply reduced availability of financing for current account deficits in developing countries.

Extreme compression of imports, however, may be a risk to recovery in individual countries and, if pursued simultaneously throughout the Third World, a threat to sustained global recovery. But IMF programs have focused more on current-account deficits than on imports, so the real blame must be placed on factors that are largely outside the control of the Fund: inadequate export promotion in the adjusting countries, external factors determining export volumes and prices, or the availability of new money.[6]

ECONOMIC PROSPECTS IN BRAZIL
AND MEXICO

Whether banks, the governments of creditor countries, or developing countries must make further changes is the more important question. Cline (1983: 121–22; 1984: 168) has been unabashedly optimistic, although his expectation that "it may not be until 1985 that Mexico and Argentina can return to normal borrowing from the capital market, or until 1986 for Brazil," has been revised slightly downward to a belief that "Mexico and Brazil could return to voluntary lending by perhaps 1986 or 1987. . . . For Argentina, however, . . . reconversion to voluntary lending may take longer." Enders and Mattione (1984: 51) are less sanguine, arguing that "the slow process of restoring growth and improving debt-servicing capabilities in Latin America will inevitably be fraught with difficulties." Finally, Dornbusch and Fischer (1984: 1) seem even more pessimistic, in their declaration that "the initial characterization of the debt problem as a liquidity problem, not a solvency problem, is becoming doubtful." Considerable disagreement remains, and some have even suggested that the current process of muddling through will have to be replaced by write-downs or interest rate caps (see, for example, Dornbusch and Fischer 1984: 48–53 and Fishlow 1984: 25–27).

Consider Mexico and Brazil, which together account for 34 percent of all developing countries' bank debt and about 24 percent of all developing countries' debt. If significant concessions are necessary to solve their problems, other debtors are likely to demand similar treatment. On the other hand, restoring creditworthiness and growth in Brazil and Mexico may make it possible to grant needed concessions to smaller debtors on a case-by-case basis without jeopardizing the international financial system.

Three scenarios will be examined for the 1984–88 period: a base case characterized by sustained growth and high interest rates in the industrial countries; a low case, driven by a runup in interest rates and consequent "growth recession" in industrial countries; and a high case conditioned on a stronger recovery with lower interest rates than in the base case. The assumptions are described in Table 2–5. All cases assume that Western recovery leads to some improvement in the nonoil terms of trade, and that dollar export and import prices

Table 2-5. External Conditions for Simulations (*Percent per Year Unless Otherwise Specified*).

Item	1984 (All Scenarios)	Average 1985–88 Value		
		Base	Low	High
Industrial countries' GNP growth	4.7	2.68	1.93	2.93
Dollar oil prices[a]	29.3	28.95	26.55	28.95
OECD inflation, in dollar terms	4.0	5.00	5.00	5.00
Interest rates[b]	13.0	10.68	11.50	10.08
Improvement in nonoil terms of trade[c]	2.0	1.50	1.25	1.50
Increase in dollar prices from dollar depreciation	0.0	1.50	1.50[d]	1.50

a. This is the predicted level of the dollar price of Saudi Arabian crude oil. Changes in oil revenues or expenditures are indexed to changes in this variable.

b. Including margin over LIBOR.

c. Ratio of dollar export price to dollar import prices in nonoil merchandise trade.

d. This part of the low scenario differs from others only in that the depreciation is assumed to be delayed; the value of the dollar against industrial country currencies at the end of 1988 is assumed to be the same in all three scenarios.

receive a boost from an expected depreciation of the dollar with respect to other industrial country currencies.

The Mexican simulations allow very little change in oil export volumes, while assuming that nonoil exports respond to continuing Western recovery and that the import-GDP ratio gradually rises toward the 1982 level. The Brazilian simulations assume a continued expansion in domestic oil production, which allows petroleum imports to fall in 1984 and grow slowly thereafter, while nonoil import volumes are assumed to move closer to trends prevailing before 1983. Exports, which were already above trend in 1983, increase sharply in 1984 before growth slows down in 1985 and 1986.

The base case is at least moderately optimistic (Table 2-6). Mexico's 1988 GDP could be 20.4 percent higher than in 1983 despite a drop in real oil prices. However, per capita GDP in 1988 would be about 4 percent below the 1981 level. Although gross debt increases

Table 2-6. Projected Economic Performance in Brazil and Mexico, 1984–88 ($ Billions Unless Otherwise Specified).

Country and Scenario	Average Annual Growth, 1984–88 (%)	Debt		Current-Account Balance		Debt/Export Ratio[a] (%)	
		1983	1988	1984	1985–88 Average	1983	1988
Brazil							
Base case	4.3	93.6	103.6	-0.82	-0.48	396	243
Low	3.3	93.6	109.4	-0.82	-1.92	396	268
High	4.9	93.6	101.9	-0.82	-0.06	396	233
Mexico							
Base case	3.7	90.7	105.9	3.71	-0.70	333	288
Low	2.1	90.7	111.8	3.71	-2.18	333	328
High	4.2	90.7	104.1	3.71	-0.28	333	280

a. Debt at the end of the year as a share of merchandise and noninterest services exports.

Source: Author's calculations.

from $90.7 billion to $105.9 billion during this period, the debt/export ratio falls from 333 percent to 288 percent. The need to build up additional reserves and to cover continuing capital flight accounts for the discrepancy between current-account deficits and net debt financing needs. Nonetheless, those needs would be modest from 1985 to 1988, lending support to bankers' hopes that Mexico could tap the credit markets for new loans.

The base case conditions would also allow Brazil's GDP in 1988 to be 23.4 percent higher than in 1983. While impressive, this growth would just restore per capita GDP to the level of 1980, before Brazil's recession began. Debt would continue to grow, from $93.6 billion in 1983 to $103.6 billion in 1988. Export growth, however, would be strong enough to reduce the debt/export ratio from 396 percent in 1983 to 243 percent in 1988. Debt would increase very slowly after 1984. The improvement might be sufficient to make the necessary financing available from the market.

A mild Western recession triggered by rising interest rates would slow progress considerably. Brazil's growth would average only 3.5 percent per year from 1985 to 1988, debt would reach $109.4 billion in 1988, and the debt/export ratio would only fall to 268 percent. The adverse effects in Brazil would be even stronger were it not for the assumption that a renewed recession would also lower oil prices, which ameliorates some of the shortfall in export revenues. On the other hand, lower oil prices would harm Mexico. Its average growth would be only 2.1 percent during the 1985–88 period, debt would reach $111.8 billion at the end of 1988, and the debt/export ratio would fall only to 328 percent. Per capita GDP would fall slightly from 1983 to 1988. Average debt financing needs would exceed $4.5 billion per year.

On the other hand, a more favorable recovery in the industrial countries could ease the pressures even further. An easing of interest rates with slightly higher growth for the industrial countries could yield 4.2 percent growth in Mexico on average from 1984 to 1988, a debt of $104.1 billion at the end of the period, and a ratio of debt to merchandise exports of 280 percent. Debt financing needs would be around $3 billion each year. Such conditions would help Brazil even more, yielding average annual growth of 4.9 percent from 1984 to 1988, debt of $101.9 billion in 1988, and debt/export ratio of 233 percent. It would also raise per capita GDP above the 1980 level.

The implications of these calculations are that a sustained OECD recovery, if supported by continuing adjustment policies in debtor nations, can be enough to rescue both Brazil and Mexico from their debt problems. It will probably be the end of the decade, however, before their growth problems are adequately solved. A more favorable OECD recovery could restore Mexico's and Brazil's access to the credit markets, which would, in turn, help to sustain future growth. On the other hand, a recession could make it difficult to sustain the current strategy for solving Mexico's and Brazil's debt problems. First, it might be difficult to find lenders for the additional funds relative to the base case. Second, the domestic political situations in Brazil and Mexico might deteriorate if per capita incomes in 1988 are still below their previous peaks.

Several factors not explicitly modeled here are important. First, while constant real exchange rates were assumed in the foregoing analysis, it is clear that exchange-rate policies can play a large role in achieving external and internal balance. The overvalued exchange rates of 1980 to 1982 were an important cause of the crisis in many Latin American nations, especially Mexico. Similarly, Enders and Mattione (1984: 34–38) demonstrated that a policy of export-led growth fueled by further small devaluations could strengthen domestic recovery, by easing the foreign exchange constraint facing borrowers. And one study recently warned that Mexico was already allowing a gradual revaluation of the peso which could harm its future performance (see Morgan Guaranty Trust 1984a: 7).

The second factor is the market's perception of creditworthiness and, in particular, the effect of repayment schedules on that perception. The original rescheduling for Mexico's public sector resulted in principal repayments of approximately $23 billion in equal installments from 1987 to 1990, in addition to some $20 billion of principal payments that had not yet been rescheduled but would come due by 1990. Even under the favorable conditions of the base case, these heavy repayments could compromise Mexico's growth prospects if smaller banks should try to bail out. A recession, by simultaneously increasing Mexico's new funding needs and damaging perceptions of its prospects, could have severe repercussions. Similar arguments hold true for Brazil.

The appropriate response to this potential difficulty is to reduce the pressures on Brazil or Mexico (or other borrowers) in the late

1980s. The recent Mexican rescheduling would help attain this goal, because it would repackage most principal payments due by 1990 into a new loan with most amortization payments due between 1991 and 1998. This could well make it easier to meet new financing needs in all scenarios by reducing the threat of a pullout by some banks. A similar financing would be helpful for Brazil, although its financing requirements may be somewhat higher than Mexico's during the rest of this decade.

Finally, if interest rates rise, for whatever reason, the clamor for interest rate caps may resume. Many sorts of caps have been proposed, but the basic purpose is to roll up any payments above a certain level into a new loan due in several years time. Some plans also forgive part of these "excess" payments, either explicitly or by applying a lower interest rate to postponed amounts.

The need for such caps could be significantly reduced by multi-year reschedulings with long maturities, which sharply lower gross financing needs for the rest of this decade. By reducing the threat that banks might bail out of reschedulings, this could ease the task of raising extra funds necessitated by any increase in the interest rate. Nevertheless it is important to realize that, should rate increases simultaneously induce a recession and thereby depress export revenues, caps alone would not cover the whole effect of the increases on the current account and on net financing needs. Automating one part of the response to external shocks would help, but alone it could be insufficient. On the other hand, it is conceivable that interest rates rise because of a stronger than expected recovery, in which case the beneficial effects of increased economic activity may outweigh the deterioration due to rising interest rates. Finally, given the reluctance of accountants and regulators to treat rescheduled loans with interest rate caps as normal loans, it is probably not worth trying to implement such schemes.

PROSPECTS FOR THE FUTURE

The future looks much more promising in 1985 than it did just three years before. It now appears that problems with bank loans have been confined largely to Latin America and to several small debtors elsewhere. A combination of improved external conditions and domestic adjustment policies have generated sharp improvements in the external accounts in Brazil, Mexico, and Venezuela. At the same time, banks have been forced to lower interest rate spreads and to lengthen the maturities available on rescheduled loans. It is possible to declare victory for the strategy of offering better terms to better behaved borrowers, but banks have extended favorable terms to Venezuela and Argentina more because of the borrowers' leverage than because of their good performance in the past few years.

It is too early to declare the debt crisis solved. If recovery in the industrial countries continues at fairly high levels, if the good export performance of Brazil and Mexico can be sustained, if high growth can indeed coexist with the current low levels of the ratio between real imports and real GDP, if interest rates do not go too high, and if borrowers pursue appropriate domestic policies, then Brazil and Mexico could restore growth while keeping their financing needs low. Per capita incomes could be restored to precrisis levels by 1988 or 1989 and continue growing, and banks would probably be willing to fund the modest net financing needs of Brazil and Mexico.

There are many conditions on that statement. A sharp slowdown in the industrial countries is perhaps most worrisome. That would bring the growth crisis to the fore, while simultaneously reducing the apparent creditworthiness of these borrowers. But the borrowers' domestic policies also remain deficient; in particular, several major borrowers have yet to solve the problem of inflation. Continuing high rates of inflation could lead to problems in exchange-rate and budget policies. Yet it is also unclear whether debtor countries can attain high growth rates over the next several years while simultaneously attacking inflation. Moreover, many smaller borrowers have found it hard to adjust either external accounts or internal policies, although problems for those borrowers are less likely to pose a threat to the financial system if Mexico and Brazil are not adversely affected.

It will be many years, probably decades, before it will be possible to write the definitive history of the debt crisis of the 1980s, its resolution, and its consequences. Considerable progress has been made, but the remaining tasks will not be easy.

APPENDIX 2A: CALCULATION METHODS

Calculations in this study are based on methods developed by Balassa (1981), as adapted by Enders and Mattione (1984), for analyzing the impact of external conditions on developing countries. The years 1976–78 serve as the base period in calculating the magnitude of external shocks received from 1979 to 1983. However, only shocks from 1979 to 1982 are reported in the tables. Four categories of shocks are calculated for each country.

The terms-of-trade shock is calculated in two parts, one due to export price shifts, the other to import price shifts. The shock due to export price shifts (XS), measured in current dollars, is

$$XS_t = (P_t^X - PB_t^X) \times XVOL_t \quad ,$$

where P^X denotes actual export prices, PB^X denotes export prices corrected for inflation, and $XVOL$ denotes actual export volumes, all in year t. Similarly, the shock due to import price shifts (MS) is

$$MS_t = (PB_t^M - P_t^M) \times MVOL_t \quad ,$$

where PB^M and P^M denote inflation-corrected and actual export prices, respectively, and $MVOL$ denotes actual import volumes. The total terms-of-trade shock (TOT) is

$$TOT_t = XS_t + MS_t \quad .$$

A positive value denotes a favorable shock, a negative value an unfavorable shock. These calculations treat current trade volumes as if they were chosen independent of prices prevailing in world markets. This estimate of the ex ante shock, however, is affected either if a country adjusted to unfavorable shocks by reducing imports or if it followed expansive policies that encouraged imports.

The effects of variations in Western demand on nonoil exports are also calculated. This demand shock (DEM) is calculated as

$$DEM_t = XVOLB \times PB_t^X \times (GR_t - GRB_t) \quad ,$$

where $XVOLB$ is the export volume in the base period, and GR and GRB denote cumulative actual growth and extrapolated cumulative growth, respectively. Extrapolated cumulative growth is based on growth rates for world trade volumes in the 1976–78 period.

The shock from high real interest rates (INT) is

$$\text{INT}_t = (RR_B - RR_t) \times \text{DEBT}_{t-1} \quad ,$$

where RR_B and RR_t are real interest rates in the base period and current year, respectively, and DEBT_{t-1} is the relevant debt variable at the end of the previous year.

Several specific assumptions were made to facilitate calculation. Real interest rates were defined as the differential between Eurodollar rates and dollar inflation and thus do not correct for changes in interest rate spreads. Only gross bank debt was used to calculate interest rate shocks; bank debt accounts for most of the debt, and most of the floating-interest-rate debt, of the particular countries analyzed. No import price data were available for Nigeria, so the terms-of-trade shock reflects only export price movements. Finally, import and export price data were unavailable in 1983 for some countries. In those cases the 1983 calculations alluded to in the text used price gaps based on 1982 data.

For compatibility with earlier calculations the current-account balance is divided into two parts. One consists of net interest payments and net earnings on foreign direct investment; the other is the nonfinancial current balance. This can be written as

$$CA = NCB - NI \quad ,$$

where CA is the current account balance, NI represents net payments on capital, and NCB includes all other current-account transactions. Normal values for these variables, labeled NCB_B and NI_B, can be constructed from the 1976–78 data. The normal position of noninterest payments in future years is then

$$NCB_t^N = NCB_B \times PI_t \quad ,$$

where PI_t is a price index set equal to 1.0 in the base period. The normal position for the net interest portion is defined as

$$NI_t^N = NI_B \times (\Delta PI_t + RR_B)/R_B \quad ,$$

where ΔPI_t is the inflation rate in year t, and RR_B and R_B are the real and nominal interest rates in the base period. Thus NI_t^N gives the position that would have resulted if nominal rates increased only as much as inflation. The normal current account position is thus

$$CA_t^N = NI_t^N + NCB_t^N \, ,$$

and the deterioration CAD is

$$CAD_t = CA_t - CA_t^N \, .$$

A positive number implies that the current-account position deteriorated less (or improved more) than expected after adjusting for inflation only. And, for example, if deterioration exceeds the amount of unfavorable shocks, then the country has amplified the effect of unfavorable external shocks.

NOTES TO CHAPTER 2

1. All these calculations use external conditions in the 1976–78 period as the basis for comparisons.
2. These calculations do not correct for the rise in interest rate spreads that occurred in 1982 and 1983; see Appendix 2A for details. Of course, high real interest rates contributed to the global recession, which reduced trade volumes and commodity prices. The combination of direct and indirect effects from high real interest rates might indeed be the largest factor adversely affecting developing countries.
3. Based on national accounts date available in IMF (1984).
4. Based on data for the narrow money stock and the consumer price index available in IMF (1984).
5. See Chapter 11, by Darity, for a discussion of models that could explain why banks were so enthusiastic about foreign lending.
6. This argument constitutes the central thesis of Margaret de Vries's chapter.

3 FUTURE CAPITAL FLOWS
Critical Improvements and the Role of Coordination

Barend A. de Vries

This chapter looks beyond the acute situation of 1982–83 and its immediate aftermath. It identifies critical improvements in future international financial practices needed to make finance compatible with development objectives without the costly interruptions of the last few years. After drawing some lessons from recent experience in the behavior of debtor nations and creditors, it clarifies the distinction between financial adjustment (or stabilization) and structural adjustment. Finally the chapter reviews the essential role of effective coordination among the various sources of capital.

SOME OBSERVATIONS ON THE 1982 DEBT CRISIS AND ITS AFTERMATH

The external causes of the debt crisis and the domestic measures taken so far have been costly in terms of foregone output. The total loss in output is equivalent to half or more of the external debt itself.[1] In part the loss can be traced to the slowdown in world trade and in the industrial economies. But delay in essential domestic structural reforms also took a large toll.

The author acknowledges useful comments received from E. M. Bernstein, Margaret G. de Vries, Richard Goode, and Guy Pfefferman.

Obviously it is to the interest of both the developing countries and the international lenders that capital should flow in the future without the interruptions in debt service and the upheaval experienced in recent years. There are several crucial elements that will help the international system of capital flows function more smoothly.

The behavior of the international commercial banks and their smaller regional and local counterparts is key. They will play a critical, if not dominant, role in any future system. Therefore it is essential that they correct the flaws exhibited in their past operations. For example, the large supply and easy conditions of project credits (including credits from export finance agencies) also obstructed essential decisionmaking in key industries and frustrated or induced postponement of essential measures to restore financial balance in the debtor economies.[2] Since substantial capital inflows tend to cause appreciation of the exchange rate and increases in real wages as well as to oppose in other ways changes in the level and structure of output and trade, it is especially important that in the future private banks collaborate with government banking officials to foster essential policy change (Harberger 1983).

Even in the narrow sense of particular projects, the banks did not apply internal measures to assure that their loans were well used. They appeared either unwilling to or uninterested in stopping loans that could not benefit their client countries' economies (as in Argentina, Chile, and Mexico, where a significant proportion of loans financed capital flight or "unrecorded" imports such as military equipment).[3]

Since the mid-1970s bank financing has been erratic. From the viewpoint of the developing countries as a whole, official credits, bilateral and multilateral, increased consistently from 1978 to 1982, and export credits grew in a sustained manner from 1973 to 1982. Bank credits were also a major factor in increasing resource flows, but they were subject to abrupt changes, and their increase was partly offset by a relative decline in private direct investment (OECD 1983).

Related to bank behavior is the fact that wide differences in developing countries' economic policies explain much of their ability to weather external shocks without interrupting debt service. Wide differences in their client countries' policies and situations provide the basis for the country-by-country approach to the debt problem adopted by the private banks and official lending institutions.

Countries that suffered debt servicing difficulties followed policies leading to appreciation in the real exchange rate, high debt in relation to exports, high inflation, excessive public sector deficits and overextended state enterprises, widespread price controls or subsidization or both, and often chaotic domestic credit markets. Their policies frustrated, indeed discouraged, coordination of external credits and the channeling of capital to investments with high economic yields. Argentina, Brazil, Chile, Mexico, the Philippines, and Peru, among others, are in this group. The domestic factors at the root of these countries' excessive external debt differ considerably, however. Argentina suffered from a lack of domestic confidence and gross overvaluation of the local currency (which caused most of the borrowed funds to be used for investment abroad). Excessively rapid buildup of public expenditures and extensive subsidization of consumption contributed to Mexico's problems. An uncontrolled budget situation in the Philippines combined with lack of confidence in President Marcos spawned excessive external borrowing. On the other hand Brazil, with one of the worst energy problems in the world, sought to restructure its economy through several public investment projects, often capital-extensive projects (with a slow payoff and often on too short financing terms). Its situation was aggravated by the manufacturing sector's inward orientation, large-scale subsidization of agriculture, and extreme credit scarcity for private industry; economic management has proven to be difficult in a highly inflationary environment. Yet Brazil enjoys a deep-seated self-confidence, has successfully controlled capital flight, and is able to manage social change while also undergoing significant political evolution.[4]

The future of international capital flows has been made brighter by the progress that some of the large debtor countries have made, more progress than many thought was possible in 1982 or early 1983. Mexico has succeeded in improving its financial position to the point that the banks were willing to restructure debt obligations falling due in 1985–91. Brazil likewise has made rapid progress; it has achieved a larger than expected trade surplus in an export-led strategy, and is once again experiencing some growth in gross domestic product. The resumption of new (voluntary) lending to Mexico and Brazil seems to require that they have a balance-of-payments surplus large enough to meet their debt obligations, especially interest payments, and that they reestablish an environment of growth and confidence in which investment projects offer attractive yields.

Nevertheless, many difficulties remain. Several debtor countries still have some way to go in financial adjustment and in meeting outstanding obligations (among these are Argentina, Chile, Costa Rica, and Peru). It is essential that their exchange rates be brought or kept in line with relative inflation, that price incentives be rationalized and controls be removed. This is particularly true in Mexico, where progress in financial adjustment must still be followed up by structural reform and resumption of a comprehensive growth strategy.

The private sector (particularly small and medium industry) has been badly affected by the high real interest rates (some as high as 40 percent) in the "free" segments of the domestic credit markets and the accumulation of dollar-denominated debt obligations. Formulation of a recovery program for the private sector awaits a fuller assessment of the damage suffered so far. Consideration of multi-year restructuring of debt obligations has *not* been accompanied by meaningful preparation for medium term restructuring of the domestic economy, especially in key manufacturing industries and infrastructure.

Little has been written about the social effects of the financial adjustment in 1982–84. One might guess that the recession has aggravated the problems of income distribution and hindered prospects for alleviation of poverty; that the middle class has suffered from the decline in real wages and salaries, particularly where food consumption is no longer subsidized and mortgage payments have become fully indexed (as in Brazil); and that the migration of rural labor to industrial regions has suffered from the severe slowdown in urban manufacturing centers. The increase of unemployment of Chile has been particularly marked.[5]

Considerable institutional innovation has taken place in the 1980s. The International Monetary Fund was able to increase its resources substantially and took the lead in organizing essential official and private financial support for adjustment programs. The commercial banks are working together reassessing prospects of debtor economies in joint economic working groups. They have launched the Institute of International Finance, which has begun to supply information and act as a forum for technical and policy discussions among bankers. And the World Bank and the regional development banks have adapted their lending operations to the recessionary conditions in debtor countries and the need for accelerating disbursements. The World Bank has taken new initiatives in expanding cofinancing with commercial banks.

Institutional change has, however, blurred the lines of responsibility among different sources of finance. The IMF has become more deeply involved in the medium-term programs, including debt restructuring; the programs it supports have longer term structural effects. The World Bank, in seeking to accelerate loan reimbursements, has left the impression in some quarters that it is engaged in balance-of-payments financing, even though its objective remains long-term structural reform and improvements in the real economy, including export and investment performance. The financing by commercial banks appears to be primarily for general balance-of-payments support (including debt restructuring), even though they have a keen interest in expending client services though trade and project finance.

DIFFERENT TYPES OF ADJUSTMENT

At present the most mentioned underlying financial objective of debt management is *adjustment.* But "adjustment," as one encounters it in the literature, is overused and too broad. Adoption of demand management policies aims at lowering temporarily excessive imports or government expenditures, a reduction that theoretically can be achieved in one or two years, but in practice may require five years or more (as was recognized in the IMF's extended financing facility, or EFF). At the other extreme, adjustment may mean a complex process of structural change affecting many countries and key sectors of their economies, involving many new sector-specific investments, and stretching over a decade or more. For example, in a 1984 paper Emminger includes in "adjustment" the postwar reconstruction of Europe and the associated changes in trade and payments patterns and arrangements, including the establishment of currency convertibility. He adds that this adjustment was not a candidate for temporary payments assistance, but instead for *long-term* "reconstruction" capital.[6] Another example is the Organization for Economic Cooperation and Development's concept of "positive adjustment," the pursuit of an industrial policy of upgrading of manufacturing industries toward more skill-intensive and capital-intensive production.

At present "structural adjustment" is most widely applied to the measures needed in less developed countries to address long-term shifts in external conditions, such as higher energy costs and the changes in the cost and availability of external credit. These measures include investment in new sources of energy, as well as conservation and industrial energy conversion, often with far-going changes in institutional finance and domestic pricing policy. Other measures, often included under World Bank "Structural Adjustment Loan" programs, include:

1. Keeping the exchange rate abreast of inflation
2. Liberalizing import regulations in line with the objectives of greater industrial efficiency
3. Helping export industries by further removing the biases against them in the incentive system and strengthening their ability to invest and modernize
4. Improving public sector management through economic evaluation of key investments, programming, macroeconomic modeling, and improving the data base; completing public sector projects with high economic returns, for example, in the steel and electric power industries.
5. Rationalizing domestic credit markets and strengthening the private industrial sector

But in many situations an export shortfall is not caused by a single temporary factor. It may be brought on by the wrong domestic pricing policies. Or the shortfall may signify a longer term weakening of the world market of a particular commodity such as copper or iron ore. Thus a very different situation presents itself when the external change is of long duration and requires structural domestic measures stretching over a period of years. In such a situation, short-term compensation, if not linked to more basic programs, may merely cover up and in fact obstruct necessary longer term structural action such as export diversification and long-term cost reduction through modernization. It is often difficult to distinguish among different external causes, and indeed *both* short- and long-term action may be called for. In many situations improvements in the balance of payments must first be brought about by a reversal in expansionary domestic policies. But such a reversal should often be bolstered, and indeed be made politically sustainable, by longer term development measures. In fact, the demand management measures lay the groundwork for longer term action and capital assistance. It is the latter, capital assistance, that may be the most essential ingredient for the long term, for it enables growth.

To sum up, in addressing various situations, it may be useful to distinguish among several types of external finance programs.

In *financial adjustment* programs that are supported by the IMF and private lenders for three to five years the underlying policies aim at restoring domestic and external balance, primarily through demand management policies, including reduction in public expenditures, increases in revenue and savings, and cuts in private credit. Balance-of-payments measures include, besides import reductions, changes in the exchange rate which eventually make possible relaxation of import restructions. The accompanying pricing measures can have deep structural implications in the long run.

The restructuring of debt, now underway, is correctly supported by financial adjustment. Most of the loans being restructured were originally made for balance-of-payments purposes and were not tied to investment. Their terms, however, were not attuned to actual or foreseeable external developments and changing them is now unavoidable. To the extent that the debtor countries had overexpanded their domestic expenditures, stiff demand management (financial adjustment) is clearly needed.

Structural adjustment finance addresses the changes in the domestic economy needed to cope with the longer term external shifts in prices and demand and supply conditions. Structural adjustment finance supports longer term policy incentives and institutional change as well as new investments in key sectors essential to the structural effort. To be effective, these loans must be an integral part of a longer term program of both sector and project finance and reform supported by official and private sources.

Long-term development finance is the range of external finance needed for the development of the economies of bc_h low-income and middle-income countries. The terms for this finance are essentially long but also depend on the present social conditions and prospects of the borrowing country.

Confusion about the nature of finance has arisen mostly in the case of structural adjustment. It may initially have to be accompanied by financial adjustment programs and requires the assistance of many different providers of external finance and capital. But it must be focused on longer term restructuring of the economy.

TOWARD MORE SATISFACTORY PROVISION OF LONG-TERM CAPITAL

A clearer vision of the future will help in dealing with the problems presently besetting the debtor countries and their creditors.[7] Capital flows must be adequate and steady, and must be compatible with growth and development, without suffering from the major interruptions currently experienced at considerable cost in loss of confidence and output. Finance and capital must be provided for clearly defined purposes. Terms of repayment should be geared to the objectives of the financing.

Market mechanisms should play a full role in achieving these objectives. Thus private bank credit and private direct investment must be given full play, supported and supplemented by official institutions. The recipient countries must undertake programs compatible with their own economic and political realities, thus subordinating any standardized approach imposed by outside agencies. National programs must provide the basis for essential coordination among various sources of capital. Finally, it must be realized that long-term capital will be scarce and will seek worldwide applications with highest returns.

Requirements of a Functional System

A variety of financial instruments (or programs) designed to meet specific objectives are required. The terms of these instruments should match their objectives. Thus balance-of-payments finance must allow for likely adversity in export earnings or the terms of trade, either by building in or permitting adjustment in the original terms, or by relying on compensatory finance (official or private). Longer term restructuring must be provided on terms suitable to the projects or programs or the restructuring effort as well as the country's basic conditions and prospects. It is of critical importance that poor and slow-growing countries receive loans with interest rates at or below their low critical interest rate.[8]

Recipient countries must play a key role in pursuing adequate policies and thereby providing a basis for international coordination. Bilateral deals between the recipient country and a single provider of capital can easily prevent the functioning of market forces, especially when conditions return to normal and credit is more amply available. Coordination must be made possible by both financial and structural adjustment in the recipient country, including rational incentive policies. Realistic medium-term development (investment) plans should be prepared. These should encourage private investment and industry (or, in the case of socialist countries, participation by private foreign investment and an increased role for decentralized small and medium industries).

Private banks should be positioned so that they can even out their lending over time, clarify their objectives, and align their operations with those of the official agencies. Their balance-of-payments finance should, as a matter of normal policy, be provided in the context of financial adjustment. Bank support for structural adjustment or development projects should preferably be made parallel or in cofinancing with the World Bank. In either case the banks should exercise more effective control over the use of their funds, for example by avoiding overuse of any one instrument (as happened with short-term finance in Brazil in 1981), by limiting the extent of balance of payments finance, by matching their terms with their objectives, and by working in coordination. Private direct investment must be in line with the debtor country's policies and plans, in particular with policies regarding foreign participation in the economy and investment objectives of specific industries.

Analysis made available by the World Bank and the IMF in the context of coordination would help in setting a proper analytic framework for lending and investment decisions. This will help the banks and the companies gear their operations more explicitly to the development requirements of the recipient country. Coordination would be particularly important were the commercial banks to contract their future operations relative to other sources, as is expected by some observers. Coordination may also help banks anticipate shocks and overcome their present myopic excessive caution. The banks would, of course retain full responsibility for their own lending decisions (see Carli and Savona 1985; Aliber 1985; Guttentag and Herring 1985).

The Fund must continue to take the lead in assisting countries in the design of financial adjustment. Its financial adjustment conditions also have implications for structural adjustment and should be coordinated with the World Bank. The World Bank and the regional development banks are better equipped to assist in the design and financing of restructuring programs.

The World Bank and the regional banks should continue to provide finance for structural adjustment, restructuring, and development. They must also continue to adjust their own operations to permit the private sector to provide finance where it is available on satisfactory terms, and indeed broaden and deepen their cooperation with the private sector. Among various institutions, the World Bank is best equipped to assist countries in coordination among principal sources of long-term finance.

A better functioning of the international capital system will also benefit from new or improved instruments. Instruments are needed to permit banks to continue lending in the face of adverse international developments, while still exercising due caution. A scheme for guaranteeing bank portfolios financed by the banks themselves with help from agencies that already have guarantee authority may be helpful (Wallich 1984). In addition some regulation of the international operations of banks may be in the interest of a more stable international system.[9] Also helpful would be new financial instruments that permit banks to adjust their lending terms, for example to lower repayment obligations when export earnings are down. It may also be useful to consider establishing a secondary market for bank loans, assuming it will be possible to find a way of stabilizing such a market (Guttentag and Herring 1984).[10]

In the event of continued relatively high real interest rates, some way must be found to compensate debtors for high market rates in selected cases. Indeed, should high interest rates prevail, many countries will have no alternative but to curtail their borrowing drastically or simply apply an acceptable form of default. High interest rates may present a more difficult problem than export price fluctuations in that when high interest cost is capitalized into excessive debt, eventual debt cancelation may be the only way out. Hence, capping of interest payments is unsatisfactory when it is applied to a large portion of the debt of countries whose critical interest rate is well below the market. It would be more satisfactory to subsidize interest on market loans. Various other forms of subsidization are possible (for example, using some of the World Bank's profits to subsidize part of its own operations, as it does now in effect by contributing to the IDA, the International Development Association). Relief may be obtained through an IMF interest rate compensation facility. In view of the cost, any scheme would have to be limited in scope and application and would have to be applied on the basis of country-by-country consideration.[11]

ESSENTIAL COORDINATION

Effective coordination among the many different sources of external finance and capital has become even more essential than it was in the 1960s and 1970s. It can be an indispensable tool in assuring that funds are provided for well-defined purposes, in amounts and on terms that are indicated by a country's present and prospective situation. In the present debt situation the amount and terms of debt proved critical in causing or avoiding costly interruption in debt servicing.

Suitable coordination can provide a basis for increased (voluntary) lending even in circumstances of scarcity and caution. But it may be even more difficult to achieve than in the past. The various debtor nations' economies, their investment programs, policy issues, and financing requirements, have become more complex. There are many more projects, sectors, and objectives to be considered. The temptation is great to proceed piecemeal, and indeed there are genuine limits to formal coordination. Moreover, the role of private banks has increased greatly and they, of course, have been accustomed to proceed on their own, providing finance for many different purposes with a minimum of countrywide conditions.

Formal aid coordination first began around 1960, with the India consortium chaired by the World Bank (1958). It was soon followed by a similar arrangement for Pakistan, and the Consultive Group for Colombia (1963). In 1981 the World Bank chaired some twenty active country groups and one for the Caribbean countries. Others included the aid groups for Indonesia and Turkey, one for Central

America chaired by the Inter–American Development Bank, and twenty-one groups, mostly for smaller countries, sponsored by the United Nations Development Project UNDP (OECD 1982b).

Essentially these groups have provided coordination of the activities of multilateral agencies and development banks and donor governments. Private banks have not as a rule participated in them. The groups continued to function in the 1970s as the private banks rapidly expanded their operations. Recipient countries either sought to limit the groups to long-term development issues and finance (as in India), or they increasingly conducted separate sessions with private banks parallel with or following the formal group meetings with official agencies (as in Colombia and Korea). As bilateral aid agencies become less important in the middle-income countries, these arrangements lose their role as a means of coordinating official finance. They can be either converted to coordination instruments with private banks or be terminated (Korea held its final meeting in 1984).

Aid coordination groups have addressed themselves to debtor countries' policy issues and prospects and to the financing of investment programs and projects. Both financial and structural adjustment are considered, with reports by the Fund and the World Bank on the agenda. At present the agenda for review of a medium-term growth strategy is substantive and timely. In both large and small countries, a cooperative approach is in the interest of all concerned: borrowers, lenders, investors, and the international financial system as a whole. In present circumstances it is of special importance that private banks participate fully. In this connection the Institute of International Finance could play a useful role. Authorities of the creditor countries (including regulatory agencies) should encourage banks to participate and generally play a positive role. Strategies for debt repayment need to focus on both financial and structural adjustment. Such an arrangement should be helpful in furthering cofinancing or parallel financing between the development banks and investing companies and should help the development banks make a greater commitment to coordinate their options with each other.

A final word on the "conditions" that must necessarily accompany coordination. In the recent past, recipient governments were often faced with competing aid agencies and official and private banks, and of course, were tempted to accept those loans that had the fewest strings attached (or, the least "conditionality"). To a large extent the present international debt situation has arisen from excessive competition under conditions of ample liquidity. It is likely that this situation has changed, but no one knows for how long.

Conditionality works best when key provisions are already in effect before the loan is signed. It is an art to seek out those sectors and countries which in this sense come closest to fulfilling acceptable policy conditions. Clearly this situation seldom exists when the IMF standby arrangements are negotiated. IMF conditions have often appeared toughest, with country policies farthest from the norm when external finance is needed most. They have been subject to much criticism, in part because of a simple and rigid IMF mold that may be prone to austerity and in each case must be adapted to the circumstances of the country in question. Such adaptation may be possible in the case of large countries (with considerable clout themselves), but may leave much to be desired in the smaller countries. In practice the standardized mold may be the only one practical, since it must be applied quickly to many different situations and be subject to monitoring. Tough demand management may be needed regardless of whether or not the Fund is involved.

World Bank conditionality is far more inclusive and diverse and often more penetrating, reflecting years of painstaking preparation and collaboration with the borrower. Its conditions have been less publicized, and the term "conditionality" is seldom applied to World Bank operations. When applied to projects, it conforms to a philosophy of good housekeeping (engineering, management, project autonomy, and freedom from political intervention), based on sound business and economic practices and rational incentives and pricing. All of these are essential to good economic management. Indeed, for more than three decades the World Bank has been engaged in a comprehensive practice of what is now called supply-side economics. Project conditions are microeconomic, applied to a specific segment of the economy; although they may have a significant impact on an institution, community, or an industry, they seldom address directly a government's overall economic management. But in its program, sector, and structural adjustment loans, the World Bank also deals with economywide issues of resource use and management and thereby is able to complement the Fund's focus on resource balance.[12] In part because of the diversity of its operations the Bank can tailor its conditions to a country's social and economic idiosyncrasies. The Bank's flexibility has been enhanced by its interest in a growing lending level and a wide geographic dispersion.

The World Bank and the Fund must clearly provide the lead in setting the conditions under which finance or capital is provided. Most other financial institutions are less capable of working out economywide conditions. It is of interest to private banks that in their own lending they adopt the same stance as the World Bank and the Fund.

The recipient countries must be at the center of the coordination process. This includes the formulation and application of the conditions and policies as well as details of the arrangements (including where possible chairing the meetings). Unless they are fully involved, they will quickly regard the conditions as hamstringing their freedom and the whole operation as a ganging up by the creditors.

NOTES TO CHAPTER 3

1. For example, in Brazil the loss in output during the period 1981–85 from a growth trend of 5–6 percent is around 5 percent per year. The loss is equivalent to around one-fourth of Brazil's gross national product, which was $268 billion in 1981, or $68 billion. This is equivalent to *more* than two-thirds of a total debt of $93 billion (as estimated by American Express Bank 1984). In Brazil the external debt is about 4 percent of GNP; in countries with a higher debt to income ratio, as in Mexico, the loss in output would be a correspondingly smaller proportion of the debt.

2. The World Bank experienced serious difficulties in the implementation of "sector conditions" in its lending for steel and other heavy industry in Brazil in the mid–1970s.

3. Staff estimates from the International Bank for Reconstruction and Development (IBRD) compare the increase in total external debt during 1973–82 with the cumulative current-account deficits (net of changes in reserves and direct foreign investment) in 1974–82. The increase in debt accounts for only 18 percent of the deficit in Argentina and 58 percent in Chile, 37 percent in Mexico—against 96 percent in Brazil. In Mexico this percentage declined rapidly, suggesting increasing financing of capital flight, in 1978–82 (according to Solis Zedillo 1984). Partly responsible for this behavior, were competition and interest in balance sheet and earnings growth, factors that may again become prominent when conditions return to "normal."

4. Bela Balassa's (1983) analysis of adjustment highlights the importance of outward orientation.

5. Scholarly analysis of the social consequences of the 1982–84 policies is as yet scarce. Roberto Macedo (1983) deals with some aspects of changes in

the conditions of the poor. He concludes that there is no clear indication the crisis has brought serious additional problems since there was no substantial indicators of worsening of the conditions of children.

6. Emminger (1984) observes: "The first major payments adjustment in Europe came to a successful conclusion when in 1958 a number of European currencies were declared convertible and the E.P.U. was dissolved as being no longer necessary." The rationale of the OECD so-called positive adjustment is explained in E. Van Lennep's statement at UNIDO IV (quoted in *B.I.S. Press Review*, August 15, 1984).

7. This observation is inspired by Cooper's remarks in his 1984 paper on an international monetary system based on a single currency some forty years hence.

8. The concept of the critical interest rate was first treated in depth by the staff of the World Bank (see Avramovic et al. 1964). It varies for different countries roughly in line with output and export growth that can be sustained over a period of years. If the interest rate actually paid exceeds a country's critical level for long and for a significant portion of the debt, the debt will accumulate out of all economic proportion and normal servicing must eventually break down. See B.A. de Vries 1984.

9. Witteveen (1983) has recommended solvency criteria (maximum ratios of categories of loans to bank capital) to international loans, which thus far have been free from regulation, and making international bank (Euro-currency) deposits subject to reserve requirements.

10. The terms of lending can be adapted to balance-of-payments fluctuations in many ways (both interest and amortization can be linked to various price or volume indexes). These links are, however, still experimental. Different types of adaptations are listed in Lessard (1983).

11. Horowitz proposed that developing countries receive loans, which are raised on the market (for example, by the IBRD) but made available at low interest rates, with the subsidization provided by governments through annual appropriations (to IDA, for example). The cost of interest rate compensation varies widely with the extent of coverage and the increase in interest rates. Cline and I have each presented calculations varying from $200 million to $7.6 billion per year. See Cline 1984: 187, B.A. de Vries 1984: 43.

12. U. Sacchetti (1983) argues that the Fund should pay more attention to resources use in its conditions.

▌▌ THE DEBT CRISIS AND U.S. ECONOMIC POLICY

Part II of this book is, in many respects, a recital of "how things really were, are, and will be" in the United States because of the debt crisis. Frank Morris provides a frank evaluation of the crisis from the perspective of the Federal Reserve System. His thesis is that the crisis is a natural outgrowth of the second stage of the disinflation process begun late in the 1970s and early 1980s. That is, the crisis was a one-time phenomenon, one that would not have occurred if the economic conditions of the 1970s had persisted. While the crisis did fray nerves and test our institutions, it proved to be manageable and to leave few if any lasting adverse effects.

Robert Jones agrees implicitly that the recent business cycle with which the debt crisis has been associated is unique. But his thesis is that the debt crisis has altered the money and credit management practices of the Federal Reserve in a way that will have a continuing influence on U.S. monetary policy. On the positive side, he argues that the threat of defaults by debtor countries, together with their related domestic banking problems, has restrained the Federal Reserve from following the procyclical policies of the past, and from subjecting the economy to record-high real interest rate levels as part of the disinflation process. However, he is concerned by actual Federal Reserve policy responses to the crisis, that Federal Reserve officials have become so concerned about the consequences of a debt

79

crisis that they are likely to pursue extreme measures in order to avoid a second crisis this decade.

Leonard Santow's view from Wall Street is not terribly reassuring. He foresees the chances of sustaining a U.S. recovery beyond 1987 as not good. If the United States does reach another cyclical peak in a year or two, the subsequent recession may be the precursor of new crisis. A recession implies a mushrooming U.S. government deficit, possibly as high as $300 billion, high real interest rates, and declining U.S. imports from debtors. Santow sees the debtors and the United States as potential victims of a time bomb that will almost certainly explode into a new crisis unless pragmatic steps are taken. He offers a list of such steps, arguing that its contents could provide the direction needed to get through the difficult times that he sees ahead.

4 DISINFLATION AND THE THIRD WORLD DEBT CRISIS

Frank E. Morris

The Third World debt crisis might be viewed as the product of the second stage of the disinflation process. The first stage, of course, was the worldwide recession of 1980–82. The second stage involves the resolution of financial commitments undertaken on the mistaken assumption that the economic conditions of the 1970s would persist into the future.

The decade of the 1970s was characterized by high rates of inflation, few and brief recessions, a flourishing world trade and a general explosion of basic commodity prices. Beginning in 1980, these conditions were dramatically reversed. The world economy suffered the worst recession since the 1930s, the inflation rate declined substantially, world trade contracted, and basic commodity prices plummeted.

The problem was further complicated by the fact that most of the debt is denominated in U.S. dollars and the interest rates on most of the debt float with U.S. interest rates. The dollar has risen dramatically against most currencies since the bulk of the debt was contracted and U.S. interest rates, while down substantially from the peak levels, are extraordinarily high both for this stage of the business cycle and relative to the U.S. inflation rate. The Federal Funds rate is 6 percent higher than it was at the corresponding stage of the expansion that began in 1975, even though the inflation rate currently is about 1½ percent lower than it was then. All of this has worked to increase substantially the real burden of servicing the debt.

It was not inevitable that these conditions would produce a major debt crisis. Most of the Third World countries did not take on so much debt as to generate extremely difficult adjustment problems, and most of the international banks do not find themselves with excessive exposure to problem borrowers. Ironically, it is the most creditworthy of the developing countries that now find themselves with the most serious adjustment problems. The less creditworthy could not borrow enough to get into major financial difficulties.

Although it is not inevitable that world disinflation would produce a debt crisis, it is probable that no major debt crisis would have occurred if the economic conditions of the 1970s had persisted. Inflation, particularly inflation of basic commodity prices, coupled with a continued growth in world trade would probably have made many marginal international loans relatively trouble free. This is not to excuse the bankers for their misjudgments. It is their job to know that the only constant in economic life is change. Their principal responsibility is to see that their banks will remain viable institutions even under dramatically changed economic conditions.

The Federal Reserve views the problem as something that can be managed, not on any grand overall basis, but on a case-by-case approach involving protracted negotiations that reflect the peculiar economic and political environment of each country.

There is a great community of interest between the lending banks and the borrowing countries. They both have a great stake in avoiding failure. Rather than face the risk of default, the banks will ultimately have to be willing to revise the terms and conditions of the loans. Rather than cut themselves off from access to international trade in a world that has become much more interdependent than at any time in history, governments will ultimately have to adopt policies that will restore the creditworthiness of the countries in world financial markets. There will be foot-dragging and procrastination on both sides, but the overriding factor is the common interest in finding an accommodation.

In the spring of 1982, Mexico was considered to have the most difficult debt problem. Mexico had run a massive current-account deficit of almost $14 billion in 1981. The adjustment problem appeared to be larger at that time in Mexico than in Brazil and Argentina, but through the application of very austere policies the adjustment was made. Mexico generated a $5 billion current-account surplus in 1983 and its debt was recently restructured into the 1990s. Mexico has turned the corner.

Substantial progress has also been made in Brazil and Argentina. Brazil's current-account deficit, which exceeded $16 billion in 1982, was reduced to less than $7 billion in 1983. Argentina reduced its current account deficit from $5 billion in 1981 to about half that sum in 1983. However, the burden is still on the governments of these countries to complete the adjustment.

Paul Volcker (House Foreign Affairs Committee 1984) recently stated in testimony before the Committee on Foreign Affairs of the House of Representatives:

> Concern is often and understandably expressed that too much is expected of these countries by the IMF in shaping its lending programs, by creditor countries or by banks. But I question whether that can be an easy, painless way to restore equilibrium, or whether failure to adjust can be in the basic interest of the borrowing countries themselves.
>
> Economic growth in developing countries over a long period ahead, and the prospects for political stability, will be dependent on their ability to participate fully in an interdependent world. In that world, credit-worthiness and credit availability will be precious, for they are essential to support trade and investment. Once lost, those qualities are difficult to restore—and democracy is not likely to flourish in the midst of accelerating inflation and economic isolation.
>
> In many of those countries, their excessive debt burdens can be traced in large part to a flight of capital by their own citizens discouraged from investing at home. To me, the ultimate test of a successful economic program will not be whether, at a moment of time, it is acceptable to the IMF or to bank lenders, but whether it in fact can restore and maintain the confidence of a nation's own citizens—and whether, as a consequence, its own savings are employed productively at home.

Nevertheless the creditor industrial countries can help the process by following policies that will contribute to the sustained expansion of world trade that is the key to the long-run ability of the developing countries to service their debts. For the United States, this means policies that are expansionary, but not so stimulative as to generate excesses that might trigger a recession in the next few years. Even a modest recession in the United States might constitute a serious set-back to the present upward momentum of world trade.

The United States could also contribute to relieving the world debt problem by changing its policy mix. A substantial reduction in the structural deficits currently projected would, with an unchanged monetary policy (defined in terms of the rate of growth of money or debt), produce substantiality lower interest rates than would other-wise be the case. This would immediately increase the debt servicing capacities of the debtor nations.

If there is one lesson to be learned from all this, it is that the high cost of disinflation is extremely high. It is high in terms of lost out-put and employment during the recession needed to get the inflation rate down. And even when the recession is over and the economy is attaining previous peak levels, there is a further price to be paid in the instability caused because debts incurred during the inflationary phase have become very difficult to service in the disinflationary era.

Recognizing from the experience of recent years that the cost of disinflation is very high will, hopefully, lead us to be more vigilant and determined than before to avoid conditions that might generate a reacceleration of the inflation rate. We can do so with the knowl-edge that any short-term costs that might have to be paid to avoid higher inflation rates are very small relative to the cost of going through the disinflationary process again.

5 U.S. MONETARY POLICY RESPONSES TO THE DEBT CRISIS

Robert A. Jones

By September 1984, fixed-income yields had either reached a cyclical peak or were very close to a cyclical peak. The current cycle of interest rate is distinguished from other postwar cycles in several ways. First, the peak is not accompanied by forecasts of a recession. Second, the cyclical peak occurred after the smallest postwar percentage increase in yields. Third, the latest cyclical upturn commenced from a record-high cyclical trough, in terms of real interest rates. Fourth, the prospective cyclical easing, which began in the third quarter, is likely to be the most gradual and long-lived of cyclical downtrends since the war.

The unique nature of the current cycle has two main causes. First is the international debt crisis and related concerns for domestic banking. The second cause is the Federal Reserve System's determination to avoid inflationary pressures arising from a weakening of the dollar. The first factor has prevented officials of the Federal Reserve from making the funds rate target significantly higher. The second factor will prevent these officials from easing their rate objectives with the speed that has characterized previous cyclical downturns.

THE FEDERAL RESERVE'S IMPATIENCE

Since the 1952 monetary accord, open market operations have been guided primarily by establishing objectives for either reserve levels or funds rates. Prior to 1970, restrictive monetary policy was aimed at limiting the general availability of reserve credit, and thereby forcing member banks to borrow from the discount window. At the window, administrative discipline was imposed on banks borrowing too frequently. Through these disciplinary measures, all banks were encouraged to preserve their needed liquidity by reducing their extensions of loans and investments. The resulting change in banks' asset management policies, in turn, reduced the rates of both deposit expansion and money supply growth. The degree of reserve restraint specified by the Federal Reserve Open Market Committee (FOMC) was heavily influenced by the growth of bank credit. Therefore, prior to 1970, money supply data were insignificant to participants in the debt markets. Instead, weekly releases of business loan data (the swing factor in the outlook for bank credit growth) had enormous effects on debt market prices.

Unfortunately, bank credit is a lagging rather than leading factor in the business cycle. The primary determinant of banks' credit extensions is the demand for credit, not the availability of reserve credit. The ratio of bank credit to domestic nonfinancial debt is surprisingly stable; its changes covary with changes in reserve availability (net borrowed reserves). This covariance has become less predictable in recent years, because the 1980 Monetary Control Act caused reserve requirements to drop dramatically.

Total domestic nonfinancial debt serves as the best available proxy of the aggregate demand for credit. Some credit sectors display immediate responses to changes in interest rates as well as in the economy. Mortgage demands, as an example, are closely associated with changes in mortgage rates and housing demand. In other sectors, credit demand lags product demand by an average of about six months. Credit demand changes in response to interest rate changes often defy traditional theory. As an example, a number of important sectors in the flow of funds picture display credit demand increases in response to interest rate increases. Public credit demands rise with rising interest rates. Business loans also rise with increased interest rates. The latter relation is true because external financing operations of corporations shift from the bond market (where existing savings credit is tapped) to the bank market (where new deposit credit is manufactured through a loan). Rising interest rates ultimately depress loan demands, but not before pushing the economy into recession.

Business and personal loan demands statistically lag behind the business cycle because of cyclical trends in business and consumer liquidity. It is a fact that liquidity is highest just after the trough of a business cycle, and lowest just past the cyclical peak. When liquidity is low, continued spending by both consumers and businesses is financed increasingly through borrowings; spending is less dependent on borrowed credit when liquidity is high. So, most credit demands generally lag behind the business cycle by about six months, and most major types of credit demands rise with increasing interest rates.

When reserve availability is being targeted, it takes about six months before a particular change in net borrowed reserves has an effect on the ratio of bank credit to total credit demands. This ratio changes because open market operations force more and more banks to the discount window, where restrictive policy is applied through administrative discipline. The forced increase of discount window borrowing, plus the threat of administrative discipline, have a measurable effect on banks' asset management policies: extensions of bank loans and investments (bank credit) are moderated. But, such a change in a bank's policy will occur only after it has incurred repeated exposure to administrative discipline. For this reason, the full effect of restrictive reserve policy is revealed only after a six-month lag.

Because credit demands lag behind the business cycle by about six months, changes in the growth propensity of bank credit (and thus monetary aggregates) will also lag behind the business cycle by about six months. Accordingly, when Federal Reserve officials were, prior to 1970, establishing reserve policy on the basis of bank credit growth, they were in effect targeting a lagging variable. One can conclude that this monetary policy would occasionally be procyclical. An even worse result, however, was that Federal Reserve officials expected immediate results from policy actions. Because of the six-month lag in response, bank credit was not likely to display at once appreciably slower growth. Federal Reserve officials then became impatient and tightened credit further. So monetary doctrine prior to 1970 was based primarily on a lagging variable and did not reflect the lag between a policy change and the resulting change in bank credit growth.

Accordingly, when a business cycle peak was reached, bank credit data continued to exhibit excessive growth, which prompted Federal

Reserve officials to tighten credit further, a procyclical move. To make matters worse, such procyclical tightening still did not affect bank credit immediately, so policymakers became even more frustrated and impatient. Further tightening thus ensued even though the economy was exhibiting clear signs of recessionary tendencies.

The effect of tightening the net borrowed reserve targets was an increase in money rates and bond yields. Net borrowed targeting produces a planned shortage of reserve credit (supplied through open market operations) relative to its demand (which is equal to the level of required reserves). Prior to 1970, procyclical tightening (produced by the Federal Reserve Board's impatience and lack of understanding) caused interest rates to increase significantly as the economy was heading into recession. Apart from earlier inventory recessions, recessions since the 1950s were caused by high interest rates; this relation indicates the procyclical nature of monetary policy doctrine at that time.

Defects of the Federal Reserve's policy doctrine were not altered during the funds rate pegging of the 1970s. During that era, the funds rate target was changed in response to any deviation of M1 growth from its targeted range. When M1 data later became distorted by deposit shifts associated with financial deregulation, its growth trends became more erratic. M1 growth is derived from trends of bank credit, and also lags the business cycle by about six months.

The targeting of interest rates, through funds rate pegging (targeting), uncoupled the funds rate from reserve availability. Traders had to quote Federal Reserve funds according to the perceived rate range pegged by Open Market Desk officials, not according to reserve availability. Whenever a bad weekly number for M1 was lifted (policy tightened), as frequently happened, to test the Federal Reserve's inclination for tighter policy, traders would arbitrarily quote the funds rate at above the known pegged range. The Federal Reserve's hours of intervention were then between 10:45 A.M. and about 1:30 P.M. If the Federal Reserve did not promptly execute repos (repurchase agreements) in response to such hesitation (only five minutes after the high quotes appeared on their screens), funds traders would immediately lift their quotes, and wait another five minutes to see whether the Federal Reserve executed repos. If not, further arbitrary increases in funds rate quotes would occur until the Federal Reserve executed repos. Whenever bad news for M1 was announced, funds traders thus forced the Federal Reserve to supply additional reserve credit whether or not policy had changed. This procyclical supply of reserve credit only served to encourage more M1 growth later.

In pegging the funds rate, Federal Reserve officials assumed that rising interest rates would slow credit demands, and subsequently slow bank credit and money supply growth. As previously explained, however, rising interest rates do not result in any predictable slowing of credit demands. After the economy has had prolonged exposure to rising interest rates, credit demands will ease, but not until the high rates have caused a recession. So, the targeting of interest rates during the 1970s was doomed to fail, especially when reserve management had to be procyclical in order to keep the funds rate within its targeted range.

Even worse than the procyclical nature of reserve management was the negative real rate of interest, which meant that nominal rates were consistently below the rate of inflation. These high rates of inflation were caused in part by such exogenous factors as the managed increase in energy costs. It was not until the return of net borrowed reserve targeting, during the 1980s, that real rates of interest became positive. In fact, the rise in real rates to a record high was almost singly responsible for pushing the economy into the Great Recession of 1981–82.

The returned use of net borrowed targeting recoupled the funds rate with reserve availability and caused the behavior of the funds rate to become more variable. But the return of net borrowed targeting was not responsible for the monetary aggregates, which lag behind the business cycle and do not immediately respond to changes in reserve policy. The Federal Reserve's impatience with the lack of desired money supply results thus continued after the return of net borrowed targeting.

A more serious mistake was made at the Federal Reserve when, in 1981, it was decided to follow monetarists' suggestions of imposing a penalty discount rate. In response to net borrowed reserve pressures, the funds rate always trades above the discount rate. So the "penalty" discount rate did not penalize banks borrowing at the window, but boosted the funds rate, to the reported surprise of FOMC members. Federal Reserve officials did not back away from a 14 percent discount rate, with its 4 percent surcharge penalty, even though the economy was clearly heading into a deeper recession; their reason was excessive monetary growth (which lagged behind the business cycle and was biased upward by inaccurate monetary accounting). The economic retreat, and the threat of a financial collapse, became so serious that in 1982 the Federal Reserve's Board of Governors had to begin lowering interest rates prior to slowing of monetary growth.

Early in 1984, Federal Reserve officials decided that reserve requirements were too low: they could not effectively use reserve management as a tool of monetary control. Reserve policy was then established to create that money rate level believed to be necessary to moderate credit demands. The policy doctrine thus mirrored the disastrous doctrine of the 1970s. As Governor Henry Wallich publicly explained, increasing rates are supposed to moderate credit demand growth, and this moderation in turn was supposed to reduce bank credit growth, deposit expansion, and monetary growth. Because reserve requirements declined so much, Federal Reserve officials believed that they had no choice but to target rates, in order to control credit demands and hence the growth of money supply. Governor Lyle Gramely also publicly explained that targeting interest rates had the advantage of directly affecting aggregate product demands in the economy and thus linked policy with economic performance more directly. His argument was so convincing that nearly all market participants soon concluded that the Federal Reserve was starting to target GNP growth.

If the Federal Reserve's policy of controlling interest rates had been directed at controlling growth of the gross national product, there would have been a much smaller lag between policy actions and the business cycle, and the GNP's response to changes in interest rates would have been much quicker than that of credit demands and credit expansion. But, the Federal Reserve was not singularly targeting GNP. In policy formulation, the monetary aggregates were to become subordinated to several factors: (1) economic growth, (2) inflationary pressures, (3) financial market conditions, and (4) the growth of domestic nonfinancial debt. The last aggregate has assumed great importance for the Federal Reserve and is worthy of a separate analysis. But attention must be focused on the second and third factors: these have been creating such a different course of Federal Reserve policy action, that the current interest rate cycle is different from all previous ones.

THE INTERNATIONAL DEBT PROBLEM

Federal Reserve officials continue to track a factor that lags behind the business cycle: total credit demands. And Federal Reserve officials continue to be impatient that credit demand does not apparently respond to rising interest rates. The July 1984 FOMC minutes, recently released in Washington, D.C. made perfectly clear that most FOMC members have been anxious to raise the funds rate. Banking difficulties related to Latin American debt were the only factor preventing further increases of money rates. All policy options were discussed not in terms of reserve effects on banks' asset management, but in terms of interest rates. I believe that money rates today would be higher by at least 3 percentage points were it not for the associated threat of international debt defaults. FOMC minutes have referred to the fact that international debt servicing has become increasingly more difficult because of high domestic interest rates and the related surge in the dollar's exchange rate.

If current money rates were 3 percentage points higher than they are, credit demands would generally be projected to rise instead of to moderate. If these demands, and the resultant monetary growth, were to continue such an upward course (increasingly due to distressed demands), Federal Reserve officials would raise their targeted rate even further. And the upward march of rates would continue once again until a deep recession ultimately weakened credit demands.

The mere threat of international debt defaults, along with related domestic banking problems, has restrained Federal Reserve officials from following the procyclical policies of the past; it has prevented Federal Reserve officials from subjecting the economy to record-high levels of real interest rates. Because of the international debt problem, one can now project some moderation in credit demands without concurrently forecasting a recession. This is a very major departure from the past.

CREDIT AND ECONOMIC DEMANDS

Every recession creates pent-up demands that a subsequent recovery can unleash. The latest near-depression created a substantial increase in pent-up demands; during the initial phase of the current recovery, the unleashing of these demands created an economic upsurge that was much greater than expected. The recovery was created primarily by a record drop in interest rates; this drop was engineered by scared Federal Reserve officials during July and August of 1982, when the discount rate was repeatedly cut. Immediately before this event, supply-side economics was enjoying a wave of political popularity that enabled President Reagan to push through Congress this century's most significant change in U.S. fiscal policy. The economic effects of this change proved to be far greater than had been initially expected. Monetary policy and high real rates of interest simply failed to offset the stimulative effects of fiscal policy.

Economic recoveries are characterized by an initial expansion fueled mainly by the consumer. The mature phase of the recovery is sustained primarily by business investments. Cuts in personal income taxes (in reality a slowing of tax increases) created sizable gains in real, disposable, personal income. These gains not only helped to unleash pent-up demands, they also sustained the initial upturn on consumption, which continued at a surprisingly fast pace. Meanwhile, corporate tax reductions increased corporate cash flows, and cash flows were significantly helped by investment tax incentives for new investments. The incentives, in turn, proved to stimulate business spending far more powerfully than had been projected. In spite of relatively high real rates of interest, a capital expenditure boom sponsored the second phase of the recovery.

This second phase of cyclical recovery has been far stronger than previously thought possible. A by-product of exceptionally strong manufacturing employment has been the unexpected but welcome gains in productivity; these gains are related to the capital investment boom. Productivity gains are always recorded in an economic upturn. Because manufacturers are typically reluctant to incur the cost of rehiring and retraining without solid evidence that the economic upturn will be sustained, rising production is not immediately accompanied by rising employment. Recent gains in productivity, however, outstrip the cyclical gains normally seen during an economic recovery.

This strong gain presents evidence that the capital investment boom is causing productivity to grow at a fast pace. This evidence, in turn, hints of a change in the secular trend of productivity, from a slight downtrend to an uptrend, which is good news for inflation fighters. Rising wages are being offset to some degree by productivity gains, and unit labor costs are not likely to rise by as much during the recovery, as they have in previous ones.

Economic growth is slowing, and widespread product-demand pressures on output capacity are not likely to develop. In turn, demand-pull inflationary pressures will likely be kept in check during the recovery. The effect of supply-side policy, moreover, has improved the outlook for inflation as much as it improved the outlook for manufacturing employment.

The effect of this policy is not short-lived; it should continue in spite of slower rates of investment growth. A gradual slowdown in investment arises from clear signs that growth in consumption expenditures is slowing. This moderation is quite normal during the mature phase of a recovery but has been furthered by high interest rates and by the dissipation of the effects of personal income tax cuts. Because most of the effects of the tax cuts have already occurred, gains in real disposable personal income have become limited; such moderate growth is expected to continue. In turn, the growth of consumption expenditures is likely to continue slowing. Of course, consumer expenditures could temporarily surge at the expense of personal savings. But the personal savings rate remains too low to expect any savings-financed surge in consumption. Slower growth of personal spending will start acting as a drag on business investments, and will gradually slow that boom to a more respectable 10 percent growth rate. So, there is an economic slowdown in progress, and real GNP growth is likely to slow to 5 percent in the current quarter, and to below 3 percent in the next quarter.

Without further increases in interest rates, credit demands are going to follow economic trends, with the usual six-month lag. The moderation of consumption slowed credit demands in the fourth quarter of 1984, and further easing of credit demands throughout 1985 can be expected. Yet, there is no prospect of recession—only the prospect that until credit demands moderate in response to slower economic growth, the international debt problems will hold interest rates in check.

MONETARY POLICY

The growth of monetary aggregates is assessed by Federal Reserve policymakers in light of its effect on these conditions: (1) economic growth, (2) inflationary pressures, (3) financial market conditions, and (4) domestic nonfinancial debt. At the July 1984 FOMC meeting, most members agreed that if monetary growth declined relative to the targeted growth for the third quarter, that decline would be tolerated and would not prompt any easing of policy. An excess of monetary growth over the third quarter's targets, however, was considered to be the justification for the immediate firming of policy. The inclination of FOMC members toward more, rather than less, restrictive policy was caused by their perceptions of the strength of aggregate product and credit demands. The strength of aggregate product demands, which had been keeping the growth rates of domestic nonfinancial debt at relatively high levels, was confidently expected to moderate. Such moderation could be expected in lagged response to slowing economic growth. But, conclusive evidence of moderating credit demands had yet to appear.

In June and July 1984, the rate of bank credit growth declined significantly, and so monetary growth since the beginning of July slowed significantly. The slowing of bank credit and monetary growth, however, was clearly not the result of any appreciable slowing in credit demands. Instead, large banks were selling nonperforming debt to thrifts under agreements to repurchase such debt. These bad debt repos can escape detection of bank examiners when sold to thrifts, which are subject to different regulatory authorities. Moreover, thrift loan totals are reported on semiannual call dates, and estimated by Federal Reserve staffers for purposes of deriving monthly bank credit data. So, bad debt repos lower weekly reporting large bank totals on total loans. In addition, the repo is executed by debiting a thrift correspondent demand deposit, which many large banks reportedly fail to report as interbank deposits (excluded from M1 data); so the bad debt repo also depresses M1 data.

July 1984 FOMC minutes indicated that when economic and credit demands both display moderating tendencies, slower growth of bank credit and money supply will not be viewed as temporary, and below-target growth of the monetary aggregates at that time will not be tolerated. FOMC members thus subordinate monetary growth considerations to perceptions of economic growth and domestic nonfinancial debt growth rates. At the present time, the trends of these two aggregates foster the FOMC's desires to make higher interest rates the goal of monetary policy.

The interest rate-related strength of the dollar has depressed commodity prices in world markets, because commodity prices are quoted in dollars. As the dollar continued to rise against foreign currencies, commodity costs to foreign bidders paying foreign currencies rose appreciably. In turn, foreign demands for commodities have eased, thereby weakening the dollar prices on commodities in world markets. This development has weakened the petroleum prices of the Organization of Petroleum Exporting Countries. That OPEC production has continued to equal or exceed demands has contributed to the weakness of crude oil's price. Deflationary pressures on commodity prices have accounted for most of the slowdown in U.S. rates of inflation, and seem to have "locked in" very low rates of gain for the consumer price index and the producer price index for the short term.

It is obvious to FOMC members that any appreciable weakening of the dollar will have the immediate effect of renewing inflationary pressures in the United States. Committee members at the July 1984 FOMC meeting therefore expressed their desire to have the dollar continue trading within recent ranges. This meeting was the first time in the history of the Federal Reserve System that policymakers publicly expressed a desire (target) for the dollar. It seemed obvious to Federal Reserve officials that the target interest rates of reserve policy cannot be reduced very quickly or the dollar will weaken. In effect, Open Market Desk officials have been instructed to manage the funds rate with an eye on the dollar's exchange value. For the first time in Federal Reserve history, the conduct of open market operations will be explicitly constrained by foreign exchange rates. This conduct is similar to the long-standing practices of other central banks. This change in American policy seems only natural because of the steady increase of the U.S. economy's exposure to foreign trade. Because of this change in policy doctrine, interest rate declines in the future will have to be far more gradual than ever before.

The FOMC's reference to financial market conditions is actually a reference to Latin American debt difficulties, and to related concern for domestic banking. Concerns about the health of U.S. banks were furthered by the Continental Illinois Bank problem. Federal Reserve officials fear that the Continental Illinois problem could occur in other large banks in the event of Latin American debt defaults or a debt moratorium. At the same time, high interest rates have been creating serious liquidity problems for a number of major thrift institutions. The perceived vulnerability of the financial system now includes both the banking and thrift sectors. The July 1984 FOMC minutes showed that the increased difficulty of nations to service their debts, associated with rising U.S. interest rates, singularly mitigated against further rises in the money rates targeted by monetary policy. More recently, interest rate-related problems in the thrift sector have undoubtedly made Federal Reserve officials even more cautious about further lifting money rates. The financial market factor in formulating reserve policy could be far more important than the July 1984 FOMC minutes indicated. Indeed, analysts are still speculating on why officials recently allowed funds to trade at $11\frac{3}{8}$ percent and did not intervene with matched sales. It could be that the Federal Reserve's concerns for the financial market have increased, especially since the International Monetary Fund announced that Argentinian loan negotiations might be delayed until 1985. Financial market conditions might make Federal Reserve officials anxious to reduce the funds rate objective of monetary policy, at the first sign of moderated growth in economic and credit demands.

THE THREAT OF DEFAULTS ON INTERNATIONAL LOANS

International debt problems have been publicly visible for so long that confidence in the survivability of large banks might be creeping upward without detection. Unless interest rates lower significantly, there seems to be no satisfactory resolution of the Latin American debt problem within the intermediate future. Should debt negotiations with Latin American countries fail to maintain debt servicing, and large banks be forced to write off nonperforming debt, several large banks could experience deposit runs. By itself, this kind of banking problem can be contained through the extended credit program managed by the Federal Reserve. However, investors and depositors have become increasingly aware of widespread liquidity problems in the thrift industry, and in the banking sector to a lesser extent. A debt-related deposit crisis at several large banks could easily spread to other financial depositories, because of the public's sensitivity to any new financial problem. FOMC minutes show that policymakers have great concern about the potentially volatile public responses to changing financial market conditions. If the worst possible scenario develops, and a sudden widespread loss of public confidence in depository institutions occurs, then the Federal Reserve's extended credit program will be inadequate as a tool to restore public confidence.

Federal Reserve officials have been considering various methods of financial rescue in the event of a widespread crisis. Until recently it was thought that drastic action would have to include a sharp cut in the discount rate, in order to push money rates and other interest rates down. Any substantial reduction in interest rates immediately builds net worth and liquidity in the financial system, and has far-reaching effects that are thousands of times more powerful than emergency extensions of reserve credit. Federal Reserve officials have acknowledged that a severe crisis would result if interest rates were regularly marked down whenever international debt problems were perceived to be worsening. If interest rates were lowered, the dollar's weakening would certainly renew privately acknowledged fears that an emergency cut in the discount rate would have to be temporary; investors would have to appreciate that temporary nature.

Because maintaining the dollar's value has become such a high policy priority, Federal Reserve officials have most recently become less willing to drastically change the discount rate if a serious banking crisis occurs. If a crisis does develop, and the Federal Reserve makes perfectly clear that any cut in the discount rate (and funds rate) will be temporary, other interest rates will not fall. The crisis would then continue. However, if the officials place a higher priority on maintaining an interest rate flooring to support the dollar's exchange value, then a debt-related banking crisis cannot be controlled.

Federal Reserve officials have become so concerned about the consequences of a debt crisis that they are likely to pursue extreme measures in order to avoid a crisis. These measures would be aimed at preventing large banks from having to write off an appreciable amount of Latin American debt as nonperforming loans. In short, the central bank's management will be basically focused on cover-up tactics, in case debt defaults become an immediate threat. This tactic does not ensure that the Federal Reserve will be able to escape the worst case. Investors and depositors have become much more concerned about potential cover-up responses to a debt crisis. The credibility of the Federal Reserve as a regulatory agency will be a key factor in the success of its avoiding a full-scale crisis. Any suspected cover-up or questionable tactic could immediately hurt the Federal Reserve's credibility and bring about a full-scale crisis. Forecasting the outcome of an international debt crisis is impossible. Nonetheless, these developments warrant close monitoring, because they could greatly affect interest rates, inflation, and economic trends.

If there is a widespread crisis, some independent commission will undoubtedly be appointed to make an exhaustive study of its causes. Inevitably, the commission's findings will turn the political tide against financial deregulation and will prompt Congress to reimpose Regulation Q limits. Congress will also be prompted to raise reserve requirements significantly, so that the central bank's control of monetary growth can be accomplished directly through reserve management. The relation between reserve management and banks' asset management provides the Federal Reserve with noncost methods of limiting monetary and credit growth. The alternative method of limiting monetary growth indirectly, through the cost (interest rate-induced) method of reducing credit demands, necessarily pushes nominal rates far above the underlying rate of inflation. This consequence was directly responsible for the record-high level of the dollar, and the growing inability of Latin American countries to maintain debt servicing. In sum, if there is a debt crisis, it might change the nature of monetary policy doctrine, and the structure of our financial system, for many years to come. Even with the lesser debt problem to date, there has been a resultant disposition against higher interest rate objectives at the Federal Reserve, which has already changed the course of the interest rate cycle.

6 THE VIEW FROM WALL STREET

Leonard J. Santow

The current economic recovery in the United States is more than two years old, but for much of the rest of the world the recovery is in its infancy. The huge increase in U.S. imports which is a by-product of the recovery has helped many other countries' exports, but the nonexport sectors for many nations have been disappointing. The hope that these nonexport areas would improve before the growth in the export sector fades now looks rather unlikely. The U.S. recovery has already moved into a phase of considerably slower growth, and one can soon expect a slowdown in U.S. import growth. This, in turn, could mean continued softness in world commodity prices, which, moreover, is not going to help many debtor nations. Finally, hopes for redressing the serious imbalance between a stimulative fiscal policy and a restrictive monetary policy in the United States seem to be fading, and the recent decline in interest rates could well prove to be transitory. It would seem, therefore, that the chances of sustaining a U.S. economic recovery for more than another year or two are not good.

If the U.S. economy should reach its cyclical peak sometime in the next year or two, it is likely that the rest of the world will be substantially affected in an adverse way. A recession in the United States should raise the budget deficit to nothing less than $250 billion and possibly over $300 billion, which could well keep an uncomfortably high floor under U.S. interest rates. Also, one has to expect that by late 1986—after four years of economic expansion—the rate of inflation in the United States will be higher than the current 3 percent to 4 percent annual rate. These items do not bode well for either the major debtor countries or other industrialized nations that have been counting (too heavily) upon the U.S. import growth to help alleviate their problems.

What this analysis strongly suggests is that even if the major debtor countries manage to hop from crisis to crisis over the next two or three years without an international debacle, their economies and the world financial system are hardly home free. The repayment problems of major debtor countries are more than likely to crop up again between 1986 and 1988, which may be the worst possible time for U.S. banks, since a recession is likely to create new domestic repayment problems in loans for leveraged buyouts, and resurrect problems in areas such as agriculture and energy.

If you hear a time bomb ticking you don't have to be a nuclear physicist to realize how serious the problem can be. One can only hope that steps will be taken in the next several years to limit the potential of this financial bomb or to reduce the effect. Supporting such a hope is the growing realization that there are no simple and magical solutions to the international debt problems, that all of the parties involved realize the seriousness of the difficulties, and that they all have a vested interest in working out solutions.

Yet, in order for pragmatic solutions to be effected, the full cooperation of governments, central banks, commercial banks and supranational organizations is needed, and while they all may have a vested interest in avoiding catastrophes, each has its own ideas of what should be done, bearing in mind its own narrow interests. Since each group has not been equally responsible for helping to create or magnify the problems, there are major differences of opinion as to how the cost and pain of suggested solutions should be divided. If these divisions continue, they could well lead to patchwork solutions that will not be able to withstand the rigors of the next worldwide recession.

It may be true that a dismal science creates dismal analysts, but the scenario just described does not have to be cast in stone. There are a combination of approaches and techniques that may help the international financial system muddle through the potential problems over the next several years. The following paragraphs are a list of suggestions that, in combination, could well be a potent force in getting through difficult times.

The United States and other major industrial countries in the world should agree to redress their domestic imbalances between monetary and fiscal policies. A major step in the right direction would be for these countries to pledge a maximum budget deficit target as a percentage of the GNP. Figures should probably run no more than 3 or 4 percent. At the same time that this occurs, the monetary authorities would need to respond by bringing down interest rates to levels that would stimulate their economies. In order to have a reasonable chance of implementing such a plan, the United States would clearly have to take the lead.

The U.S. budget deficit is the key place to start. Because of the magnitude of the problem, it must be attacked through a dual approach—increasing receipts and reducing the growth in spending. Tying budgetary reform to methods of substantially reducing the deficit is a mistake, since it can easily lead to a political stalemate or ineffective actions. A national sales tax on the receipts side used as a surcharge when the deficit exceeds certain targets and a ceiling on expenditures rather than a ceiling on debt would be a good combination with which to start.

The Federal Reserve and other major central banks could place the international debt crisis on close to an equal-policy footing with domestic economic considerations and the growth of the monetary aggregates. The thought is that if the international debt crisis has close to an equal-policy footing, then the monetary authorities would try to limit upward interest rate pressures. This greater emphasis on international factors would likely limit the strength of the dollar, limit the size of debtor countries' interest payments, and allow debtor nations to keep their interest rates lower. It would also help stimulate the economies of both the United States and the major debtor countries, and through increased exports allow the latter to meet their international interest and principal payments more easily. At the same time, the commercial banks that have lent substantial funds to these debtor countries would probably receive a steadier stream of payments and would have less reason to write off or write down loans.

Major industrial countries and their central banks should follow domestic policies that reduce the possibility of recessions. The key factor is not to maximize economic growth but rather to minimize economic adversity and economic variability. What really hurts major debtor countries are swings from feast to famine in world economic activity. Even if such activity is too robust, as long as there is a steady, reasonable, and relatively predictable growth rate, it allows debtor countries to better manage their economies. It is very difficult for these countries to control inflation and have a steady growth in exports when their economies fluctuate in a substantial way due to outside forces that are beyond their control.

Implementation of the previous suggestions should reduce the outside buffeting for major debtor countries. It should allow them a greater opportunity to work on domestic solutions for domestic problems. After all, it can be strongly argued that many of their problems are of their own doing—that is, reflecting improper domestic policies and attempts to create unreasonably high standards of living. If this statement is valid, it also means that all of the help from the outside will do little good in the long run unless major changes are made inside these major debtor countries.

The IMF, instead of telling debtor countries the specific economic goals they must achieve—suggestions that often lack political and social practicality—should base its assistance on whether the debtor countries have stayed current on their interest and principal payments. Let the debtor countries choose the internal and principal payments. Let the debtor countries choose the internal sacrifices they want to make. As for the IMF's ability (or lack thereof) to obtain funds, practical realities dictate that much larger subscriptions by major countries are needed. The IMF could also take the lead international role in the areas of countertrade and barter agreements, possibly even setting up an organization to develop and operate such facilities.

The role of the World Bank in lending to, or investing in, major debtor countries must increase substantially. The World Bank has an advantage over the IMF in that it can directly tap the financial markets around the world and does not have to depend upon the generosity of various governmental bodies. One possible suggestion is for governments to be allowed to match the amount that the World Bank invests or lends, with the proviso that these governments would receive the same rates of return as the World Bank. This approach could substantially enhance the availability of funds to be placed internationally.

Cooperation and coordination between the regulatory authorities of the various industrialized countries must improve. Even though the various countries do not have to handle their respective programs, rules, guidelines, penalties and inducements in exactly the same way, they should not work at cross-purposes. Most important, individual debtor countries or groups of countries should not be viewed as either a "U.S. problem" or a "European problem." To avoid such potential conflicts, the central banks that regularly meet in Basel should try to develop a series of common ground rules for dealing with major debtor countries.

The Federal Reserve could allow commercial banks to borrow under the "extended credit" category at a rate below the market rate in order to make additional funds available to major debtor countries, *but only* if the banks set up larger loan-loss reserves, write down more of their loans, and meet more stringent capital requirements. Since such extended-credit borrowings would provide many billions of dollars of reserves to the banking system, equal amounts of funds would need to be taken out by the Federal Reserve through open market operations.

On new loans to be made by commercial banks, the debtor countries could have the option of making their repayments based upon the value of the dollar, mark, yen, or ECU. The major central banks would at the same time set up a pool of funds that would compensate the commercial banks for any foreign exchange losses incurred in such loan operations.

The commercial banks could devise a plan whereby they would offer major debtor countries the opportunity to receive either an interest rate discount on outstanding loans or the opportunity to receive additional funds at favorable rates. These opportunities would exist only as long as the debtor countries were current on their payments of interest and principal. The key here is to use the carrot rather than the stick in order to induce debtor countries to stay current on payments. This approach is entirely different from one where debtor countries, often unilaterally, try to seek repayment moratoriums, capitalization of interest charges, and similar readjustments. The problems with this adjustment approach are that it does not add discipline, it creates uncertainty, and it places emphasis upon ad hoc solutions.

All of the previous suggestions should either directly or indirectly help commercial banks gradually come out from under their major international debt exposure. The price to be paid by the banks for this help should be dear. As a start, they should more accurately portray their accounting circumstances. They should be severely limited in their ability to avoid classifying loans as nonperforming simply by making new loans to countries which will allow the latter to pay the interest on the old loans. Such an approach allows major debtor nations to borrow additional funds often without attacking their basic problems, and puts them further into debt with maturities and terms that often complicate future repayment problems. For the banks, this situation creates an even larger exposure to loss, as well as distorts their balance sheets and income statements. It makes other types of window dressing look like child's play.

The relationship between the Treasury and the Federal Reserve should be changed so that the central bank has more operating flexibility in the foreign exchange market. At the moment, the Treasury totally dominates the relationship to the degree that very seldom is the Federal Reserve allowed to intervene in the foreign exchange market. While one can hardly argue with the concept that the Treasury should be the institution that has prime responsibility for basic U.S. foreign exchange policies, the Federal Reserve should be given additional latitude to operate, especially in holding more foreign exchange reserves and in combined intervention efforts with other central banks. The primary purpose of coordinated and combined efforts would be to reduce unjustifiable market aberrations but not to fight basic underlying forces. One can argue that anything that lends some stability to the foreign exchange market will be of help to major debtor countries that traditionally suffer from highly volatile currencies and exports.

The restrictions the Federal Reserve places on banks with respect to the amount of loans that can be made to various classes of borrowers should be tightened appreciably. It is not sufficient to have the restrictions apply merely to the amount that can be lent to one borrower. Rather, restrictions should be placed upon the amount that can be lent to different categories of borrowers. For example, the amount of loans that a bank can make in any one country, or in any single region, should be limited to a certain proportion of capital. Or, banks whose international loans as a percentage of total loans exceed a predetermined percentage would need to have larger capital requirements. Because of the problems that such a plan might initially create, the restrictions would have to be phased in over a number of years. Clearly, this type of approach would do little to solve current problems but would be a way of limiting banks from getting into future difficulties.

The Federal Reserve should reconsider its approach with respect to reserve requirements as changes here could help limit future loan problems for banks, especially with respect to major debtor countries. The large reserve requirements on demand deposits and the negligible or nonexistent reserve requirements on interest-sensitive deposits should be reversed—the highest requirements should be placed on the most interest-sensitive deposits such as large CD accounts. Moreover, a reserve requirement surcharge could be placed on deposits where a bank has exhibited excessive loan growth, especially in high-risk areas.

The Federal Deposit Insurance Corporation should reconsider this approach to insurance premiums. It is painfully clear that the insurance premium should not be uniform but rather commensurate with the risks involved. Moreover, one can argue that since the largest banks apparently have full protection for their depositors irrespective of deposit size, while the small banks do not, the FDIC should insure all deposits but substantially increase the insurance premium for the larger banks. Insuring all deposits would also reduce the nervousness of foreign investors, an important factor since such balances are growing rapidly because of the U.S. trade deficit and capital inflows. The larger these inflows, the greater the potential vulnerability to outflows.

The Federal Reserve could use a more imaginative approach with respect to the discount window. For example, if bank credit expansion is growing below the bottom end of the Federal Reserve's acceptable range, the base discount rate could be set below the funds rate; if it is growing in the acceptable range, it could be placed at about the funds rate; and if it is growing above target, it could be set above the funds rate. Moreover, access to the window could be considerable when bank credit expansion is weak and limited when it is strong. Moral suasion and the rate penalties charged for frequent use of the window would be the primary methods used to induce or restrict such borrowing. The purpose of this proposal is that if the Federal Reserve is able to react more quickly to the need for a policy change, it will not have to move as aggressively later on. This should moderate interest rate swings, which should make the interest payment situation more manageable for major debtor countries.

There may well be some technical changes in Federal Reserve policy implementation procedures that could minimize the fluctuations in interest rates and still allow the Federal Reserve to meet its economic activity and monetary aggregate goals. For example, in September 1984 the Federal Reserve Open Market Committee (FOMC) stated that it had a 4 percent acceptable band on federal funds rates, but seems to have a much narrower acceptable band for operating purposes. That band, which often is 1 percent or less, is usually pressed against one end or the other of the broader band. One can argue that this approach creates undue fluctuations in short-term rates since market participants regularly test the Federal Reserve with respect to funds-rate intervention points, especially at the high end of the range. It would be interesting to see whether the average funds rate might be more stable if, for example, the FOMC were to take the approach of setting the acceptable funds band at say 1½ percent above to 1½ percent below the going funds rate.

Finally, as a last and least preferred alternative (but one that might prove necessary if suggestions such as those just mentioned are not accepted), governments may have to fill the breach, in particular the U.S. government. The latter could be faced with a variety of alternatives it would implement in trying to stop an international debt crisis. One approach would be for the Treasury to get more involved in the loans made abroad to major debtor countries by U.S. banks. The assistance could take such forms as buying foreign loans made by U.S. banks, lending additional funds directly to countries that are in difficulty, giving the banks special incentives to make additional loans to foreigners, and pressuring the banks to renegotiate the loans so that the terms to foreigners are less onerous.

Besides the practical realities, the justifications behind the U.S. government taking an active role are that there could be an unacceptable level of bank problems and failures leading to major difficulties for the U.S. economy, that the degree of the problem is so large that only the government can help out in a meaningful way, and that many of the major debtor countries are political and military allies. Also, the argument can be made that the government left the recycling of petrodollars up to the commercial banks and, therefore, the government should share in the responsibility for many of the foreign loan problems.

The reason such an approach should be used as a last resort is that once the government gets involved in such assistance, it is almost impossible to determine how large the involvement will become and how much it will cost. Then there is the question of the "bail-out" precedent and how it would relate to other areas of the U.S. economy. Also, while the banks may have had the recycling responsibility, that does not condone excessive amounts lent to individual countries at inordinately low interest rates in cases where the banks did not do all of the necessary homework on political and economic risk. Finally, the point can be made that the U.S. taxpayers should not take on this major burden, since they were not responsible for the financial difficulties—an argument that would carry considerable weight in Congress.

These arguments against additional government involvement could well cause further government assistance to be mainly in the form of behind-the-scenes activities. The purpose would be to help out banks and large foreign debtors in ways that are as indirect and discreet as possible. Nevertheless, it is strange how indirect involvements tend to become direct and moderate involvements tend to become major.

The suggestions offered here are not meant to be considered as an overall solution to international debt problems. Rather, they are items that should be analyzed separately and pursued or discarded based upon their individual merits. It is hoped that this chapter will induce further ideas and suggestions in a similar vein. Unfortunately, many analysts continue to look for the great master plan in the sky to avoid a full-blown international debt crisis while a much more fruitful approach would be to develop individual pragmatic suggestions that limit the degree of the problem, cushion the adverse shocks, and set the foundation for a more stable financial future.

III ▐▐▐ MULTINATIONAL INSTITUTIONS IN THE GLOBAL DEBT CRISIS

This part opens with a paper by International Monetary Fund historian Margaret Garritsen de Vries. Her contribution is to offer an unflinching interpretation of the IMF's role in the debt crisis from the IMF's perspective. She provides a detailed look at the pre–August 1982 period, the events of 1982, and their immediate aftermath. The Fund's responses reflected its view that the crisis was real, but that it was largely a matter of financial imbalances that could be remedied with the appropriate management. De Vries argues that the IMF strategy, which, as she notes, has been termed "muddling through," has been largely successful in dealing with financing emergencies and thwarting the cessation of credit flows.

Robert McCauley does not share Margaret de Vries's optimism. He is concerned about what he calls the increasingly problematic relation between IMF and bank lending. Has the IMF conditioned its own assistance to major troubled borrowers on banks' (and governments') committing further resources to them? McCauley tests the hypothesis implicit in this question by analyzing ninety-nine IMF programs over the period 1976–81. His central conclusion is that locked-in banking has largely replaced the IMF's former arm's length relation to commercial banking, and that it is very likely that locked-in banking will continue for the foreseeable future.

Philip Wellons's chapter deals with multinational institutions' performance as international lenders of last resort (ILOLR) during the

109

crisis periods. The focus is on how a system of independent nations affects crisis management, especially in providing ILOLR services. Wellons's contention, one that will be repeated in Larry Sjaastad's paper, is hardly optimistic. The optimal resolution to the debt crisis lies in establishing a multinational institution that can act as ILOLR. Unhappily, the world is organized by nations, which poses a seemingly insurmountable obstacle to creating a multinational ILOLR. Powerful nations simply will not give an ILOLR a broad enough mandate to allow it to deal effectively with crises growing out of North-South financial relations. The result: instability, and unwieldy crisis management.

7 THE ROLE OF THE INTERNATIONAL MONETARY FUND IN THE WORLD DEBT PROBLEM

Margaret Garritsen de Vries

The developing world's external debt problems have been the International Monetary Fund's main occupation since mid-1982. After briefly reviewing the world economic setting in mid-1982 when the "debt crisis" suddenly erupted, as background for understanding the Fund's actions, I will explain what the Fund has been doing, and then describe how the Fund views the prospects for debt management.

THE SETTING OF MID-1982

The story begins in 1979, by which time "stagflation" had become a commonly used term. Industrial countries' output had not fully recovered from the oil price rise of late 1973 and the subsequent 1974–75 recession. Despite unemployment that remained notably higher than in the early 1970s and a stagnant world economy, inflation persisted. Average annual increases of domestic prices in industrial countries were still in the range of 7 or 8 percent as 1979 opened.

Early in the year, and even before the impact of the second round of oil price rises, another upsurge of inflation in industrial countries took place. As higher prices for oil and for many foodstuffs and other primary commodities were passed through to final product prices, rapid inflation plagued all industrial countries. By late 1979

111

consumer prices in many industrial countries were rising by over 10 percent — 15 percent in the United States — the highest level ever in peacetime. Combatting inflation became the central theme of the annual meeting of the IMF and World Bank governors in Belgrade in September 1979. Indeed, Paul Volcker dashed home even before the meetings ended to introduce a major package of anti-inflation measures, notably the introduction in the United States of short-term monetary targeting.[1] Abatement of inflation had become the prime objective of virtually all industrial countries' authorities. It was widely believed that inflation and inflationary expectation had to be ended before growth could be resumed. The priority of controlling inflation as a prerequisite for stimulating growth and employment dominated the meetings of the Interim Committee of the IMF Board of Governors.[2]

To this end, monetary policies in the industrial countries became decidedly more restrictive after late 1979 and remained so through the middle of 1982. The rate of inflation in industrial countries did fall, especially by 1982. In 1982 consumer prices in the industrial countries rose on average at an annual rate of 5 percent, lower than for some years. Nominal interest rates rose considerably, however, and although down somewhat by the end of the year as monetary policies were again relaxed late in 1982, they considerably exceeded the rate of inflation. Thus, real interest rates became positive, about 8 percent per annum, in sharp contrast to several years prior to 1979, when real interest rates were low or even slightly negative. By 1982 the world economy was in a recession more severe than that of 1974–75 and, in fact, the deepest and longest in fifty years. Real gross national product in the industrial countries, which had grown weakly in 1980 and 1981, fell in 1982, especially in Canada, the United States, West Germany, and Italy, for the first time since 1975. Unemployment rates soared to the highest level since the 1930s. Instead of rates of inflation in double digits, rates of unemployment were in double digits in nearly all the major industrial countries, except Japan. The volume of world trade, which had continued to rise even during the 1970s except for 1975, despite the disruptions of the decade, actually fell in 1982.

IMPACT ON BORROWING COUNTRIES

Many nonoil-producing developing countries had been borrowing heavily after 1973, especially from commercial banks, to finance their balance-of-payments deficits. By mid-1982 their aggregate external debt was estimated at over $600 billion. Moreover, over half of this debt was in commercial terms. Readily available credit at interest rates that came close to inflation rates had helped induce countries to borrow. Steadily rising deposits, particularly as oil-exporting countries deposited their vastly enlarged oil revenues in U.S. banks, induced creditors to lend.

Borrowing countries' payments positions suddenly became extremely difficult. Furthermore, the virtual cessation of credit expansion posed a broader threat. The inability of some major borrowers to "roll over," or refinance, maturing loans threatened a major crisis of confidence with respect to the banking system and a cumulative contraction of credit-financed imports that could seriously damage world trade and the prospects for world economic recovery.

At the 1982 Annual Meeting of the International Monetary Fund and World Bank governors in Toronto in late September, Prime Minister Trudeau, in his opening remarks, stated that "These hard times, and these perceptions of looming crisis are generating fear" and "frustration and confusion" (IMF 1982b:1). J. de Larosiere, the Fund's managing director, called the world economic situation "very complex and difficult, perhaps more so than at any time in the postwar period" (IMF 1982:13).

This background highlights the setting in which the finance minister of Mexico told monetary authorities in mid-August 1982, just a few weeks before the Fund-Bank Annual Meeting in Toronto, that Mexico could no longer meet its debt servicing payments. This was the crisis to which the Fund was asked to respond. The prospects for developing countries managing their debts looked dismal indeed.

THE FUND'S RESPONSES

Mexico's circumstances are worth noting in some detail. From 1977 to 1981, greatly expanding petroleum production helped Mexico to achieve economic growth rates of more than 8 percent a year. But growth was accompanied by accelerating inflation and a weakening of the country's external situation. The expansion of the public sector, which registered a deficit equivalent to 15 percent of gross domestic product during 1981, was the most important factor behind these worsening trends. To help finance the expanding public sector deficit, Mexico had contracted a substantial amount of external debt in 1981, much of it short term, at rising interest rates. By early 1982, as confidence eroded, capital flight began to occur and Mexico's exchange reserves were being rapidly depleted. The Mexican authorities allowed the peso to depreciate sharply, introduced some measures of fiscal restraint, imposed import restrictions, and received several large loans; but because of a widening public sector deficit, the situation continued to deteriorate. Then in mid-1982 capital inflows virtually ceased.

In a rescue operation, the U.S. Treasury and the Federal Reserve announced on August 30 their participation in an arrangement—in cooperation with the central banks of the other Group of Ten countries, Spain, and Switzerland, under the aegis of the Bank for International Settlements—to provide $185 billion in short-term financing to the Bank of Mexico. In addition, the U.S. government lent the government of Mexico $1 billion in credits for imports of agricultural products and provided $1 billion as advance for payment for purchases of Mexican oil by the U.S. Strategic Petroleum Reserve. These "bridge" loans were to allow time for a program supported by the use of the International Monetary Fund's resources to be developed.

After a protracted negotiation, at the end of 1982, the Fund approved Mexico's use of the Fund's resources for SDR 3.6 billion. SDR 0.2 billion was in the first credit tranche, while the remainder was to be drawn by Mexico over three years. The public sector deficit was to fall gradually from about 17 percent of 1982 GDP to 3.5 percent in 1985. Public institutions' prices for government-provided goods and services were to increase so as to bring them more in line with market prices. Tighter monetary policy was mandated so as to curb excessive private spending. A flexible exchange rate was to be introduced initially to help correct the peso's severe overvaluation and then to help the exchange rate adjust to domestic price changes. The program's intent was to lower Mexico's reliance on external financing over the next few years, to contribute to an easing of Mexico's debt servicing problems, and to foster renewed growth of output and employment.

It was not possible for the IMF managing director to go to the IMF executive with an adjustment program for which financing, both for new lending and for debt restructuring, was incomplete. Therefore, the managing director and staff of the Fund played a central role in Mexico's negotiations with the international banking community. An estimated $7 billion in net new financing would be required in 1983, $5 billion of which was sought from commercial banks and $2 billion from official sources. To encourage financing of this amount, and in a sharp departure from past practice, the Fund made the granting of its own financial support conditional upon commercial banks and official creditors themselves providing the required financing and to making this commitment *before* the Fund approved the country's program and the associated use of the Fund's resources. In the end, the financing was arranged, with as many as 530 commercial banks participating in the $5 billion raised from commercial banks.[3]

In the next few months, other debtor countries, especially in Latin America, also came to the Fund for assistance. The Brazilian case, for example, received the Fund's approval to use nearly SDR 5 billion of its resources to try to reduce the external and internal imbalance and to bring about important structural changes so as to resume growth. The goal of the Fund was to halve the public sector's financial requirement from 1982 to 1983 and a further halving by 1985. Achievement of the targets was to be facilitated by depreciation of the exchange rate, the implementation of substantial fiscal measures and of more rational financial and pricing policies by state enterprises, and a restrictive monetary policy.

It was clear that even after the Fund's lending there would still be a sizable gap in Brazil's balance of payments. After much discussion with government officials and private bankers, in which the managing director again played a central role, Brazil obtained new long-term financial loans of $4.4 billion for 1983, a rollover of $4 billion of amortization of medium- and long-term debt falling due in 1983, and a rollover of some $9 billion in trade-related short-term lines of credit.

Under the new reality, debtor countries could obtain new loan commitments, especially from private creditors, only as part of a comprehensive, Fund-supported financing program aimed at restoring the debtor country's viable external payments position within a few years. Thus, the Fund has adopted what it calls a cooperative strategy. It is a country-by-country approach, in collaboration with all the interested parties. This strategy, which J. de Larosiere described in June 1984 in an address to the International Monetary Conference in Philadelphia, comprises two elements—adjustment and financing.[4]

Adjustment

Helping members design and implement adjustment programs is a central responsibility of the Fund. However, the Fund has proceeded in part on the conviction that weak domestic policies and delays in adjustment measures have at least in part been made possible by relatively easy access to foreign borrowing under favorable conditions at least until the middle of 1982. Demand-management policies had been lax. In particular, the nonoil developing countries' median fiscal deficit as a proportion of GDP, which was 3½ percent in the late 1970s, increased steadily to nearly 6 percent in 1982. This average conceals some extremely high deficits in a number of countries. In the three major Latin American countries, for example, budget deficits jumped from a range of 7 to 8 percent in 1979 to a range of 14 to 18 percent in 1982. Such large budget deficits had to be reduced.

There were also policy weaknesses on the supply side in the countries that had run into external payments deficits. Because of high rates of inflation, officially set prices had frequently moved far out of line with market realities, leading to distortions and excessive subsidy (which added to budgetary deficits), as well as weakening incentive for producers, exporters, savers, and investors. Moreover, many developing countries failed to adjust nominal exchange rates to differences between domestic and foreign rates of inflation, causing their currencies to appreciate in real terms. Overvalued exchange rates weakened the trade account, necessitated imports restrictions that caused distortions in domestic production, and led to massive capital flight from some countries. This drain on savings limited the capacity to import and also the scope for investment.

The objective of adjustment programs is thus to achieve a viable balance of payments in the medium term and a more efficient use of scarce resources by introducing a number of incentives and measures to generate more domestic savings, more investment, and more exports.

Financing

The second element of the strategy has been to keep financial flows moving. In the years since the middle of 1982 the Fund has lent some $22 billion in support of adjustment to sixty-six members, several of which have had debt problems. A further $8 billion of commitments are outstanding in support of the thirty-four programs that are presently in place.

In addition to providing direct balance of payments financing, the need to obtain agreement on the provision of additional bank and official loans *before* approval of a Fund arrangement has altered the role of the Fund in relation to commercial banks in the management of the debt problem. To the Fund's certification role, in which the Fund's willingness to lend to a country acts as a seal of approval inducing other creditors to lend, has been added a catalytic role: actively helping to mobilize funds from other lenders. A key aspect of the Fund's facilitation of this "nonspontaneous lending" from commercial banks has been to explain the debtor countries' adjustment policies and how additional private funds are necessary if the adjustment programs are to succeed.

The Fund's catalytic activities have resulted in net new lending from commercial banks on a much larger scale than was thought possible in 1982, and a rescheduling of official and commercial debt for an unprecedented number of countries and on an unparalleled scale. During 1983 alone, some thirty developing countries, including eleven of the twenty-five largest borrowers, completed or were engaged in debt rescheduling with official or commercial creditors. The Fund estimates that debt restructuring arrangements eased the cash flow situation of the nonoil developing countries by some $40 billion in 1983, equivalent to about 8 percent of their exports of goods and services. Restructurings agreed to in the first four months of 1984 are projected to result in a further reduction of debt service payments by at least $10 billion. It has also been possible to muster the essential commercial bank lending to support countries' efforts to adjust, a prospect that was in real jeopardy in late 1982. The indications are that commercial bank exposure in nonoil developing countries increased by some $25 billion in 1983.

Net new lending, together with restructuring, has helped to bring about a considerable improvement in the maturity profile of outstanding debt. The share of short-term debt in total external debt for the nonoil developing countries declined to some 15 percent at the end of 1983 from almost 20 percent at the end of 1982. As a result, the average debt service ratio of the nonoil developing countries, though still high, fell from 24½ percent in 1982 to 21½ percent in

1983, and for Latin American countries, from 54 percent to 44 percent.

In addition to pursuing this cooperative strategy as debt problems arise in individual countries, the Fund has been acting to prevent future debt crises arising by strengthening its surveillance over the external debt policies of members. A new technical assistance program to help members monitor external borrowing has been launched. The Fund's work on compiling and publishing statistics on debt has been expanded. The Fund's consultations have been broadened to go more into review and analysis of external debt, especially over the medium term.

THE FUND'S VIEW OF THE PROSPECTS FOR DEBT MANAGEMENT

In the Fund's view, the strategy has been working well. By mid-1983, it appeared to have averted the threat of a crippling cessation of international credit flows and to have brought about a considerable easing of tensions in international financial markets. By October 1984, a number of encouraging developments had occurred so that debt problems could be viewed with greater confidence than in a year before.

The Fund's resources have been reinforced by a a nearly 50 percent increase in members' Fund quotas so that the aggregate of Fund quotas is now just below SDR 90 billion. Agreement has been reached on a threefold increase in the resources available to the Fund under the General Arrangements to Borrow (GAB), a line of credit with the major industrial countries. This GAB has been enlarged from SDR 6.4 billion to SDR 17 billion. Saudi Arabia has agreed to lend the Fund SDR 1.5 billion under an associated arrangement with the GAB. The GAB may now be used by the Fund not only for the benefit of Fund members among the Group of Ten major industrial countries, but under certain circumstances, for the benefit of any member country. Finally, the executive board has approved other borrowing arrangements, totaling SDR 6 billion, with the Saudi Arabian Monetary Agency, the BIS, Japan, and the National Bank of Belgium.

The commercial banks, with the assistance of central banks, have developed and expanded their cooperation through advisory committees and regional groupings. The Paris Club has also demonstrated remarkable efficiency in handling the rescheduling of loans from official sources.

In addition, the external adjustment that has taken place, both as a result of the adjustment programs and the pursuit of more appropriate macroeconomic and exchange rate policies by debtor countries and as a result of renewed world economic growth, has been dramatic. Countries in Latin America with Fund-supported programs saw their combined external current account deficit reduced from $41 billion in 1981 to $11 billion in 1983, while their trade accounts shifted from a deficit of $7 billion to a surplus of $24 billion. The nonoil developing countries taken together cut their combined external deficit by half during those two years—from a record high of $109 billion in 1981 to less than $53 billion in 1983. While this adjustment involved sharp cuts in imports and domestic activity in many countries, it is the Fund's firm conviction that in their absence much larger cuts would have had to take place.

Now, however, as many of these countries are beginning to experience increased exports and a resumption of growth, activity in some sectors is accelerating sharply—for example, Mexico and Brazil, both of which are likely to record positive growth rates in 1985 after a period of stagnant or falling output. A resurgence of imports is projected from the great majority of countries implementing Fund-supported programs. For the nine largest countries with such programs, the value of imports is projected to increase by 12 percent in 1984, compared with a decline of 9 percent in 1983, which amounts to a turnaround of nearly $25 billion.

It is, moreover, particularly to be stressed that by late 1984 and early 1985, recovery in the industrial world was also changing somewhat the contours of the adjustment and financing problem facing developing countries. For nonoil developing countries as a group, the Fund staff estimated a current-account deficit for 1984 still lower than that of 1983, about $45 billion for 1984, expected to stabilize at about the same magnitude in 1985. Deficits of this magnitude would represent 9 percent of exports of goods and services in 1984 and just over 8 percent in 1985. Viewed in these terms, prospective deficits among the nonoil developing countries are the lowest in twenty years. Perhaps more significant is that nonoil developing countries have passed from the import-compression phase of adjustment to the export-expansion phase. As a result, the Fund believes that it should be increasingly possible to combine the restoration of external creditworthiness with the resumption of more satisfactory domestic growth. The Fund stresses repeatedly that restoring growth in developing countries on a sound basis is one of the most pressing objectives of international economic policy.

The Future

Despite all these encouraging developments, the Fund continues to stress the need for vigilance and determination to consolidate and extend the progress to date as well as the need to avoid pessimism or wishful thinking. It also stresses that the "crisis" is not of a global nature—that is, that generalized solutions are not the answer. The Fund believes that the case-by-case approach in which individual debtor countries undertake adjustment programs supported by the Fund should be continued. This approach aims at restoring the confidence of the financial community in each country through a re-orientation of policies by the debtor country that is seen to be a credible and enduring effort toward restoring the country's external financial viability and its capacity to service its external debt. At the same time, while the intensity of the debt crisis has receded, more needs to be done by all parties—industrial countries, debtor countries, and commercial banks.

In the Fund's view, industrial countries need to strengthen their financial policies in order to bring about a lowering of their interest rates but still maintain noninflationary policies. They must keep a firm rein on monetary policy and also reduce their structural budget deficits. They need to roll back their trade restrictions, reversing the protectionist tendencies of recent years. Third, industrial countries' governments must provide the necessary financial backing for adjustment efforts, particularly in the form of guaranteed export credits and long-term capital, either bilaterally or channeled through multilateral organizations such as the World Bank. Here, the balance-of-payments adjustment programs that are being implemented by developing countries, often at high social cost, must receive greater backing by longer term capital in order to tackle the fundamental obstacles to growth. To this end, the Fund has been working to strengthen its close cooperation with the World Bank.

Debtor countries will have to continue to implement adjustment programs. The impressive gains that have been realized in decreasing external deficits need to be followed by more vigorous and determined efforts to remove the obstacles to domestic growth. There is considerable scope for developing countries to do more in the way of tackling rigidities in their economies that have for years been stifling growth and increasing their vulnerability to external shocks. Though progress has been made, much more flexibility is needed in prices, particularly interest rates and exchange rates and wages, so as to keep these prices in line with market realities. Only through such policies, backed by counterinflationary demand management, can debtor countries achieve the expanded savings, investment, and exports they need to generate productive employment and to fuel their growth and development. The Fund has also been emphasizing that it is also very much in the interest of debtor countries to do more to attract foreign capital, especially in the form of direct investment.

As far as commercial banks are concerned, the Fund emphasizes that there is a crucial role for them in the future, as in the past, in helping to cope with debt problems and the provision of new finance. A longer perspective may be particularly desirable for rescheduling in cases where heavy amortization payments due by some debtor countries over the next few years—countries that otherwise are performing well—impede a return to more normal market conditions. The commercial banks, moreover, will have a vital role to play in channeling new money to debtor countries implementing adjustment policies. Projections made by the Fund staff in the 1984 *World Economic Outlook* document envisage a rate of growth of such lending that is much lower than in the years leading up to the 1982 crisis, and one that is consistent with the gradual decrease in the proportion of banks' assets committed to developing countries and a significant decline in their capital exposure to those countries. In addition, reliance on "nonspontaneous" flows will decline as the adjustment process continues in debtor countries. It will also be important to see that the terms and conditions of restructuring and new lending are such that a self-defeating impact on the balance of payments and debt service capacity of debtor countries is avoided.

Within this framework, the Fund is increasingly confident that what others have sometimes called "the muddling through strategy" is the best strategy for dealing with the debt problem.

NOTES TO CHAPTER 7

1. The press release issued by the U.S. Federal Reserve Board on October 6, 1979 is reprinted in IMF 1979: 330.
2. See, for example, the communiqué issued after the May 12–13 meeting of the Interim Committee, para. 2; reprinted in IMF 1982a: 146–47.
3. Further details of the Mexican operation can be found in Kraft (1984).
4. Reprinted in IMF (1984b: 178–82).

8 IMF Managed Lending

Robert N. McCauley

On November 15, 1982 the managing director of the International Monetary Fund told a roomful of bankers that they would have to agree to extend fresh credits to Mexico and Argentina in order for him to recommend to the executive directors of the IMF a loan for either country. Formerly the IMF had tried to predict bank lending and then to build a package of policy measures for its borrowers around the expected volume. Now the IMF was calling for a certain level of bank lending as a condition of its own lending. Thus, the IMF was trying to lock in bank lending. Chairman Paul Volcker of the Federal Reserve underscored this change during testimony (House Banking Committee 1983: 101) defending public efforts on behalf of the developing countries in debt to banks. These efforts do not, he held, bail out banks; rather the insistence on the future extension of commercial credits bails *in* banks.

Chairman Volcker's turn of phrase was well directed. Congress has been concerned for some years over the relation of IMF to bank lending. Thus Senator Jacob Javits, no enemy of the IMF, asked the under secretary of the treasury in 1977 (Senate Foreign Relations Committee 1977: 31):

Aren't you really saying that when a country has reached the limit of its credit worthiness, where the banks now have reason to fear that loans they have made will not be repaid or any further loans ought not to be made, or where their judgment has let them go too far, that this is where IMF comes into the rescue mission? It extends public credit which in turn enables that country to start repaying on private loans.

More recently, the debate over whether or not IMF lending relieves commercial banks of their loans to foreign countries stalled approval in the U.S. House of Representatives of a bill providing for an increase in the U.S. commitment to the IMF in 1983. In order to secure the votes to pass the bill, the Treasury agreed to an eleventh-hour amendment titled, "Opposing Fund Bailouts of Banks." The amendment, now law, requires the U.S. executive director of the IMF "to oppose and vote against any Fund drawing by a member country where, in his judgment, the Fund resources would be drawn principally for the purpose of repaying loans which have been imprudently made by banking institutions" (*Congressional Record* 1983: S16698).

In fact, the IMF's command over resources is not of a scale to replace much bank credit. Under normal circumstances, an IMF member cannot borrow much more in a year than its quota. And the quota of the largest debtors amounts to no more than a few percent of their bank debt. Not one of the top twenty debtors to banks in the reporting area of the Bank for International Settlements (BIS) has an IMF quota that reaches 15 percent of its bank debt. So the idea that IMF lending can relieve banks of the bulk of their claims on major foreign borrowers can be put aside.

While Congress fears that IMF and bank credit are substitutes, the usual view is that they are complements. The IMF's role is often viewed as the catalyst in a member's working out of its balance of payments and debt problems. Before the member country enters an IMF program, it builds up its debt rapidly but encounters increasing difficulty borrowing from banks, supplier corporations, and governments. It may switch to short-term bank borrowing, experience domestic capital flight, and fall behind in contracted payments. With the announcement of the IMF program and associated changes in policy, banks once again make long-term loans, corporate suppliers reopen credit lines, governments offer guarantees and loans, and residents of the country repatriate their funds. The reaction of other creditors multiplies the modest resources at the disposal of the IMF.

This chapter examines the facts of IMF and bank lending in the years 1976 to 1981 to determine how consistent they are with the model that IMF lending catalyzes bank loans. However the loaf is sliced (and here the data are analyzed two ways), broad support for the catalytic model emerges. But reduced bank lending associated with increased IMF lending did become more common toward the end of the period.

The increasingly problematic relation between IMF and bank lending provides a new vantage on the IMF's change in practice in 1982. The IMF has conditioned its own assistance to major troubled borrowers on banks' (and governments') committing further resources to them. According to J.J. Polak (1984: 256-7), the IMF's former head of research and a current executive director, the IMF "accepted a new international role for the institution: the role of the leader of coordinated balance of payments assistance." In its expanded role, the IMF has in practice "determined . . . the indispensable contribution of other groups of providers of funds," including commercial banks. Perhaps in taking on this role the IMF was not simply responding to the extraordinary strains in financial markets in 1982; the experience of its own lending not catalyzing bank lending may have also prepared the IMF to expand its role.

ANALYSIS OF NINETY-NINE PROGRAMS, 1976-81

Data and Procedures

One way to examine the relationship between the IMF and bank lending is to compare snapshots of each before and after every IMF program of conditional lending. More precisely, one may compare the conditional IMF credit and bank credit to a member at the end of the last full quarter prior to a program's inception conditional IMF credit and bank credit one year later.[1] Rises in both sources of credit are consistent with the view that IMF lending catalyzes bank lending or that the two complement each other. Conversely rising IMF credit and declining bank credit suggest substitution of official for private credit. These comparisons will be made for all the ninety-nine IMF programs that had quantitative policy conditions attached in the years 1976-81.[2]

In order to perform the test ideally, one would bring more complete data to bear than those available. Figures for each foreign bank's claims on a given country could answer questions about how many or which kind of banks lent more or less. In addition, it would be useful to know in what currencies claims on each country are denominated, whether in dollars, deutsche marks, sterling, yen, French francs, or some other currency. Finally one would want to know which bank claims were guaranteed by, for instance, the export credit agencies of the U.S. or other governments. With all this information, the evolution of each bank's exposure to each country borrowing from the IMF could be traced.

Unfortunately, such precise data are not available. The BIS quarterly international banking data are commendable for their comprehensiveness[3] and their frequency. But they are reported in highly aggregated form, as total claims of banks in the whole reporting area. Conclusions drawn from such aggregates may not be true of many or a majority of reporting banks.

In addition the BIS data are reported in dollars, with foreign currency claims converted to dollars at an exchange rate at or near that prevailing on the reporting date. As a result, when the dollar strengthens, the nondollar portion of claims shows a decline as expressed in dollars even when they actually remain static. The analysis of all ninety-nine cases will take this valuation effect into account only to a limited extent; the case studies of Turkey, Romania, and Yugoslavia will address the problem more directly.

Finally, the BIS data do not adjust for external guarantees of bank loans. This problem is particularly acute for countries that host a great deal of offshore banking and shipping business: the United Kingdom, Liberia, and Panama. The explosion of British reserves in 1977 may be taken as prima facie evidence that private agents, including banks, eagerly placed money in Great Britain after it entered an IMF program. For Liberia and Panama, data on U.S. bank claims that are adjusted for external guarantees are used.

With these data limitations in mind, consider the ninety-nine cases displayed in Tables 8A–1 through 8A–4. Note that some IMF members appear repeatedly on the tables. Indeed, only fifty-six countries account for ninety-nine programs. Some, like the Philippines, entered and drew down several programs in a row; others cancelled programs that had gone off track to embark on new ones.

Tables 8A–1 and 8A–2 list the seventy-four programs during which the member increased its conditional borrowing from the IMF; Tables 8A–3 and 8A–4 list the twenty-five programs during which the member held steady or decreased its conditional borrowing from the IMF. For cases like the latter to happen, the member must borrow little or nothing during the course of a program and meanwhile perhaps even repay previous IMF loans. Often this happens because a member does not have much use for the IMF's funds. For instance, Italy experienced such a rapid turnaround in its balance of goods and services after entering a standby program with the IMF in 1977 that it was able to cease drawing, to exceed the agreed limit on governmental borrowing, and to repay earlier IMF loans. Gabon's 1980 program represents an even more felicitous outcome: it met all the IMF targets, actually borrowed nothing under the program, and repaid both IMF and commercial-bank loans. A less felicitous possibility is that of a member who needs the IMF support but does not meet the conditions and must repay earlier IMF advances.

Results

The comparison of IMF and bank lending snapshots before and after the ninety-nine conditional IMF programs finds that two-thirds conformed to the catalytic model (Table 8A–1) or showed no increase in conditional IMF credit (Tables 8A–3 and 8A–4). Only one-third were followed by decreases of bank credit in conjunction with increases in conditional IMF credit in one or more years (Table 8A–2). Of the programs followed by an increase in IMF lending (seventy-four), the majority (forty) conformed to the catalytic model. Declines in bank credit were more common in association with extended arrangements than with standby arrangements.

Much more striking, however, than the differences between standby and extended arrangements is the increasing likelihood over the 1976–81 period that IMF lending not catalyze bank lending. In 1976 there was no instance of reduced bank credit to a country that was increasing its conditional borrowing from the IMF. By 1981, however, half of the countries entering IMF programs appear to have experienced some cut in bank credit.

It was not only the *frequency* of observations of increased IMF credit in conjunction with decreased bank credit that rose over the period. The *amounts* of money involved in some such cases also rose. The sums involved for Yugoslavia, Romania, Turkey, and Zaire are not insignificant.

Qualifications

Recognizing the valuation problem compels at minimum a sharp qualification of the findings reported in the preceding paragraphs on bank lending to Francophone Africa. Consider that the French franc fell from about 4 francs to the dollar in 1980 to about 8 francs to the dollar by the end of 1983. Even if a moving average of the dollar/franc exchange rate has been used to convert franc claims to dollars, the dollar value of the stock of franc claims must have fallen sharply. For this reason, the apparent declines in bank credit around the six IMF programs for Mauritania, Senegal, Togo, and the Ivory Coast in 1980–81 are suspect.

Problems in the data force one to qualify the results for Liberia and Pakistan as well. In the first case, Liberia's difficulty in servicing its debt in recent years has led to U.S. banks' taking a hard look at their Liberian claims. The banks have found that more carried external guarantees of, for instance, Greek shipping companies. The drop in bank claims may thus reflect more a secular change in reporting standards than anything else. In the case of Pakistan, close examination of the BIS data shows that the drop in claims reflected changes in the position of U.S. banks' home offices vis-à-vis their branches in Pakistan. Home offices' claims on and liabilities to branches in Pakistan declined. Such reductions of gross positions are not consistent with the notion that funds drawn from the IMF repaid bank loans.

What is left of the results after putting these qualifications in the balance? The effect of the fall in the French franc against the dollar makes suspect the six instances of lower bank lending to the Mauritania, Senegal, Togo, and the Ivory Coast, mentioned previously. The data for lending to Liberia yield no reliable clue as to bank behavior there. And Pakistan's program was followed by no great change in the country's net position vis-à-vis banks in the major industrial countries. In all, nine instances of reduced bank lending to borrowers from the IMF are doubtful or do not lend themselves to the view that IMF credit repays bank loans.

The results as qualified may be restated: some twenty-five of ninety-nine IMF programs were followed by withdrawals of bank credit. That is over one-quarter of all programs and over one-third of programs that were followed by increased IMF lending.

Bear in mind that the reduction in bank lending after some of these programs reversed itself in short order (for example, in the early programs for Egypt, Burma, Sri Lanka, and Peru). Furthermore, some of the declines in bank credit were of minimal size. For instance, how much significance does one attach to the $3 million drop in bank credit in 1981 to Sierra Leone, a country that relies overwhelmingly on multilateral and bilateral sources of official finance in any case?

All of that having been said, one is left with a number of debtors of some significance that reduced their bank credit while drawing on the IMF. The next section gets down to cases.

Case Studies

This section steps behind the analysis of the universe of IMF programs to spotlight the fourteen large debtor countries that borrowed from the IMF in the period under review. It gives particular attention to the three of these that showed up in Table 8A-2, namely, Turkey, Romania, and Yugoslavia. But it will be shown below that they accounted for only a small share—less than 10 percent—of the debt of the top fourteen debtors.

The record of IMF and bank credit to most of the large debtors generally corresponds to the catalytic model. Mexico and Portugal briefly borrowed from both sources when they experienced current-account deficits, then repaid both sources after their accounts moved into surplus. Korea, the Philippines, and Thailand drew on both sources over several years. As shown in Table 8A-2, Peru and Egypt experienced difficulty in retaining bank credit for a time, but reestablished their credit and repaid IMF loans. For two quarters in 1976, Argentina reduced its debt to banks while drawing credit from the IMF. But by meeting all the conditions attached to its 1977 standby arrangement, the country so reestablished its creditworthiness that it could readily borrow from banks but did not need to borrow from the IMF.

The three countries for which the catalytic effect was not in evidence were far from the largest debtors. Table 8A-5 displays the largest gross debtors to BIS area banks among the net debtors to the same banks that borrowed conditionally from the IMF in 1976-81. The fourteen countries owed $221 billion to banks at the end of

1981. The three countries discussed in greater detail below, Yugoslavia, Romania, and Turkey, accounted for $20 billion of that debt, or less than 10 percent.

Common among the three cases is the protracted nature of the negotiations between banks and borrower on the restructuring of debt. And, partly in consequence, in all three cases the banks found scheduled payments in arrears over a likewise protracted period. The reasons for the prolonged negotiations varied from case to case. But in all three cases, the accumulation of the arrears of payment stood in a reciprocal relation to the banks' inclination to cut back lending. On the one hand, bankers take arrears as a signal of the capacity or the willingness to pay and move to reduce exposure in response. On the other hand, it is often only when banks attempt to reduce exposure to a borrower that the latter shows itself to be illiquid and falls into arrears on its payments.

Turkey

Turkey's debt crisis of 1977–79 had its roots in expansive fiscal policy, protected, inefficient state enterprises, and an increasingly overvalued exchange rate. The way Turkey borrowed left the country exposed to any change in its creditors' willingness to lend, and it also contributed to the length and difficulty of ensuing negotiations with them. Public policy had encouraged the buildup of high-interest, short-term credits, and the authorities' information on the debt was scant. Lack of information together with the Turkish perception that foreign bankers had profited handsomely from their short-term lending made the debt restructuring negotiations long and difficult.

Turkey entered two abortive standby arrangements in 1978 and 1979. After a military coup in 1980, a three-year standby arrangement with the IMF was fully implemented. World Bank teams helped restructure state enterprises. Unconstrained by labor unrest, the government devalued the Turkish lira to boost exports. As a result, exports boomed, Turkey's current-account deficit shrank (see Figure 8–1) and Turkish workers abroad resumed their repatriation of funds. There was some slippage on the monetary policy in connection with a 1983 standby agreed with the IMF, but the government elected in late 1983 gives every evidence of its commitment to the basic policy pursued since 1980.

Figure 8-1. Current-Account Balances of Romania, Turkey, and Yugoslavia.[a]

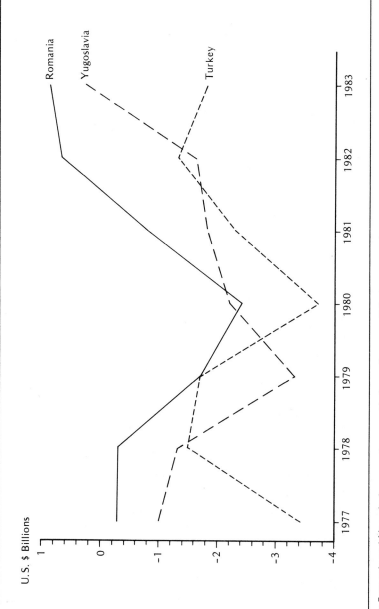

a. For Romania and Yugoslavia, current-account balances in convertible currency only.
Source: IMF.

In the face of the performance under the 1980 standby, IMF credit might have been expected to catalyze bank lending. But not-withstanding an injection of funds from the IMF, the World Bank and an Organization for Economic Cooperation and Development consortium, such catalysis is nowhere in evidence (see Table 8A–2). To be sure, some of the decline since 1980 in Turkey's bank debt as measured in dollars should be ascribed to the rise of the dollar against such currencies as the German mark and Swiss franc, as ex-plained previously. But surely there was little increase in bank credit to Turkey before the end of 1983, when Turkey regained regular access to the syndicated credit market. And the U.S. Country Expo-sure Lending Survey (CELS) data show that American banks actually reduced their claims on Turkey by $160 million, or more than 10 percent, between end-1978 and end-1981. It is clear that the re-sponse of BIS area banks to Turkey's three-year program did not conform to the catalytic model.

The protracted rescheduling negotiations may explain the banks' behavior. Turkey fell behind on payments to its creditors in 1978, did not come to terms with its bank creditors until 1981, and only cleared up its arrears in 1982. Again, these arrears both furthered and reflected the unwillingness of Turkey's bank creditors to lend. But the lengthy negotiations and the long-standing arrears with which they were associated may have neutralized the catalyst.

Romania

In common with many other borrowing countries, Romania faced adverse external developments in 1980–81. Higher oil prices, high interest rates, a drop in demand for exports, and a deterioration in the rate of exchange between exports and imports all strained Romania's external accounts. In addition, Romania's foreign borrow-ing in the 1970s financed an overambitious program of investment. It also financed oil processing and petrochemical manufacturing, which, in terms of world prices, were money-losing activities.

The management of its external debt left Romania vulnerable to a change in sentiment among its foreign creditors. Over four-tenths of Romania's debt to BIS area banks in mid-1980 was short term, much of it contracted in the interbank market, where foreign banks re-garded their claims as readily realizable. This reliance on the interbank market reflected the authorities' reluctance to pay higher rates in the syndicated credit markets for medium-term funds. This same reluctance left Romania's international reserves at a low level. Thus, Romania was not in a position to weather a storm.

The storm came with the rise of Solidarity, the workers' union, in Poland in the summer of 1980 and the subsequent break in Poland's debt service in the beginning of 1981. Romania's debt to BIS area banks peaked in the third quarter of 1980 and fell rapidly thereafter as banks cut back on interbank credit lines and trade credits.

Romania compounded its difficulties with banks by assuming an awkward stance in the negotiation for a rescheduling agreement. Arrears in payments arose in 1981, but the Romanian authorities were slow to start the negotiations. Once negotiating, the two sides had difficulty speaking the same language. In part because it had not fulfilled its commitment to eliminate its payments arrears, Romania lost access in the second half of 1981 to IMF credit under a standby agreed in June of that year. It was not until the second half of 1982 that Romania agreed to a rescheduling with governments, commercial banks, and suppliers. Arrears were not eliminated until 1983.

The decline in bank claims on Romania departs sharply from the catalytic model. The valuation effect could account for the drops in bank claims in 1981 and 1982, over 10 percent each year, only if none of Romania's bank debt were denominated in dollars. A better estimate is one-half; thus banks succeeded in reducing their claims.

By the end of 1982, Romania had slashed imports to achieve a current-account surplus in convertible currency. Thus, the reduction in debt to BIS area banks from 1982 on can be ascribed to the striking turnaround in the trade account. But the reduction in bank debt in 1981 occurred notwithstanding a continued deficit in convertible-currency trade. The drop in bank credit was associated instead with the buildup of arrears in payments of interest, a decrease in reserves, and an increase in borrowing from official sources, including the IMF.

Yugoslavia

Yugoslavia on the face of it is the most puzzling of the three cases. After years of rapid economic growth it entered first a one-year standby program in 1980 and then a three-year standby program in

1981. Its performance in closing its fiscal deficit, making its exports more competitive and restricting credit qualified the country on balance to draw down its IMF lines of credit fully. Cutbacks in imports led to a much improved current account (see Figure 8-1).

Yet Yugoslavia lost access to medium-term bank credit in 1981. The decline in BIS area bank claims (see Table 8A-2) is not easy to interpret. The behavior of European banks is obscured by the valuation effect, but the CELS data show clearly that U.S. banks reduced their claims by over 13 percent, some $300 million, in 1982. By the end of 1982 the country was negotiating with banks for a rescheduling, with governments for a package of export credits, with the BIS for a bridge loan and with the World Bank for fast-disbursing credit.

Yugoslavia had had some difficulty borrowing medium-term in 1981 owing to the difficulties of its neighbors. Financing was shifted to short-term interbank credits. But with limited means through which the several republics shared foreign exchange, continued interbank financing depended on the weakest link. When a major bank in one republic, which had been financing oil imports at a loss, ran short of foreign exchange, foreign creditors started cutting back lines of credit. The illiquidity of other Yugoslavian banks became manifest, and arrears began to accumulate in 1982.

The process of negotiation was prolonged in part owing to the same decentralization that had set the stage for debt crisis. Foreign banks wanted central government guarantees to cover restructured debt. But this required constitutional change and entailed the extension of central bureaucratic control over foreign exchange allocation. Continued errors and omissions outflows suggest that this effort has produced mixed results.

The failure, then, of IMF credit to catalyze bank credit was associated with the appearance and persistence of payment arrears. These reflected both caution on the part of foreign creditors and defects in the country's management of its debt and foreign exchange. In common with Turkey and Romania, lengthy negotiations over the restructuring of Yugoslavia's debt let the payment arrears persist and nullified the catalytic effect of the IMF's lending.

Drawing Some Lessons

The answer to the question whether the facts are consistent with the claim that IMF lending catalyzes bank lending is, in general, yes. This conclusion holds for the years 1976–81 whether one examines comparisons of lending before and after IMF programs or individual cases. This finding confirms that of the U.S. Treasury in its analysis of the 1970–75 period: increased bank credit to a country drawing IMF credit is the norm (House Banking Committee 1977: 80–84).

IMF lending to Turkey, Romania, and Yugoslavia, among others, did not catalyze increased bank credit. But, after some time working out its debt problems, Turkey may be regaining its access to bank credit. At this stage Romania is pursuing a positive policy of reducing its commercial indebtedness. And the decline in bank credit to Yugoslavia appears to have stopped. Furthermore it is important to keep these cases in perspective. Turkey, Romania, and Yugoslavia accounted for no more than 10 percent of the commercial bank debt of the fourteen largest borrowers at end-1981 that had entered IMF programs in the preceding half decade.

Nevertheless, the second conclusion is that this rare event—banks' cutting their lending to a country that is borrowing from the IMF—became markedly less rare toward the end of the 1976–81 period. Again, this conclusion emerges from the before-and-after snapshots and the case studies. The explanation for this observed shift in bank behavior lies in changes in the global economy, in the business of banking, and in the performance of particular borrowing countries.

The deterioration in global conditions, first, comprised prolonged recession, consequently depressed world trade, low commodity prices, and record rates of short-term interest rates. These conditions raised the risks associated with outstanding international loans.

Next changes in the business of banking affected banks' response to these heightened risks. While the recession of 1975 raised the risks of international lending, banks proved quite willing then to accelerate it. By the end of the 1970s, however, international loans bulked larger on the books of commercial banks both in relation to total assets and bank capital. Consequently, an obvious risk probably induced more caution in 1980 than in the mid-1970s. And, as pointed out previously, the risks were also higher in the latter period.

A change in the industrial organization of international banking between the middle and the end of the 1970s likewise affected the banks' response to the risks posed by recession in the world economy. In the mid-1970s the "who's who" of international banking was expanding rapidly. By the end of the decade the entry of new lenders had slowed. This meant that one bank trying to reduce its lending to a country was less likely to be balanced by another bank trying to increase its market share.

Third, in addition to these general circumstances, the particular performance of certain countries induced banks to reduce their exposure to them and perhaps to think twice about other countries. Not only macroeconomic performance—the growth of output and exports, for instance—but also track records in two matters important to bank creditors sometimes did not inspire confidence. First, some countries repeatedly approached the IMF, announced changes in policy, but then did not sustain them. Second, some countries fell into arrears in the payment of principal and interest to banks. To the extent that such cases occurred more frequently than expected, banks may have adopted a more aggressive strategy of reducing exposure to countries in actual or potential difficulty.

It may seem a paradox that even as banks followed the IMF lead less consistently, they signed loan contracts that linked their lending to IMF lending more closely. The integration of commercial loan contracts and IMF lending has gone beyond an informal understanding that a loan contract will not be signed until the borrower has arranged a conditional loan with the IMF. It has also gone beyond "technical assistance to a member, at its request, in its efforts to negotiate loans that will augment the resources available under a standby arrangement" (Gold 1982: 11). According to the IMF's counsel, commercial banks have at times made draw-downs of syndicated credits contingent on a country's borrowing conditionally from the Fund or on the IMF's certifying that the member was able to borrow under a conditional arrangement.[4]

In this matter, the relation in law may be getting stronger because the relation in practice is getting weaker. If many lenders, especially among smaller banks, have become more inclined to reduce exposure to troubled borrowers, then the stage is set for legal linkage of IMF and bank lending. For one thing, such an inclination makes for a lenders' market in which terms and conditions can be tightened. In this light, contractual linkage to IMF lending is of a piece with pledges of assets and increases in spreads.[5] For another, reluctant lenders, persuaded not to withdraw credit if a country is borrowing from the IMF, are likely to insist on contractual linkage.

What are the consequences for the IMF of the banks' disinclination to follow the IMF's lead? Most directly, it reduces the confidence the IMF can have in any prediction it makes of private capital inflows for a country under a conditional program. A recent IMF study acknowledged, "In some stand-by arrangements in the past, the bank financing that was assumed to be available did not materialize" (Mentre 1984: 26). This forces the IMF to arrange programs for its members in an increasingly uncertain financial environment, even apart from widespread crisis conditions. And the IMF's job is made more difficult in another, more telling fashion. IMF programming starts with the expected capital inflow to arrive at a target for a member's current-account balance. The lower the expected capital inflow, the smaller the current-account deficit can be. Holding other things equal, the smaller the financeable current-account deficit, the more restrictive the monetary and fiscal policy or the larger the real depreciation of the currency. Thus, to accommodate the inclination of banks to reduce lending to a member, the IMF must design a tougher program. This jeopardizes the chances for getting broad and stable political support for any program of austerity in the borrowing country.

One may ask why the IMF itself does not lend more under such circumstances, if it finds a greater capital inflow desirable. The answer is twofold and simple. Not only do the IMF Articles of Agreement preclude the use of Fund resources to finance a capital outflow, but the IMF does not even have the resources to offset much of a reduction in bank lending to many of its members.

The difficulty the IMF experienced in keeping banks lending to its borrowers before 1982 has informed its practices since then. It seems likely that the approach the IMF adopted in 1982 for Mexico and Argentina reflected not only the immediate seizing up of the international credit market and the scale of the debts in question but also the strains already evident before 1982 in the relation between IMF and bank lending. In early 1983 an unnamed IMF official was quoted (in Kaletsky 1983: 12) as saying:

> We learned a lot of lessons in 1979 and 1980. . . . We found that relative to the enormous efforts that we and the World Bank and the various governments were making, some of the countries ended up with relatively little extra. We lent them the money, but instead of staying in the country, the private banks got all their interest out and some got out their capital as well. When we went to Mexico we knew this had to be avoided.

The IMF has worked to keep Mexico from following Turkey by, in effect, requiring commercial banks to lend the bulk of sums owed for interest. First for Mexico and Argentina, then for Brazil, Chile, and Peru, the IMF has made it clear that it would lend only after commitments by commercial banks to expand lending were in hand. The IMF has sought to avoid the risks of the drawn-out negotiations that occurred between banks and Turkey, Romania, and Yugoslavia. Thus, banks' following the lead of the IMF has ceased to be a market outcome with at most some quiet official encouragement. Instead, the IMF now requires bank lending directly as a precondition for its injection of credit. Indeed, the frequently used metaphor of catalysis—a reaction induced by, and therefore following, the introduction of a chemical agent—is no longer strictly appropriate.

The compelling question is: Will the historically "normal" role of IMF lending as a catalyst for private bank finance reemerge? At the American Economic Association meetings in December 1982, an IMF official was asked whether he anticipated that insistence on further commercial bank lending would become a regular feature of IMF efforts on behalf of its members. He answered no, that he understood the practice was an extraordinary response to the equally extraordinary conditions of 1982. But if the strain in the relation between IMF and bank lending that began to show before 1982 is a change in the structure of international finance, the return to an arm's length relation seems less likely.

There are several alternatives to continuing locked-in bank lending. First of all, global economic conditions and the performance of debtor countries may succeed in restoring the confidence of commercial bankers so that they resume lending spontaneously. Second, the private flow of capital from sources other than banks, especially foreign direct investment, may respond to global economic recovery and greater receptivity in debtor countries. Third, governments of creditor countries might increase their lending through bilateral or multilateral channels. Finally, in the absence of more locked-in lending and any of the three alternative sources of capital, the debtor countries could find it necessary to accentuate the already politically difficult compression of income and restraint on economic growth.

These four alternatives to locked-in bank lending range between the barely possible and the just plain unlikely. If locked-in bank lending continues, no one should be surprised.

NOTES TO CHAPTER 8

1. Conditional credit is defined as net advances in the upper credit tranches (usually lending above 25 percent of quota) and in connection with extended fund facilities. Actually, the IMF attaches quantitative conditions to first credit tranche drawings that are part of an upper tranche standby. Not taking this practice into account results in fewer positive and more zero changes in conditional IMF credit.

2. Included in this analysis are two types of IMF programs: standby and extended arrangements. They share the feature that under them the IMF actually lends only if a borrower respects specific, quarterly limits. If a member does not meet a condition, it loses access to IMF credits unless the IMF waives the condition. Extended arrangements, instituted in 1974, give countries a longer period over which to raise their production of traded goods, both exports and imports. Accordingly, extended fund facility (EFF) loans have longer maturity than standby loans, ten years instead of five years. The two kinds of programs appear together because the differences between them in practice are less than in theory. On the one hand, a standby arrangement can run for two to three years; in any case successive programs can run back-to-back to approximate a longer term program. On the other hand, the quantitative conditions attached to extended arrangements are set for but a year at a time. Furthermore, if a member does not satisfy by a wide mark the conditions attached to an extended arrangement (or multiyear standby), it may cancel the arrangement to enter a new one.

3. Included are claims of banks in Austria, Belgium-Luxembourg, Denmark, France, West Germany, Ireland, Italy, the Netherlands, Sweden, the United Kingdom, Canada, Japan, and the United States and of certain offshore branches of U.S. banks.

4. Note that the IMF counsel's account of these legal developments appeared before mid-1982. Since mid-1982, of course, loan contracts for troubled borrowers like Brazil, Mexico, Argentina, Chile, and Peru have contained explicit links to IMF lending.

5. By contrast, the contract recently signed by banks and Portugal after Portugal entered a standby with the IMF did not contain contractual linkage, called for a narrow spread, contained no asset pledges, and was oversubscribed (that is, banks collectively offered to lend a sum greater than the borrower sought).

APPENDIX

Table 8A-1. Yearly Changes in Conditional IMF and BIS Area Bank Credit after IMF Arrangements, 1976–81, Showing a Rise in Both Conditional IMF Credit and Increases in Bank Credit.

Country	Date	Change in Conditional IMF Credit (SDR Millions)[a]	Change in Bank Credit ($ Millions)
Philippines (EFF)	4/76	90	138
Second year		70	976
Third year		57	685
South Africa	8/76	116	987
Israel	10/76	12	1,706
United Kingdom	1/77	1,325	—
Mexico (EFF)	1/77	100	1,446
Zaire	4/77	5	317
Jamaica	8/77	14	280
Peru	11/77	10	723
Jamaica (EFF)	6/78	56	175
Burma	7/78	20	22
Egypt (EFF)	7/78	43	810
Guyana (EFF)	8/78	16	44
Haiti (EFF)	10/78	0	5
Second year	—	0	0
Third year	—	11	5
Sri Lanka (EFF)	1/79	72	2
Second year	—	-4	66
Third year	—	147	109
Sudan (EFF)	5/79	30	53
Second year	—	121	58
Third year	—	170	88
Guyana (EFF)	6/79	7	15
Peru	7/79	122	172
Turkey	7/79	420	356
Bangladesh	7/79	32	25
Malawi	10/79	8	52

Table 8A-1. continued

Country	Date	Change in Conditional IMF Credit (SDR Millions)[a]	Change in Bank Credit ($ Millions)
Philippines	2/80	158	1,528
Second year	—	193	1,084
Korea	3/80	231	3,714
Yugoslavia	6/80	307	2,192
Equatorial Guinea	7/80	15	23
Mauritius	9/80	23	24
Tanzania	9/80	9	71
Morocco (EFF)	10/80	275	197
Pakistan (EFF)	11/80	344	31
Korea	2/81	577	2,939
Morocco (EFF)	3/81	136	270
Madagascar	4/81	32	18
Central African Republic	4/81	4	62
Grenada	5/81	2	0
Ethiopia	5/81	42	7
Thailand	6/81	301	221
Burma	6/81	22	43
Somalia	7/81	38	43
Senegal	9/81	20	19
India (EFF)	11/81	1,500	380
Second year	—	1,600	1,772
Third year	—	800	581
Mauritius	12/81	15	17

a. IMF loans are denominated in Special Drawing Rights (SDRs), defined as 54 U.S. cents, 46 German pfennigs, 34 Japanese yen, 74 French centimes, and 7.1 British pence. The dollar value of the SDR thus varies day to day; at end-1983 it stood at $1.04.

Sources: IMF, *International Financial Statistics*; BIS, *International Banking Developments* and *Maturity Distribution of International Bank Lending* (for Thailand); Federal Financial Institutions Examination Council, *Country Exposure Lending Survey* (for Panama and Liberia).

Table 8A-2. Yearly Changes in Conditional IMF and BIS Area Bank Credit after IMF Arrangements, 1976–81, Showing a Rise in Conditional IMF Credit and a Decline in Bank Credit.

Country	Date	Change in Conditional IMF Credit (SDR Millions)[a]	Change in Bank Credit ($ Millions)
Egypt	4/77	30	−50
Burma	5/77	22	−7
Sri Lanka	12/77	41	−3
Turkey	4/78	40	−49
Zambia	4/78	73	−22
Second year	—	114	−19
Peru	9/78	70	−126
Jamaica (EFF)	6/79	99	−34
Honduras	6/79	16	52
Second year	—	−4	41
Third year	—	8	−52
Zaire	8/79	29	−50
Mauritius	10/79	55	−3
Sierra Leone	11/79	10	−5
Bolivia	2/80	31	−91
Malawi	5/80	17	38
Second year	—	16	−56
Turkey	6/80	371	476
Second year	—	395	−258
Third year	—	346	−121
Mauritania	7/80	11	−28
Guyana (EFF)	7/80	34	8
Second year	—	16	−24
Senegal (EFF)	8/80	41	−89
Liberia	9/80	20	−630
Kenya	10/80	68	−145
Bangladesh (EFF)	12/80	189	−5
Yugoslavia	1/81	556	275
Second year	—	554	−579
Third year	—	460	−161
Togo	2/81	7	−67
Dominica (EFF)	2/81	3	−17
Second year	—	3	5
Third year	—	2	3

Table 8A-2. continued

Country	Date	Change in Conditional IMF Credit (SDR Millions)[a]	Change in Bank Credit ($ Millions)
Ivory Coast (EFF)	2/81	177	63
Second year	—	115	154
Third year	—	153	−249
Sierra Leone (EFF)	3/81	33	−3
Jamaica (EFF)	4/81	178	−28
Second year	—	142	16
Third year	—	86	−10
Zambia (EFF)	5/81	301	−142
Uganda	6/81	65	−13
Mauritania	6/81	23	−17
Romania	6/81	59	−909
Second year	—	305	−638
Third year	—	132	−404
Costa Rica (EFF)	6/81	23	−87
Zaire (EFF)	6/81	165	−66
Liberia	8/81	55	−347
Pakistan (EFF)	12/81	445	−260
Second year	—	285	88

a. Special Drawing Rights.

Sources: Same as Table 8A-1.

Table 8A-3. Yearly Changes in Conditional IMF and BIS Area Bank Credit after IMF Arrangements, 1976–81, Showing No Change or a Decline in Conditional IMF Credit and a Rise in Bank Credit.

Country	Date	Change in Conditional IMF Credit (SDR Millions)[a]	Change in Bank Credit ($ Millions)
Zambia	8/76	0	70
Argentina	8/76	0	210
Pakistan	3/77	−27	118
Italy	4/77	−639	1,756
Romania	9/77	−11	1,130
Argentina	9/77	0	2,577
Gabon	5/78	0	219
Panama	6/78	0	644
Portugal	6/78	0	755
Panama	3/79	0	904
Congo	4/79	0	68
Nicaragua	5/79	0	44
Togo	6/79	0	59
Philippines	6/79	0	1,409
W. Samoa	8/79	0	2
Kenya	8/79	0	199
Somalia	2/80	0	2
Costa Rica	3/80	0	168
Panama	4/80	0	936
Madagascar	6/80	0	140
Laos	8/80	0	0
Solomon Islands	5/81	0	10

a. Special Drawing Rights.

Sources: Same as Table 8A-1.

Table 8A-4. Yearly Changes in Conditional IMF and BIS Area Bank Credit after IMF Arrangements, 1976–81, Showing No Change or a Decline in Conditional IMF Credit and a Decline in Bank Credit.

Country	Date	Change in Conditional IMF Credit (SDR Millions)[a]	Change in Bank Credit ($ Millions)
Haiti	8/76	0	−211
Ghana	1/79	0	−79
Gabon (EFF)	6/80	−7	−10
Second year	—	0	−122
Third year	—	0	33

a. Special Drawing Rights.
Sources: Same as Table 8A-1.

Table 8A-5. Fourteen Largest Debtors That Borrowed Conditionally from the IMF, 1976–81.

Country	BIS Area Bank Claims, End-1981 ($ Billions)
Mexico	$57.1
Italy	54.0
Argentina	24.8
South Korea	19.9
South Africa	11.2
Yugoslavia	10.7
Philippines	10.2
Portugal	7.7
Thailand	5.1
Romania	5.1
Peru	4.4
Turkey	4.2
Morocco	3.7
Ivory Coast	3.2
Total	$220.9

Source: BIS, *Maturity Distribution of International Bank Lending* and (for Italy) *International Banking Developments*.

9

MULTINATIONAL INSTITUTIONS IN THE DEBT CRISIS
National Interests and Long Term Consequences

Philip A. Wellons

In October 1976 the government of Peru negotiated a $386 million syndicated loan to help it restructure its problem debt, then promptly announced the purchase of $250 million in military equipment from the Soviet Union (*Institutional Investor* 1976). Far from easing Peru's debt crisis, the credit appeared to have financed imports the lenders found least desirable.

Embarrassed, the governments and banks of the West, including the United States, West Germany, and others, learned their lesson for the next restructuring. They wrung from Peru's government an agreement not to buy more military equipment.

Soon after that agreement, a representative of one of the three big German banks visited a senior Peruvian official with an offer. As part of the effort to increase exports, a major German customer could provide military equipment, which the German bank would finance at good terms. Was the Peruvian government interested?

"Have you forgotten our agreement not to buy that sort of thing?" asked the Peruvian official. "Ah," was the reply, "That was another part of the bank."[1]

Not far below the surface of this vignette lurks the message of Rousseau's fable of the stag and the hare.[2] Despite the efforts of the

I would like to thank Dwight Crane, Stephan Haggard, Robert Keohane, and Charles Kindleberger for their comments.

147

group to work together, the immediate needs of its members can work at destructive cross-purposes.

This chapter examines the international lender of last resort (ILOLR) as a function that has been performed in debt crises at least since the mid-1970s. The crises occur when countries lack the exchange to service residents' foreign debts as they become due. The task of a lender of last resort during such a crisis is to provide liquidity needed to maintain or restore market confidence, keeping creditors from hasty withdrawal that could make the crisis worse. The ILOLR must do this without jeopardizing the financial system over the longer run.

Any international lender of last resort faces the central political fact of the twentieth century: despite the apparent intergration of the global economy, the world is organized by nations. This poses an apparently insurmountable obstacle for efforts to resolve the debt crisis in what appears to be the optimal manner, establishing an institution that can act as ILOLR (Kindleberger 1978a: ch. 10).[3] In practice during the recent debt crises, the ILOLR function has been performed mainly by governments of the Group of Five helped by the major banks in those countries (France, West Germany, Japan, the United Kingdom, and the United States). They negotiate each debt problem case by case.

For this chapter, I assume that a more formal international lender of last resort is not politically feasible, either in the form of one central institution or as one of a range of proposals designed to create a proto-ILOLR.[4] My central question is how the nation-based system, built around five industrial countries, affects debt crisis management and future lending. The literature suggests three important conclusions.[5]

1. The national interests of the members of the Group of Five determine who takes responsibility for the system. While this organization by nations gives a rationale for rich countries to share responsibilities, conflict about who performs the ILOLR function arises since nations have different perspectives.

2. This organization by nations permits creditor nations and banks to be free riders but also introduces the uncertainty of a bailout for every country and hence is a stabilizing force over the long run.

3. Since national interests of the Group of Five define the public good, more than just the stability of the financial system is a goal of intervention. Other goals, including growth and power, qualify the ILOLR actions.

The action of the ILOLR in crisis shapes the way banks allocate credit long term. Simply put, despite the forces for integration, the ILOLR today ties the banks more closely to their home countries, which in turn play an important role in defining risk and return on future cross-border loans. To reach this conclusion, this chapter examines the process by which the Group of Five governments and banks have managed debt crises since the mid-1970s.

WHO ACTS IN INTERNATIONAL CRISES?

Despite the ad hoc appearance of efforts to resolve the debt crises, there is a management system decentralized to the level of states. Instead of relying on a global institution, the creditors that are party to a debt crisis coordinate their response through one of the Group of Five powers and its major banks.

An alternative view exists. In this view, the increasing integration of world financial markets placed the job of managing the crises in the hands of the banks themselves and the IMF. On the surface, international integration in world finance would appear to have grown by leaps and bounds over the last fifteen years. Among private sector entities, principally banks, the uniquitous syndicate and the newer restructuring committees for each debtor country suggest a high level of integration. The Institute of International Finance (IIF) gives intimations of a still higher circle. Among creditor governments, the Paris Club and the Bank for International Settlements, with its Cooke committee, provide forums for coordinated inter-government action. Among multilateral institutions, the IMF would seem to be the linchpin in a complex system.[6]

My view is that this surface cooperation masks underlying national forces of great tenacity. Syndicates and restructuring committees are organized by home country, while Japan has organized its own IIF, in part to give Japanese banks more clout in the original IIF. The Cooke committee and the Paris Club are cautious forums for negotiating rather than transnational actors in their own right. The strength of the IMF varies with the support of its principal shareholders, the governments of the Group of Five. In this sense, the IMF is a player with independence at the margin, powerful when the country it deals with is not important to the Group of Five, such as a Sri Lanka, or when the Group of Five governments are not united.[7]

The real ILOLR consists of some combination of the five major industrial nations aided by their major banks. One of the governments of the Group of Five, with one or two of its banks, acts as leader in a particular crisis. Two questions arise. How is the status of leader achieved? What does the ILOLR do to keep the players in the game?

Leadership is important. The more successful restructurings take place under the leadership of one of the Group of Five governments. Success consists of keeping creditors and borrowers from withdrawing, eventually returning the country to a position in which it can raise net new funds in private financial markets. Examples of success include Turkey (Germany took the lead); Egypt in 1977 (the United States took the lead, helped by Saudi Arabia); Gabon (France led); Indonesia's Pertamina in 1975 (the United States was helped by Japan); and Mexico in 1982 (the United States was leader). The notable failures have occurred in the absence of such leadership: Zaire (which no major power led); Peru in 1977 (where the banks tried to impose a discipline alone); and Brazil and major U.S. banks (trying to organize over 700 private creditors).[8] The leading government turns to its major banks for help leading private creditors.

Banks, presumably those with the most at stake, become crisis leaders[9] according to criteria that include exposure, nationality, and strategy. Yet the largest banks' major criterion is simple exposure, other than the better one, loans to the problem country as a share of capital.[10] Banks act as leaders at two levels. At the global level, one bank, or a small group, coordinates banks from all countries. An example is Morgan Guaranty Trust Company, seeking to lead 700 banks to a free market solution in Brazil in December 1982. At the national level, in each home country one bank or a small group coordinates all banks from that country, acting as a liaison with the global leaders. Thus the Bank of Tokyo coordinated the Japanese banks in any number of reschedulings.

The leaders and the other Group of Five states act to keep the players in the game, by providing liquidity. An analysis of the bal-

Figure 9-1. Nonoil Developing Countries, Banks, and the Balance of Payments.

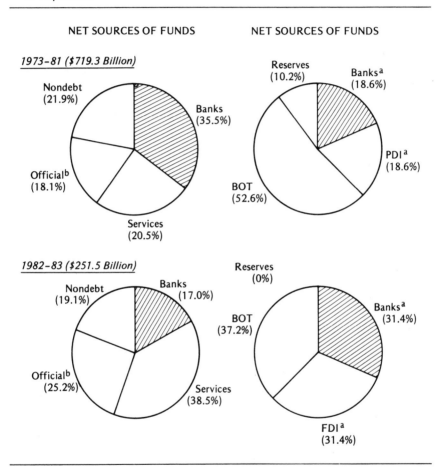

a. Reported as "investment payments," banks and other investments (FDI is foreign direct investments) are separated here 50/50, a conservative estimate of the banks' role.

b. Official includes errors and omissions and long-term nonbank flows.

Source: IMF Staff. 1983. *World Economic Outlook, Occasional Paper* no. 21, International Monetary Fund, Washington, D.C., May, Tables 21, 25, 28.

Figure 9–2. Biggest U.S. Banks Gain Share as Small Banks Pull Out of Latin America after 1982 Crisis.

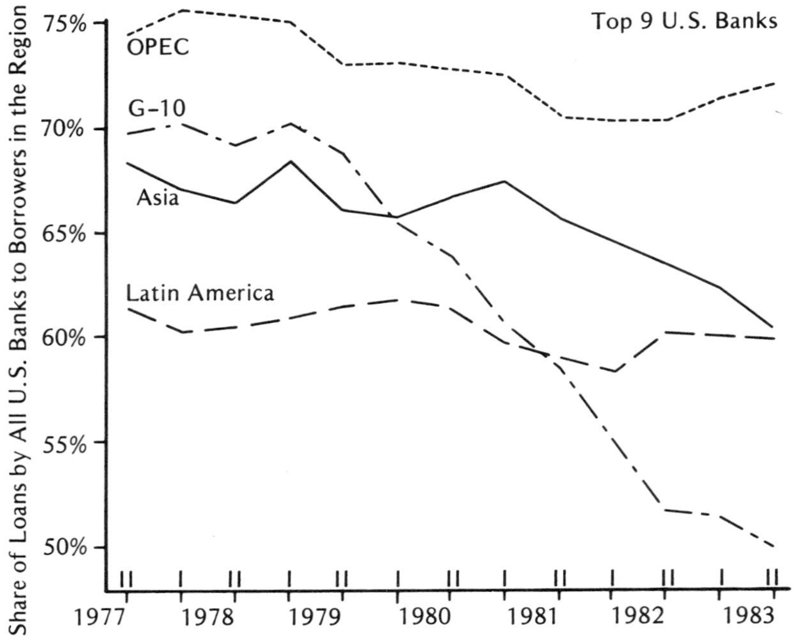

Total Credit by U.S. Banks ($ Billions)

End of Year	OPEC	Growth Rate
1977	$14.1	—
1978	19.4	36.8%
1979	18.9	12.5
1980	19.0	7.6
1981	22.4	10.0
1982	24.4	8.9
1983	25.1	3.0

End of Year	ASIA	Growth Rate
1977	$11.0	—
1978	13.9	26.7%
1979	18.1	29.7
1980	22.5	24.5
1981	27.5	22.0
1982	32.7	18.8
1983	33.2	1.7

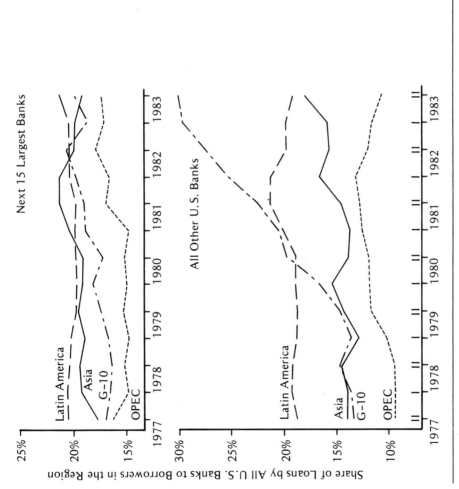

End of Year	Latin America	Growth Rate
1977	$31.9	—
1978	33.8	6.1%
1979	39.6	17.2
1980	51.1	28.9
1981	62.8	23.0
1982	70.6	12.4
1983	71.2	0.8

End of Year	G-10	Growth Rate
1977	$81.0	—
1978	91.0	12.4%
1979	101.8	11.9
1980	122.3	20.1
1981	150.2	22.7
1982	161.9	7.8
1983	164.3	1.5

Source: Federal Reserve System, *Country Exposure Lending Survey.*

ance of payments of nonoil developing countries reveals a fundamental shift in the sources and uses of funds. After 1981, governments and official agencies have borne the greatest share of the burden, while the banks benefited, reversing the pattern of the preceding eight years.

As Figure 9-1 illustrates, commercial banks' share of the funds provided dropped from 35.5 percent in the 1973-81 period to 17.0 percent in the watershed years of 1982-83, while the use of funds shifted dramatically from financing the trade deficit to servicing investment by banks and others. The banks supplied about twice as much as they drew during 1973-81, but then received about twice as much as they supplied in 1982-83. The net effect is that official agencies were funding the withdrawal of funds by the banks as a group after the crisis began.

Within the banks as a group, the big banks provide some liquidity by slightly increasing their exposure in crisis countries relative to other banks. As Figure 9-2 shows, when the crisis hit Latin America, the largest U.S. banks increased their share of U.S. exposure there as many small banks reduced theirs. Although the direction of the shifts in Latin America is important, their size is marginal: the small banks merely return to their 1977 share of 19 percent, down from about 22 percent in 1981. Escape is very difficult.

HOW WELL DOES THE SYSTEM PROTECT
ITSELF FROM FREE RIDERS?

The system just described is a mess. The result is moral hazard: the system may encourage single players[11] to act to the detriment of the group before, during, or after a crisis. For at least a decade, the U.S. Congress and the press have rung with cries that the banks were lending imprudently on the expectation that the government would bail them out. If this view is accurate and the system persists, we could expect to see more of this behavior by banks.

Today's ILOLR, however, seems to provide the commonly accepted prerequisites to moderate moral hazard: a qualified uncertainty over the long run about the actions of the ILOLR and penalties for invoking its aid.

Uncertainty about Aid in a Crisis

Over the long run, to the extent a bank is uncertain of a bail-out, its risk and cost rise and, one presumes, it hews closer to the strait and narrow of prudent lending. To estimate the uncertainty, a banker might adopt implicit guidelines about the ILOLR. From the behavior of the major players in the debt crises of the last several years, a bank strategist could reasonably draw the following guidelines for future crises:

1. Official aid will come, but a bank cannot be certain about the volume, timing, terms, and immediate recipient (bank or countries).
2. The composition and leadership of the multiple ILOLR will vary among borrowing countries. In many cases a bank cannot be certain in advance about the extent of the leader's or the other members' commitment.
3. The most exposed big banks will increase their share of credit to the problem country marginally as smaller banks pull back after the crisis. While the outflow is limited at the aggregate level, a bank cannot judge in advance the degree to which the smaller banks will escape in particular problem countries.
4. Since leadership among the banks will be defined not only by their relative exposure but also by their long-term interests in the country, a bank cannot be certain how dedicated other major banks will be in a debt crisis.

Each creates uncertainty over the long run. Guideline 1 is self-evident. For guideline 2, evidence of uncertainty about the ILOLR itself abounds: one multination study "found considerable controversy over what the LLR [lender of last resort] facilities are, let alone which banks had access to them" (Guttentag and Herring 1983a: 31). Guideline 3, is consistent with the documentable behavior of banks. As to guideline 4, a bank's long-term interests in a problem country vary with its strategy, which may shift, so even bank leadership in crisis is unclear in advance.

Since domestic politics determine aid to the debtor country, variations in the political processes in the Group of Five countries create uncertainty. In differing amounts, domestic politics constrain the Group of Five government from bailing out the banks directly, causing official aid to typically go to the debtor rather than the banks. The banks, in turn, must typically collect from the debtor.

Individual Group of Five countries have unequal political and economic interests among debtor countries, which undermines a bank's ability to estimate the likelihood and volume of aid. Japan is an example. Imagine debt crises in South Korea, Indonesia, and Malaysia. Given South Koreas's proximity to Japan and its long history as a recipient of substantial Japanese aid, a bank might expect Japan to take the lead if South Korea were to restructure its debt,[12] but expectations would be less clear for Indonesia or Malaysia. And in Japan, the political process for assistance to developing countries is bureaucratic rather than parliamentary,[13] so when we know the administrative position, the outcome is more certain than in the United States, where legislative scrutiny can change the executive's plans after the bureaucracy hammers out its stance.[14]

Penalties That Accompany Aid in a Crisis

The ILOLR must penalize those who use its aid in order to discourage them from relying on that assistance over the long run. A lender of last resort commonly assesses penalty rates against banks that draw on it, though it is uncertain that the present ILOLR system reduces the economic value of the loans.[15] The effective penalty banks pay for ILOLR help in reschedulings consists of the costs they cannot escape. Administrative costs and the cost of making provisions for problem loans arise as banks negotiate acceptable terms not only with the borrowers, but also with creditor governments and other banks. Thus, multiple reschedulings are expensive. Opportunity costs are incurred as funds are frozen. And administrative and opportunity costs arise as banks lose power to their home regulators. Of these, the final point is least noticed. The crises enable banks' regulators to consolidate their control even in areas not linked to the particulars of a crisis. In 1974, just after the first oil shock, Japan's finance ministry reined in its banks' overseas activities and kept firm control into the next decade. In 1983 and again in 1984, U.S. regulators increased the capital requirements for U.S. banks (see "Minimum Capital Guidelines Amendments" 1983: 539). German regulators are finally on the verge of forcing their banks to consolidate accounts, a major step made possible in part by the financial crisis.[16]

Other costs are a function of the home environment. For banks based in a country with a strong capital market, capital costs may rise dramatically. In the United States, bank stock prices have collapsed, in part because of the debt crisis and more so for banks highly exposed relative to capital.[17] In the other countries, capital markets are less able to distinguish among banks since hidden reserves make it difficult to determine the effect of the debt crises.[18]

Though in total these costs can be quite high, the penalty evaporates if banks can pass them on. The administrative costs are easiest to pass along. Much of the maneuvering in the political arena concerns these costs. At first the banks won, making some Latin American countries luminous profit centers in their darkest hour.[19] Spreads for Latin American countries began to fall only after the governments of the Group of Five, led by the Federal Reserve Board, intervened.[20] It would appear that while the roughly 0.75 percent decline in spreads for Mexico erased the profit incentive, the lower spread still met the higher administrative costs, since it was 0.25 percent to 0.50 percent above precrisis margins.

Less easy to pass on are the other costs associated with the crises. Banks must absorb the opportunity costs of greater regulation and of having their assets frozen in countries for years to come. Placing a value on these costs is difficult, but Group of Five countries with strong capital markets have done this in valuing the banks' equity.[21] Since 1982, U.S. bankers have commonly explained their unwillingness to increase cross-border exposure in many countries in terms of the adverse effect on their stock. In other countries, where share value is less important to the bank, the finance ministries play a more direct role in adjusting the banks' balance sheets. The German banks have tried self-regulation to preserve their independence.

Decentralization—Key to Dealing with Free Riders in a Crisis

To a financial crisis, this nation-based system shifts to more manageable groups. In a crisis involving 300 to 1,400 banks from dozens of countries, most banks have a small stake in the particular country.[22] In the Mexican rescheduling after August 1982, the two banks with the largest exposure had respectively only 3.8 percent and 3.5 percent of all bank loans. Only twenty-two other banks had between

1 percent and 25 percent each.[23] At a global level, many players are potential free riders.

The system's solution to this problem is to shift the players from the international ocean to their home ponds. There, global free riders become integral. In Mexico, Dresdner Bank of Germany had only 1 percent of loans by all banks, but 25 percent of loans by German banks, which alone would not keep such a bank in the rescheduling. But as the second largest bank in Germany, Dresdner had a position to maintain.[24] The process of international syndication contributes to this. Lead banks often recruited participants from their own homes. Dresdner's creditability in home markets would be affected by the success of the foreign restructuring. By the same token, Dresdner could exercise its power on smaller banks that might be less responsive to the entreaties of the U.S. banks with the largest stake in the Mexican rescue package.

That other possible forms of crisis management were not employed suggests the power of the home country as an organizing principle. In the abstract, other types of decentralization were possible. For debtor countries, one alternative would have been to organize by syndicate, relying on lead banks to do all the work; other types of lenders could act as blocs.[25] Industrial governments could still have been lenders of last resort, providing liquidity to the borrowers as they do now. More was needed, however. Today only the home country provides the multiple ties that keep the players in the game during a crisis.

Decentralization to the home country increases stability for several reasons. First, home is where the oligopoly is, in banking. The big three (in France and Germany), the big four (in the United Kingdom), the big eight (in Japan) all have a dominant stake in the home system.[26] At the national level, decentralization to the home country affords more opportunities for tradeoffs among the players. Not only can they bargain about international issues, but even unrelated issues in domestic markets may be part of the deal. Finally, national commonalities make it easier to ride herd on the free rider. At home, bankers speak the same language, are part of the same culture, and apply the same standards for success (earnings per share or market share, for example). Leaders at home are established, permitting market discipline. Relations with the home authorities are established, increasing the predictability of official action.

Precisely this dynamic worked in the Mexican case immediately after August 1982. In the United States, for example, banks with very little exposure in Mexico threatened to make waves if Mexico did not let them out fast. The big banks and the U.S. authorities both pressed them to stay in. In each region of the country, a major regional bank[27] worked to persuade the smaller banks to stay on as lenders. The Federal Reserve Banks did the same.[28]

In this sense, national ties act to shore up cooperation and confidence. The nation-based ILOLR is more than just an administrative convenience. Its multifaceted nature, however, contains destabilizing elements.

Limitations of a Decentralized System

Inherent in the nation-based ILOLR is a form of decentralization that is its weakness. For some lenders and their home government, like Swiss banks and the Swiss government, syndicated loan markets are more important than the medium-term or sovereign risk markets, particularly for developing countries. The Swiss' successful efforts to distinguish the treatment of short-term interbank lenders from that of medium-term lenders had a debilitating effect on Brazil and on the management of the Brazilian crisis. In this sense, a creditor nation chose to be a free rider and won.

A second weakness exists from the perspective of the debtor nations. Some receive much help, others very little. If an Egypt had debt problems, it would quickly attract the attention of the Group of Five nations. If a Sri Lanka had similar problems, it would not get similar help.

Finally, this system gives individual players the opportunity to take advantage of the group over the long run. Banks and national governments recognize and anticipate the effect of this system of crisis management. As Darity argues in Chapter 11, banks appear to have anticipated the national dynamic just outlined, as evidenced by their lending practices prior to 1982. To document this, one should find banks lending to countries likely to have the support of a Group of Five government and particularly to those supported by the banks' home government. Conclusive evidence is marred by noise, however. The developing countries that were major Eurocurrency borrowers in the past were indeed strategically important by virtue of their size, resources, or location—South Korea, the Philippines, Indonesia along the edge of China; Brazil, Argentina, and Mexico as the major countries of Latin America. These were also, however, among the fastest growing, most industrial, and apparently best managed of developing countries. Another measure is needed. At the aggregate level, U.S. banks have had a greater market share in countries and regions that are important to the United States for political or economic reasons. These are Latin America and Pacific Asia. Are the banks simply following trade? While the relation between trade and debt is relatively close for U.S. banks, it has weakened slightly in the past years. At the aggregate level, however, the data are so general that we cannot capture the significance of political factors in the banks' allocation of credit.

WHAT PUBLIC GOOD DOES THIS SYSTEM SERVE?

So far, this chapter has assumed that the ILOLR benefits the world at large by providing more *international financial stability* than we would otherwise have.[29] Yet there are two other systemic functions it could perform. One is to promote *economic growth.* The ILOLR may promote the growth of developing countries (Kuczynski 1983b: 17) in the interest of the Group of Five nations or the growth of the Group of Five countries themselves.[30] The other is *power maximization.*[31] Perhaps the ILOLR benefits the security interests of the Group of Five governments.

The nature of the three systemic benefits and their overall mix should affect lending by the banks. For example, suppose the only benefit is to the financial system. To fit such a system, banks would be well advised to lend on the traditional "good security" that a lender of last resort is supposed to demand of banks. On the other hand, if economic growth alone is maximized, banks should lend to countries that are well managed, regardless of external shocks. If the ILOLR promotes only security interests, banks should make a careful study of those interests before they lend.

An ILOLR could serve stability to reduce the extremes of the peaks and troughs in the cycle of international financial flows. The ILOLR now addresses the troughs but ignores the peaks. In crisis, the decentralized system permits the bigger players to keep others in. Over the long run, no mechanisms deflate euphoria; the link between domestic stability and international instability must be obvious to the Group of Five government before it acts in the ILOLR.

If the benefit of the ILOLR is to promote growth in output, the system now does not push far in that direction. It crudely distinguishes among countries' economic performance but offers no way to spark growth. One might say, however, that the existence of the ILOLR encourages gradual adjustment of disequilibria. The standard example is the oil shock and the so-called petrodollar recycling. Without the tacit support of the multiple ILOLR, banks would have been loath to lend to oil-importing countries, Here again, however, is the short-run fix without the long-run solution. The IMF's adjustment measures rest on macroeconomic policies, giving limited attention to underlying structural problems. One example in Mexico is corruption, which could cripple recovery over the long run even if macroeconomic policies meet medium-term goals.

The ILOLR could serve to augment the political power of Group of Five countries. A long tradition supports this function. It is debatable whether over the long run, the management of recent debt crises reduced the power of problem countries against the Group of Five.[32] It does emphasize the relative importance of various nations in different regions: the United States in Latin America and, with Japan, in Pacific Asia; West Germany in Eastern Europe; France and the United Kingdom in their former colonies; and a mix in strategic countries around the Mediterranean. In this sense, it reinforces the regional hegemony among the Group of Five powers that has evolved since World War II.

Mutant forms of these benefits spring from the ILOLR. They may reinforce one another: security requires some economic growth, which in turn benefits from a stable financial system. The three also conflict, so a natural question is which takes precedence. U.S. national security interests mean the United States will not want the ILOLR to push Mexico to address its problems of corruption even if that is needed for long-term growth and stability. The goal of export-led growth prompted the Group of Five to use credit to promote sales to developing countries, thus adding to the instability of the financial system (the opening quotation about the German banks in Peru gives an example). Obviously, as debtor countries adjust, deflation slows their growth to a standstill.

Several points emerge. Economic growth in developing countries has the lowest priority. Even though the crisis spokesmen for Group of Five governments are the financial authorities, one cannot assume that either domestic or international financial stability is dominant. Thus ILOLR is essentially conservative. Its goal seems to be to maintain the political and economic balance.

THE EXTREME CASE: MANAGING MEXICO's 1982 DEBT CRISIS

Mexico is the extreme case of the ILOLR at work today. By virtue of its importance to the United States, Mexico and its creditors received special treatment after the August 1982 crisis. That the U.S. government accorded Mexico special treatment is evident when compared to the assistance given to Brazil. By many financial measures, the two countries are roughly equivalent, yet the U.S. government helped Mexico much more than Brazil. As Table 9-1 shows, the absolute volume of funds in the first year was twice as high in Mexico as it was in Brazil. Moreover, the help came much faster. For Mexico, these funds were arranged over a weekend, compared with

Table 9-1. U.S. Help in Rescheduling: Volume and Timing in the First Phase (*$ Billions*).

Mexico	*(Started 9/82)*	*Brazil*	*(Started 9/82)*
Funds			
CCC	1 one weekend 8/82	.25	(6/83)
Swap/BIS	1	1.23	(9/82)
Oil reserve	1.00	—	
Eximbank	—	—	(promised mid-1983)
Pressure			
International, mobilized other OECD countries		Failed to get much new money from other group of five governments	
Domestic, fast and thorough		Informed from start, no active pressure on smaller banks until after 5/83	

many months for Brazil. By a more qualitative measure, the pressure the U.S. government exerted on behalf of the rescheduling process in the two countries was much greater for Mexico than for Brazil at both the international level and the domestic level.

The ultimate question is the cause of these differences. The conclusions that banks draw about the cause may affect their lending in the future.

Several explanations for U.S. behavior exist. The first is that Brazil wanted the United States to go slower. Because the Brazilians did not want to be treated like the Mexicans, they did not take the route of official rescheduling. Related to this is the view that others did not recognize the Brazilian problem as fast as the Mexican. It is true that Brazil did not give even its own bankers as much information about the country's performance as it had in the past. But for several years leading up to the crisis Brazil's problems had been obvious.[33]

U.S. acquiescence in a do-little policy toward Brazil appears to have occurred because the U.S. government was more concerned about the impact of a crisis in Mexico than in Brazil—the impact on the U.S. financial system, on U.S. economic growth, and on U.S. national security. Table 9-2 captures some of the U.S. interests in both countries.

Table 9-2. Economic Measures of U.S. Interests (*End-1982*).

	Mexico	Brazil	
All U.S. Banks' Exposure			
$ billions	$25	$19	
Market share	39%	34%	
Exposure/Capital			
Top 9 U.S. banks	60%	54%	
($ billions)	($14)	($12)	
U.S. Foreign Direct Investment			Total
$ Billions (stock)	$ 5.6	$ 9.0	$221
Share	2.5%	4.1%	100%
U.S. Exports			
$ Billions (Flow)	$17.8	$ 3.8	$224
Share	7.9%	1.7%	100%

Sources: FEEC, IMF, Salomon Brothers Inc.

The U.S. financial system was not substantially more exposed in Mexico than in Brazil at the end of 1982. The market share of U.S. banks in both countries was about the same, as was the exposure of the biggest banks, according to Salomon Brothers: lending as a share of capital in Mexico was 60 percent and in Brazil was 54 percent. This is a lot of money in both countries. The differences for the U.S. financial system are not large enough to justify a substantially different response by the U.S. government.

Differences in equity interests also do not help to explain U.S. policy. In fact, direct U.S. investment in the two countries suggests the United States would move more quickly for Brazil.

U.S. domestic politics and national security policy emerge as most important. Enormous differences exist in U.S. trade with the two countries. U.S. trade with Brazil was a much smaller share. The clear balance in favor of Mexico on trade translates into jobs, and so into domestic political issues. If one adds to that the fact that Mexico is a neighbor whose own political stability seems endangered by war in Central America as well as the facts of the long border, the large number of Mexican immigrants in the United States, and the consequent cultural connections, one concludes that very close security and economic ties to Mexico shape domestic U.S. politics and explain this treatment. These U.S. interests—security, trade, and culture—are outside the financial system. Yet they explain differences in the treatment of the two largest debtor countries, both of which threatened the U.S. financial system equally.

Banks anticipated this special help for Mexico. From 1978 on, Mexico was the darling of the banking club, yet it was Mexico that precipitated the crisis in Latin America. Evidence of the collective euphoria (Kindleberger 1978a: ch. 2, n. 4) surrounding Mexico appears in Table 9-3. The growth of banks' assets in Mexico far exceeded that in comparable countries, whether one chooses other oil-producing countries outside the Mideast, other Latin American countries, or even the newly industrializing countries of Pacific Asia. What prompted banks to pump so much credit into Mexico?

Mexico's proximity and importance to the United States appears to have encouraged banks to lend so much, so liberally, at such favorable rates. Other explanations are not adequate. Euphoria surrounding oil, and the associated high demand for credit to finance fast growth of output, cannot alone explain the jump in bank credit to Mexico, since loans to other high-growth, high-absorbing oil pro-

Table 9-3. Euphoric Lending: The Growth of Banks' Assets in Mexico Compared with Other Areas, 1978-81.

Bank Assets in	The Base Year: Bank Assets at the End of 1978	Percentage Growth from 12/78 to		
		12/79	12/80	12/81
Mexico	$23.3 billion	32%	76%	138%
OPEC (non-Mideast) [a,b]	31.1	28	44	51
Latin America [a]	55.9	28	58	84
Pacific Asia NICs [c]	14.8	31	66	97

a. Excludes Mexico.

b. Algeria, Brunei, Ecuador, Gabon, Indonesia, Nigeria, Trinidad/Tobago, Venezuela.

c. Malaysia, South Korea, Taiwan, Thailand.

Source: Bank for International Settlements, International Banking Statistics, 1973-83, April 1984, Table 5.

ducers fell far short. That there were limited opportunities elsewhere does not explain Mexico's spectacular growth. The tar baby effect— banks lend to protect outstanding loans—did not apply, since banks financed much more than debt service through 1981. Ignorance of other banks' lending also was not the cause, despite the claims of some banks; the high growth and increasing short-term portion of Mexican debt was visible in public data (from the BIS) by 1981 at the latest.

The impulse to lend against the security of Group of Five interests implicit in the system was realized during the years building up to the crisis. It occurred in Mexico. We know of Mother Russia's umbrella over Eastern Europe. The same principle applies wherever else a powerful nation's interests are perceived.

CONCLUSION

It is useful to think of the ILOLR as a device for system maintenance where the system extends far beyond finance. This helps to answer the question: who benefits? Behavior that is anomalous in terms of the international financial system makes more sense against a broader canvas. The Group of Five countries seek to maintain a set of political and economic relations in which finance is only part. A multiheaded ILOLR with such a broad mandate cannot coordinate beyond its abilities. An ILOLR that contributes to financial instability does not necessarily carry within it the seeds of its own destruction. Without arguing that instability in itself carries political advantages, it is possible to say that the costs of instability may be offset by benefits elsewhere in the system.

The ILOLR does not extend beyond maintenance, however. While the Group of Five countries may augment their power over debtor countries, they do not seem to try to maximize power toward one another. For example, one might expect Japan to continue its strategy of export promotion through the activities of the ILOLR. In practice, Japan has drastically limited the credit its export-import bank may extend to countries in trouble. The Group of Five also do not appear to have tried to change the system. The U.S. government rejected proposals to press Moscow by declaring Poland in default, for example. Indeed, little direction is given.

A strength of this decentralized system should be its ability to manage international debt crises that occur within the Group of Five nations. The debt of developing countries involves borrowers outside the jurisdiction of the Group of Five governments. If the next crises arise because of lending to borrowers in the major industrial countries, they should be easier to manage.

NOTES TO CHAPTER 9

1. Interview, Lima, Peru, February 1978.

    Subsequent to this incident President Bermudez denied that Peru had been forced to dampen its "friendly relations with the other major power bloc." His carefully chosen words, however, do not refute the assertion that Peru had agreed to end military purchases as part of the help it received. (See "How Peru's President Views the IMF and the Banks" 1978: pp. 28, 29.)

2. The fable sets five hungry men who cannot communicate well to hunt a stag they can catch if they all cooperate. But a hare darts by, one catches it, and defects, and the stag escapes. In one view, "In cooperative action, even where all agree on the goal and have an equal interest in the project, one cannot rely on others" (Waltz 1965).

3. When it appears that debtor may not be able to service all its debt, a creditor will try to get the debt owed to it paid before other claimants deplete the debtor's treasury. As confidence ebbs, a destructive stampede of creditors could occur. By assuring liquidity, the lender of last resort maintains confidence.

4. Dean and Giddy (1981) review four proposals: (1) global supervision, (2) country risk guarantees, (3) an international deposit (this seems least unlikely), and (4) a single ILOLR. They advance a fifth proposal: incentives for an interbank safety net.

5. In the argot of the trade, these questions are stated as follows: When does the lender of last resort act? How is the moral hazard resolved? What is the public good?

6. Some might argue that the U.S. Federal Reserve System is the lender of last resort to the system. This argument simplifies the way in which liquidity is provided to the system, as I describe below.

7. For a view that the IMF plays a much more important role, see Lipson (1981: 603).

8. Some problem countries shift in status: Poland in 1978 had the active leadership of the West German government but lost it later when it outlawed the Solidarity movement.

9. I use "leader" to denote an active player that provides policy direction as well as administrative services. Not even all members of the restructuring committees are active.

10. For example, in Latin America, where big U.S. banks took the lead, several large British banks had loaned a higher share of their capital to Latin countries than had the most exposed U.S. banks.

11. Among the creditors, the single player includes not only a bank but a national government.

12. For many years, Japan has provided massive amounts of rice to South Korea whenever that country was unable to feed itself.

13. Japanese aid is provided by the Overseas Economic Cooperation Fund, which is not part of the general budget and is funded by the postal savings system.

14. The most recent example is the IMF quota increase, but aid funds are notoriously subject to congressional intervention.

15. On whether banks lose part of the economic value of their loans when restructuring, see Guttentag and Herring (1983b: 209). In the abstract, a restructuring increases a loan's present value by making its terms more realistic while at the same time reducing the present value by lengthening the time for repayment. Data are not adequate to permit empirical analysis.

16. The West German authorities proposed laws that would require banks to consolidate their accounts as early as 1975. Domestic factors also played

a role in bringing the bill to law in 1984, but the world debt crisis was a stimulus.

17. For example, relative to the Standard and Poor 500, the price/earnings multiple of twelve U.S. money-center banks fell from a ratio of 77.1 in June 1979, just as the second oil shock was appearing, to 45.6 in June 1983. See Hanley and Christian (1983).

18. Both Japanese and German banks continue to carry hidden reserves. In Japan, for example, Sumitomo Bank was able to absorb the debts of the bankrupt trading company Ataka in 1975 and still declare its largest dividend at the end of the year. In Germany, Commerzbank and Dresdner Bank have been forced to show their provisions more than in the past, presumably because their reserves have not been adequate to the task. (See, e.g., "Dresdner Tops Up Its Reserves," 1982: 22).

19. It is no secret that in 1983 profit centers within U.S. banks wanted responsibility for rescheduling. High margins passed the administrative costs on to the borrower and, indirectly, to creditors advancing new funds, while at the same time allowing the bank officers to reach their earnings target.

20. Note that the Federal Reserve intervened again on behalf of a country of major economic and political importance to the United States, Mexico.

21. For the effect of the debt crisis on the stock price of U.S. banks, see Kyle and Sachs (1984).

22. International credit markets are highly concentrated. According to one study, "about 25 large banks based in OECD countries" make up the inner circle, accounting for some 60 percent of lead managements and over 50 percent of all bank lending. These banks could be presumed to have a stake in the system as a whole. See Mentre (1984): 5–6). Some bankers, drawing the circle a bit wider, refer to the Apex 40 banks. Obviously, the precise number is not important.

23. 1983 Credit Agreement for $5 billion between the United Mexican States and Banks, Schedule 5.

24. One might say that Dresdner Bank had little choice but to cooperate, given its worldwide exposure and its interest, as a lead bank, in the stability of the market for international syndications. In fact, after its recent experience with what it might have considered the intransigence of the U.S. banks in the Polish rescheduling, it could well have adopted a tougher line.

25. This was tried in the early Brazil rescheduling and it failed.

26. Even in the United States, with over 14,000 banks, the largest nine banks account for a large share of the market.

27. In the big U.S. market, regional banks occupy a position that is analogous to that of major banks in other countries.

28. Interviews, Boston, New York, and Washington, D.C., 1982–84.

29. This view is implicit in the work of many economists. See Kindleberger (1978a) and Dean and Giddy (1981) for example.

30. See arguments that the recessions in developing countries hurt U.S. trade (Brock 1984: 1037).
31. This view is implicit in the analysis of Diaz–Alejandro and Bacha (1982).
32. Large debtors often have power in dealing with their creditors.
33. Hindsight suggests Brazil was less able than Mexico to take good corrective action. At the time the U.S. government helped Mexico, however, the political will to act was absent in both countries. President Lopez Portillo of Mexico opposed stringent measures in August 1982, while Brazil's government delayed imposing such measures until after elections in November 1982.

IV MODELING CRISIS-CREATING AND CRISIS-RESOLVING BEHAVIOR

This part of the book models bank and borrowing nations' behavior prior to and during the Latin American debt crisis, and the contending strategies for solution. Magee and Brock see the evolution of the debt crisis as the product of rent-seeking behavior by both borrowers and lenders. Because equity holders' risks from making bad loans were covered politically, U.S. banks concentrated their loan portfolios in high-risk, potentially high-return Latin American loans. The less developed countries (LDCs), in turn, were stimulated by the redistributive political activity to allow their debt-to-equity ratios to rise above prudent levels.

William Darity's thesis echos that of Magee and Brock. He also concludes that U.S. banks made poor lending decisions. However, where Magee and Brock paint U.S. banks as rational players in a political redistributive game, Darity argues convincingly that they knowingly engaged in self-victimization by pushing bad loans on Latin America. Darity closes on a pessimistic note, commenting that it appears that the loan pushers, whose bad loans have been ratified by public authorities, will survive to push again.

Lance Taylor builds a formal model aimed at enhancing our understanding of the concentrated Latin American debt crisis and of how it might be resolved. His North-South model indicates that the revulsion period that typically follows a lending boom, especially if a severe crisis is involved, can take years to overcome. What is novel

171

about Taylor's model is his contention that Latin America's difficulties are a natural consequence of the U.S. foreign payments position. In particular, he suggests that interest payments associated with the United States' own growing foreign debt portend a second debt crisis during the 1980s.

Larry Sjaastad's chapter provides a fitting conclusion to the book. He recognizes the Latin American debt concentration as a given, and then models the determinants of the magnitude of debt service and examines the real interest rate issue. His model concludes that little relief is in sight. Simply put, the debt crisis is unlikely to fortuitously disappear. Given that Latin America's debt service will most certainly continue to exceed its capacity to pay on a sustained basis, how might the debt issue be resolved? Sjaastad's suggestions are both disquieting and controversial. There is no magical strategy for solving the problem of international debt. "Bailing out" debtors and the banks via further transfers from the international financial institutions would only confirm the Magee–Brock political redistribution hypothesis and would invite renewed loan pushing, because it would erode the discipline that ordinarily governs financial transactions. The alternative market, or in some circles, Chicago school solutions are also fraught with difficulties as well. It is hard to mark the debt to market when many Latin American financial assets are of little market value. Banks will resist the only viable market solution, renegotiating the debt with debtor country governments, in the hope that the transfer solution may be invoked. Resolving the debt problem requires nothing short of creating an elaborate set of guidelines, which would surely run afoul of national sovereignty in much the same fashion that IMF conditionality does.

10 THIRD WORLD DEBT AND INTERNATIONAL CAPITAL MARKET FAILURE AS A CONSEQUENCE OF REDISTRIBUTIVE POLITICAL RISK SHARING

Stephen P. Magee and William A. Brock

Over the past decade, we have witnessed an increase in the integration of capital and goods markets of the northern and southern hemispheres and an increase in the severity of shocks to world markets. How then do we explain the puzzle of the decline in North–South risk sharing and, as Lessard (1983) suggests, international capital market failure? His data show that the percentage of less developed country (LDC) risks shared with developed country (DC) foreign direct equity investors declined from 31 percent in 1973 to 17 percent in 1981. In other words, the external debt/equity ratio of the nonoil-producing LDCs increased from 2/1 in 1973 to 5/1 in 1981. Because of this increase in leverage, the LDCs became more vulnerable to external shocks and the entire world economy is subject to greater systematic (nondiversifiable) risk.

In this chapter, we explore political answers to the Third World debt/equity question. Behavior that is economically puzzling becomes clearly rational when the endogenous political elements are considered. In earlier work on endogenous redistribution theory in general equilibrium, we found that redistributive political investments can lead to destabilizing increasing returns to political activity and endogenous redistributive equilibriums with potentially large fractions of an economy's resources wasted in political activity (see

173

Magee, Brock, and Young 1983). Application of endogenous redistribution reasoning to the Third World debt problem yields the perversities described in this chapter. In the 1970s, rational redistributive political activities by both DC bank lenders and LDC borrowers induced governments in both the advanced countries and the LDCs to share in the systematic risks of these economic agents. One of the consequences of this behavior is the current debt-rescheduling exercise.

The hypotheses and results in the chapter can be summarized as follows. Large U.S. banks are more active in the U.S. political system and obtain greater benefits from it than the U.S. multinationals (benefits such as regulatory favoritism, lender-of-last-resort benefits, and other activities of the Federal Reserve System). This has had three consequences.

1. The differential political protection of U.S. banks may have allowed them to take greater systematic risks than the multinational corporations. As a consequence, external debt is crowding out equity in multinational firms as a source of external LDC funding.

2. Because their big risks were covered politically, the large U.S. banks concentrated their loan portfolios in high-risk, high-return LDC loans.

3. Bank loans to borrowers with high moral hazard (see Arrow 1970) usually require collateral. This effect encouraged bank loans to those capitalists and redistributors of wealth in the LDCs who are better at accumulating collateral outside of their country than at investing in projects in their country.

LDC political insider manipulation of LDC governments into guarantees of external borrowing, combined with behavior of the International Monetary Fund, had three effects.

4. LDC borrowers took greater risks and increased their leverage (proportion of debt financing) in the past decade. When debt payments are guaranteed by one's government, a borrower cannot have too much debt.

5. The moral hazard problem of deliberate default is a more serious possibility in LDCs in which the borrowers are especially powerful; in extreme cases, the borrowers retain the wealth acquired

by the loans and the repayments are transferred to taxpayers in adverse states.

6. The actions of the IMF also encourage moral hazard behavior by LDC governments. The IMF lends funds to countries that have been economically irresponsible and imposes stringency programs on LDC taxpayers which the government can blame on the IMF.

The world redistribution of wealth caused by OPEC had three effects.

7. OPEC's actions transferred financial intermediation from equity markets and small banks to large money-center banks. Because of the sizable sums involved, this biased world investment toward large projects. The world's largest investment projects are politically controlled development projects in the LDCs; hence, much of the money went to them.

8. Because of the importance of speed in moving the massive inflow of petrodollars, the banks transferred their normal economic functions of project appraisal and risk screening to LDC governments through government guarantees. Again, this biased loans toward political operators and away from economic projects.

9. Thus, one consequence of OPEC was adverse selection in LDC bank lending toward LDC political insiders. While the petrodollar recycling exercise of the 1970s has been labeled a macroeconomic success, the adverse selection effect might be counted as a microeconomic failure.

All of these political, redistributive and free-riding effects contribute to the LDC debt problem being one of insolvency rather than illiquidity. The political elements in the Third World debt problem imply regressivity of adverse states of nature. That is, the political investments of large DC banks cause DC citizens to cover the losses of large bank equity holders in adverse states (Federal Deposit Insurance Corporation coverage, macroeconomic policy, etc.); and the political investments of large LDC borrowers cause LDC citizens to cover their payments in adverse states.

Redistributive political activities increase the moral hazard problem in Third World lending and reduce international capital market efficiency. As a result of their political activities, the equity holders in large banks do not lose when the banks make bad loans and large

LDC borrowers do not lose when they fail to repay. Insurance companies control such moral hazard problems by coinsurance: in the event of loss, the insured individual bears part of the cost. Unfortunately, redistributive political investments generate negative coinsurance schedules for some LDC borrowers: their wealth is greater with adverse states and public bail-out than without.

The voters' perception that an "economic crisis" is at hand is an important device for enlisting their participation in political risk sharing and facilitating the redistributive transfer. The role of economists in these proceedings is partly ceremonial: we discuss policy options, Pareto optimality, and other matters although, frankly, these frequently appear to be of coincidental relevance to the resulting political equilibrium.

The policy paradox is that public policy is partially outside of public control in a democracy. In redistributive political equilibriums, democracies balance the generalized efficiency interests of voters against the particularized interests of the large players (see Magee, Brock, and Young 1983). The endogenous redistribution arguments in this chapter are a general equilibrium parallel to agency problems and strategic redistributive games that are played over control of firms (on the latter, see Jensen and Meckling 1976).

We present stock market data at the end of the chapter which is consistent with our hypothesis that largest U.S. banks were not harmed by their loans to Third World countries.

The chapter is arranged in order of the following major actors: the Organization of Petroleum Exporting Countries (OPEC), the LDC governments, the U.S. Federal Reserve System, the large banks, the international organizations, and the LDC borrowers. We examine the strategic and political behavior of each of these actors in the Third World debt game.

THE ROLE OF OPEC

The U.S. money-center banks are not primarily responsible for the rapid growth in LDC lending in the 1970s, even to Latin America. OPEC had an even larger role. Following the rise in oil prices in 1973, the LDCs approached OPEC for loans and aid but were rebuffed. OPEC invested most of the funds in Europe, and the big banks lent the money to the LDCs. As a result, European debt grew

Figure 10–1. Guaranteed LDC Debt, OPEC Current-Account Surplus, and Annual Changes in U.S. Direct Foreign Investment in the LDCs.

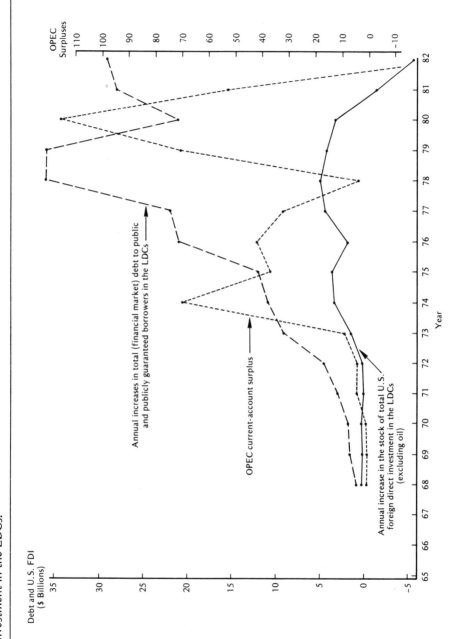

more rapidly than U.S. bank debt. From 1975 to 1981, U.S. bank debt to the non-OPEC LDCs grew 3 times while non-U.S. debt grew 6 times; over the same period, U.S. bank debt to Argentina, Brazil and Mexico grew 2.5 times while non-U.S. bank debt grew 7 times (Barth and Pelzman 1984: table 4). The softening in world oil prices and the declines in the OPEC current-account surpluses from 1980 to 1982 were one cause of the repayment crisis because they reduced new lending of petrodeposits (see Figure 10-1); the 1982 world recession was another; a third was the increase in the fiscal deficits in the advanced countries in the 1980s, which reduced the net funds available for LDC lending (Sjaastad 1983). The change in Third World debt (from financial market lenders to public or publicly guaranteed borrowers in all LDCs) and the OPEC current-account surpluses are shown in Figure 10-1. Although the annual comovement between the two series is not strong, Cline (1982) and others argue correctly that Third World lending is partially a recycling of OPEC current-account surpluses. OPEC looks smart for refusing to lend directly to the LDCs, and the world's largest banks do not. From an international capital market perspective, however, bank lending makes more sense since it permits superior financial market allocation of moral hazard risk. Banks have centuries' worth of experience in making loans to people who are skillful at not repaying.

THE STRATEGY OF THE LDCs TOWARD EXTERNAL EQUITY VIA THE MULTINATIONAL CORPORATIONS

Why would the Third World increase its external debt/equity ratio at the same time that shocks to world markets were increasing? Part of the answer lies in the LDC treatment of multinational corporations. The strategy of the LDCs in the 1960s and 1970s was to finance their development partially by encouraging multinational firms' entry but preventing repatriations of earnings by the multinationals. This attempted appropriation of the multinationals' wealth is explained by moral hazard; by political learning by LDC special interests leading to Olsonian sclerosis (Olson 1982); and by political compensation effects for declining terms of trade, high oil prices, and so forth. The compensation effect in endogenous redistribution theory refers to substitution into lobbying and political activity when the rate of return from economic activity declines (see Magee, Brock, and Young 1983). Some of the techniques used by the multinationals to cope with their political vulnerability included investing in politically stable LDCs or those that received aid from Western governments (see Schneider and Frey 1984). Redistributive activity in LDCs directed at multinationals included limitations on repatriations, increased taxes on dividend remittances, forced sharing of equity with local partners, and had other effects. A counterstrategy of the multinational firms was to move new external equity investments into the Third World indirectly through parallel loans from large money-center banks, since the latter were more likely to be repaid. The effect of both the LDC redistributive behavior and the counterstrategies of the multinationals was an increase in the external debt/equity ratio of the LDCs. New foreign direct investment (equity) financing in the Third World has been less than reinvested retained earnings since the late 1960s, and has declined in real terms since the early 1970s (see Figure 10–2).

Notice that the behavior just described causes the LDC financing ratio to go in the wrong direction: Lessard's (1983) debt/equity data imply that the percentage of LDC risks shared with foreign direct equity investors declined from 31 percent in 1973 to 17 percent in 1981. Given the increased magnitude of world market shocks in the last decade, capital market theory would lead us to expect an increase in the proportion of equity funding. Developed country evidence for the normal result is provided by Bradley, Jarrell, and Kim (1984: 869), who found that the higher the variability in the value of a U.S. corporation, the more it tends to rely on equity financing. As an aside, the debt/equity ratio for U.S. corporations has also risen in the past decade: the ratio of corporate debt to equity for the United States rose from 0.85 in 1975 to over 1.05 in 1982 (*Chase Economic Observer* 1984). Thus, there may be larger forces at work.

A number of countries, such as Mexico, chose to fund their development with debt instead of equity so they would not have to share the anticipated rents from increases in the future price of oil with foreign investors. Oil price expectations were bullish at the time the debt was acquired; also, the Mexican government committed Mexican taxpayers to share the risks. When oil market expectations reversed and the unanticipated world recession of 1982 occurred, the foreign investors were also not there to share the losses.

Figure 10–2. U.S. Direct Foreign Investment in LDCs.

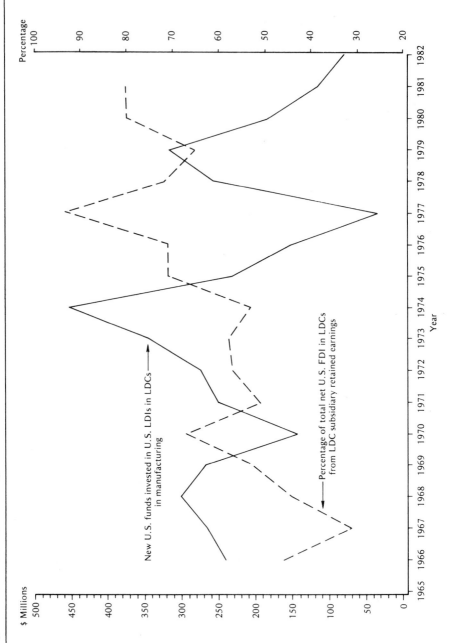

It is our belief that the median voter in the typical LDC would prefer to repudiate the external debt of the country because (1) large foreign creditors are politically unpopular; (2) the IMF austerity programs for LDCs in arrears are painful and regressive; and (3) in some cases, the present discounted cost of repudiation would be less than the current value of the debt. Wriston (1984) notes that Mexico has experienced declines in its public sector from 18 percent of gross national product in 1982 to 8.5 percent in 1983 and possibly to 6.5 percent in 1984 and a swing in its current account of $18 billion in two years, partially at IMF insistence. The IMF stringency programs appear to be more constrictive than the British provocations that led to the American revolution. How do we explain the docile behavior of LDC governments when it comes to paying off unpopular foreign banks at IMF insistence? First, endogenous redistribution theory and capture theories of regulation suggest that this behavior is explained by the disproportionate political influence exerted by large actors (such as the LDC borrowers). Second, even within stable democracies, politics is a constant-sum game: except in neutral cases, every economic shock makes one political party better off and the other worse off (Brock and Magee 1978). Ironically, one of two political parties in an LDC will favor debt repayment.

THE STRATEGY OF THE FEDERAL RESERVE

One of the Federal Reserve's concerns is financial panic. Wriston (1984) reports that with seventy commercial satellites now in space, banks can move money around the world at the speed of light; that the cost of communicating electronically has fallen 20 percent per year for the past decade; and that the cost of storing information has fallen 40 percent per year for the same period. It is amazing that these innovations have not generated more bank panics. G. William Miller, former U.S. secretary of the treasury and chairman of the Federal Reserve Board, has described the run on Continental Illinois as "silent, dustless and technical." A second consideration making the confidence problem appear to be serious is that until recently, no single central bank was the lender of last resort for the hundreds of billions of dollars transacted in the unregulated Eurocurrency markets. Only in the early 1980s (after Banco Ambrosiano) did the DC central banks agree to make good the external deposits of their member national banks. A priori, the world's largest banks would thus appear to be more vulnerable than before to bank runs. Given this vulnerability, why then would the large banks lend excessive amounts to the LDCs?

Appearances notwithstanding, the risk of runs on large banks is now lower than a decade ago because of three factors: the homogeneity of the assets in the world market in liquid funds, the absence of significant alternatives to Eurocurrency deposits (gold is relatively small and market price changes would limit wholesale substitution), and floating foreign exchange rates (which make flight among currencies self-limiting). Ritter and Urich (1984) report that there is about 1.4 billion ounces of gold in the world in private hands: at $300 an ounce, this gold has a value of $420 billion. This contrasts with world bond and equity totals of over $5 trillion and U.S. demand deposits of over $1.3 trillion in 1980. These economic factors reduce the likelihood of runs on large banks and they have the same effects on Third World lending as political risk sharing: the reduction in risk allows the banks to take greater risks in their lending.

Walter Bagehot argued in the last century that a banking system could weather financial crises only if there were a lender of last resort. He recommended that the Bank of England supply reserves to the banking system at a penalty rate (a rate higher than the banks earned on their assets). The purpose of such an arrangement is to prevent a liquidity shortage caused by a short-run crisis of confidence to escalate into a solvency problem for the entire banking system. As the "lender of last resort," the Federal Reserve is responsible (along with the FDIC) for avoiding widespread bank failure and maintaining public confidence in the banking system. According to William Miller, the U.S. political division of labor is as follows: the FDIC protects depositors while the Federal Reserve protects the banks. Since the large money-center banks are the most important focus of public confidence, the Federal Reserve will go to some lengths to prevent their failure. Even though only deposits (not equity) need to be protected to maintain public confidence, the U.S. political system also appears to provide some protection of large bank equity holders. This is a partial explanation for why bank owners would allow heavy lending to LDCs at low risk premiums in the 1970s (at only about 2 percentage points over the rates charged to General Motors). For political analyses of public interest versus capture versus bureaucratic models of Federal Reserve behavior, see Kane 1980 and Beck 1984.

THE STRATEGY OF THE BANKS

Starting in 1974, the world's largest banks suddenly faced the situation of having to lend tens of billions of dollars more than normal. OPEC increased the world concentration of savings and the resulting increased concentration of deposits in large banks had five interesting effects on the composition of world investment. First, since the effect of OPEC was to transfer financial intermediation from many small banks to a few large ones, the desired size of the average bank loan investment project increased. Second, the composition of world investment shifted from the DCs toward the LDCs. Since massive economic development projects were underway in the Third World, they were ideal targets for large banks that needed to lend a lot of money; hence the geographic shift in investment. Third, large projects in the LDCs, even those with low returns and high risks, will be favored over small projects with high returns and low risk. Fourth, LDC investment projects are more likely to be public rather than private and more likely to be coordinated by individuals with political rather than economic skills.

A fifth point and unfortunate consequence of the preceding points is a phenomenon that we shall call political adverse selection: the need to intermediate such large new deposits so quickly biased investment toward politically controlled and possibly economically inferior projects in the LDCs. Given the sums involved, LDC talent would substitute from economic activity into political, redistributive, and large-scale activity. It is conceivable that the negative redistributive effects of adverse political selection could offset the benefits of bank lending and cause welfare declines in the LDCs. While we have no clue as to the size of these effects, the redistributive costs contribute to the repayment problem being one of insolvency rather than the illiquidity. We are less optimistic than other experts, who see the repayment issue as one of illiquidity rather than insolvency (see Cline 1983 and other authors in this book).

The world's money-center banks wished to avoid the exploitation that befell the MNCs. One of their techniques was the creation of self-enforcing loan strategies: the situation would be structured so that the LDC borrowers would lose more if they did not repay than if they did (through loss of collateral). While this technique operated on desire of an LDC to repay, other techniques focused on its capacity to repay when adverse states of nature materialized. For example, a borrowing LDC would have to rely on sharply increased domestic tax collections if its exports dropped unexpectedly. Moreover, an economy's ability to increase tax collections will increase with the diversity of revenue sources in a politically modified Ramsey tax model. For example, starting from a political equilibrium tax rate, the expected rise in tax revenue from a marginal increase in tax rates will be low for an economy with only one sector (such as copper in Chile some years ago) while it will be higher for an economy such as Brazil which has many revenue sources. This will be anticipated by the money-center banks and they are likely to lend more to Brazil.

The banks institutionalized other strategies to cope with possible repayment problems: (1) they formed syndicates of many lenders to spread the risk and (2) they charged countries markups over the London Interbank Offered Rate (LIBOR), the rate at which the large European banks lend to each other, which compensated them for expected nonpayment. Notice that these premia would exist even in a world of risk-neutral lenders if there were identifiable classes of nonrepaying borrowers. For example, assume that loans to DC borrowers have an expected repayment rate of 97 percent while loans to LDC borrowers have an expected repayment rate of 90 percent. Even risk-neutral banks would charge LDC borrowers higher borrowing rates to equate the expected returns across loans. If banks are even mildly risk averse, they can eliminate unsystematic loan risk almost costlessly through syndicated loans. (By definition, unsystematic risks can be eliminated by portfolio diversification while systematic risks cannot.) If loans to LDCs carry greater systematic risk than those to DCs (because of higher world income elasticities of demand for primary products, for example), then a portion of the premium over LIBOR will reflect this as well. The premiums over LIBOR are good, though not perfect, predictors of relative country risk since (1) they do not incorporate some front-end fees and (2) they vary with the degree of liquidity in the Euromarkets and hence are not comparable through time (see Saini and Bates 1984). Note that loan diversification through syndication does not bias the supply of capital to the LDCs toward debt even if firms are risk averse, since most individual multinational firms have country diversification of their foreign direct investments through their many subsidiaries in the LDCs.

Bennett (1984) suggests the following portfolio considerations in large bank lending to the LDCs. Banks should not diversify loan portfolios because this reduces their specialization gains from information (there are economies of scale in gathering product-specific and country-specific information) and because bank shareholders can provide their own portfolio diversification almost costlessly. However, arguments for world loan portfolio diversification include the following:

1. Simulation studies reveal that there are large reductions in risk starting from low levels of loan diversification.
2. Industry-specific human capital depreciates dramatically with bank failure.
3. Bank auditors and regulators are risk averse.

Diversification of bank loan portfolios is more complex than for equity portfolios because loan contracts do not allow the banks to share in the upside returns.

It has been argued that the premiums over LIBOR charged by the large banks on their LDC loans are abnormally low. For example, in 1983, well after the LDC repayment crisis was underway, only Brazil was being charged premiums over LIBOR consistently in excess of 2 percentage points: all other LDCs were paying less (when they could find lenders). The same phenomenon had existed for almost all of the LDCs for the previous decade. How can we explain these low premiums? Stiglitz and Weiss (1981) suggest an adverse selection theory: banks charging low interest rates to low-risk borrowers and high interest rates to high-risk borrowers can have perverse results. In the spirit of Akerloff's lemons model, only borrowers willing to pay the high interest rates will have a low probability of repaying. Stiglitz and Weiss conclude that the equilibrium in such a market will display credit rationing and lower risk premiums on high-risk loans than might appear reasonable (see also Eaton and Gersovitz 1981a). Quite apart from its value in explaining the low risk premiums, the credit rationing story does not generally appear plausible in Third World lending during the 1974–81 period because of the massive volume of petrodollars which the large banks had to move. The banks were probably aware of the adverse selection problem and coped with it in other ways, including insistence on political risk sharing (with both LDC and DC governments). Lessard's (1983) data indicates that government guaranteed debt increased sixfold while nonguaranteed debt increased only fourfold from 1973 to 1981. Figure 10–3 shows that public or publicly guaranteed debt as a percentage of all LDC debt (including OPEC) rose from 75 percent in 1972 to over 82 percent in 1980.

We advance two arguments for the low-risk premiums charged by the banks to the LDCs. The first is economic: the current pricing of the premium on a loan by the lead bank must reflect the option value of future right to be the lead bank in another loan to the same LDC. For example, if Chase Manhattan charges a slightly lower premium (than an economic assessment of the risks) on a syndicated loan to Brazil, it is more likely to be chosen by Brazil to be the lead bank on future loans. Since the lead bank role carries large fees (from 0.5 to 2 percent of the value of the loan), the lead bank will bias the premium over LIBOR downward. In equilibrium, it will balance the expected value of these future lead-bank fees against the risks that its underpricing of the current loan premium will, first, discourage other banks from participating in the current syndication, and, second, hurt the brand name of Chase Manhattan with other banks in future syndications.

Our other explanation of the low premiums charged to the LDCs is political. They are low because the systematic risks of the LDC loans are covered politically, either with DC governments, LDC governments, or both. Let us examine each of these possibilities.

Consider first risk sharing with LDC governments. The large banks wanted and (in many cases) obtained guarantees from LDC governments on LDC borrowing for two reasons. First, quite apart from the risk issues, government guarantees increase the expected value of the repayment on a loan and are valuable for that reason. Second, guarantees may have low intrinsic value (LDC governments have short half-lives) but they are valuable because unpaid government guaranteed debt permits DC government to freeze the assets of the nationals of the LDC (as in the case of Iran). While the assets cannot be confiscated, they can be tied up legally so that their owners cannot use them, and this is troublesome. Thus, the external assets of the elite of the LDC become implicit collateral for the country's borrowing. This is also important because these elite have considerable local political influence in their LDC and usually greater continuity than the government itself. Notice that this consideration also helps ex-

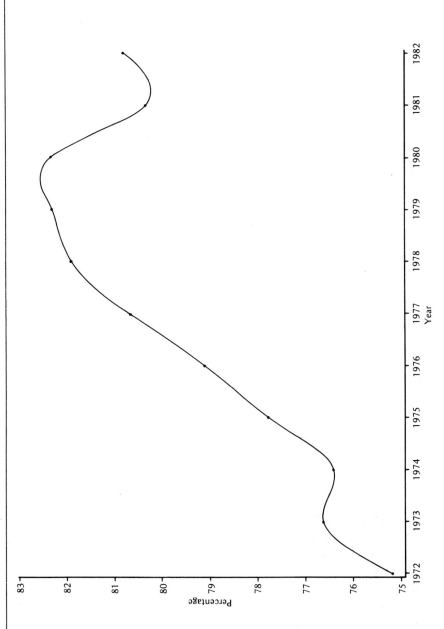

Figure 10–3. Stock of Public and Publicly Guaranteed Debt as a Percentage of Total LDC Debt (*including OPEC*).

plain the alacrity with which LDC governments adopt politically unpopular IMF stringency measures.

Consider now the desire of the large banks to engage in risk sharing with their own DC governments. Loan syndications, efficient market pricing of loan premiums over LIBOR, LDC government guarantees, and other devices all provide good coverage of the unsystematic risk that an individual LDC will be unable to repay. However, the risk of massive nonrepayment by many LDCs at once (which was the situation in 1982) cannot be handled by loan diversification: it must be borne by equity holders (and compensated by higher returns paid to them on bank stocks) or shared with the public through political activity. Our hypothesis is that the largest U.S. banks have the Federal Reserve, the FDIC, and possibly the Congress to protect their equity holders against the systematic (nondiversifiable) risk of large-scale nonrepayment by many LDCs at once. This political subsidization of world systematic risk induced the largest banks to lend to the highest risk, highest return LDCs. The smaller banks are probably not so covered (despite the political activities of the American Bankers Association and their political action committees): they invested much smaller proportions of their portfolios in syndicated Third World loans. (There is no institutional reason for the latter: small U.S. regional banks participate actively in syndicated loans to LDCs.) For an analysis of the political interests of U.S. banks, see Ferguson and Rogers (1981). If large-bank political power increased substantially in the United States in the 1970s, an alternative and provocative explanation of the expansion and contraction of their Third World lending is provided by Kindleberger's (1978a) mania-and-panic thesis.

Consider now some economic reasons why the large U.S. banks might concentrate their lending in Latin America, the location of most of the problem borrowers. For example, Eaton and Gersovitz (1981b) argued that such geographic specialization would emerge for two reasons: there are economies of scale in gathering information about borrowers and in monitoring economic conditions that affected loan repayment; and geographic specialization does not mean economic specialization, since the export experiences of Mexico and Brazil have historically been uncorrelated (coincidence caused this to be untrue in 1982). However, these arguments apply equally to large and small U.S. banks. More is needed to explain why the largest U.S. banks devoted larger proportions of their loan portfolios to Latin America than the small banks.

Why do the large U.S. banks have greater access to systematic risk sharing with the U.S. political system and hence why did they take bigger risks than the small banks in their LDC lending? Olson's (1965) lobbying theory, the theory of regulation, and endogenous redistribution theory all predict that the largest banks will be disproportionately represented in democracies for three reasons. First, large U.S. banks are insiders in the American political system (relative to smaller banks) because they are not as plagued by free rider problems. The larger the actor, the larger the fraction of its political investments which can be considered private goods; the smaller the actor, the larger the fraction of its political investments which are public goods and accrue to others in the industry. This public goods nature of lobbying leads to free riding and underprovision of collective activity in large-member groups. Second, there are catastrophic (major systematic) threats to the wealth of bank equity holders on a large scale only occasionally; and during these periods, actors who have always been politically active receive more from the political system than those who have not. By definition, financial crises are the realization of the worst possible state of systematic risk. Third, for small banks, the high political organization costs are in the present, whereas the expected benefits are far into the future (because of the infrequency of financial crises), so that the present value of obtaining political subsidization of major systematic risks may be negative. When the same calculation is made by the large banks, their lower political organization costs apparently make the present value of political investments positive.

These observations are consistent with greater political involvement by the large banks and hence lower systematic risk for them. An example of differential big bank political access is the recent coverage of deposits of all large as well as small deposits in Continental Illinois Bank by the FDIC, and not just deposits up to $100,000. A sizable number of the large Continental Illinois deposits were from other banks. Such coverage helps large banks relative to small ones since deposit size diversification is no longer necessary. Another implication of the political clout of the large banks is that U.S. government policies proposed as "solutions" to Third World repayment problems will not be hostile to the economic interests of the large money-center banks. Maverick or irresponsible members of the cartel will have to be disciplined or discarded occasionally (as in the cases of the First Bank of Chicago and Continental Illinois), but this will be primarily for public consumption. Finally, the DC borrowers and the LDC lenders are locked into what appears to be a constant sum game over repayment: one's gain is the other's loss. However, both wish to avoid the noncooperative prisoner's dilemma outcome of default by the borrowers and heavy sanctions by the lenders and their governments (see Young and Magee 1982 for examples of prisoner's dilemma outcomes in tariff lobbying equilibriums). Rationality would dictate the more cooperative payment rescheduling outcome, or the muddling through approach described by Dornbush (1984c).

An economic effect of differential political treatment of large versus small banks will be the emergence of two systematic risk clienteles: a more risk-averse small bank group and a less risk-averse large bank group. The larger banks will hold larger proportions of riskier LDC debt while smaller banks will hold larger proportions of safer U.S. debt. In equilibrium, the desired holdings of U.S. and LDC debt by the two lending clienteles will just equal the desired level of borrowing by the two borrowing groups at the market risk premiums.

Sjaastad (1983) reports that a significant amount of the international borrowing of Argentina and Mexico may have been redeposited in banks outside of the country. Does it make sense for sophisticated money-center banks to allow this chicanery? In some cases, the answer is "yes." The strategy of all banks is not to lend to projects that have the highest expected economic returns, but to individuals or groups with the greatest likelihood of repaying. This practice encourages redistributive loans to "flight capitalists" rather than to LDC capital development: collateral outside of the LDC is safer than capital inside it. (Diaz-Alejandro 1984 argues that much private wealth was also transferred out of Latin American countries because of overvalued foreign exchange rates, the latter partially due to the foreign debt inflows.) If the loans do not go to flight capitalists, the next best thing is a loan to a political insider who can force through tax increases to make repayments following an unanticipated economic downturn.

A public discussion of the "economic crisis" is an important political marketing device during such a transfer of wealth from taxpayers to political insiders (both in DCs and LDCs). Expert economists, the

IMF, and others lend credibility to the existence of a "crisis" and generate public acceptance for a new tax equilibrium. The role of economists in these proceedings is largely ceremonial: that is, to legitimize the process by discussion of Pareto optimality and other matters of marginal relevance to the resulting political equilibrium.

Consider now the effects of bank lobbying in the United States. Thanks to unanticipated inflation, the U.S. banks had loans on their books which were earning negative real rates in last half of the 1970s. Since their economic returns were down, they demonstrated the compensation effect of endogenous redistribution theory and substituted into lobbying activity in the late 1970s. Their goal was reduced money growth, lower inflation and (it was hoped) higher real interest rates. The large U.S. banks used the argument of their growing LDC debt vulnerability and their superior access to the American political system to obtain all three of these goals from the Federal Reserve starting in 1979. While these policies are attributed to Federal Reserve Chairman Volcker, we suspect that his personal role has been overstated. The resulting unanticipated decline in inflation increased returns on outstanding fixed rate loans and the increase in real rates also made new floating rate loans more profitable. An unrelated point is that the negative real U.S. interest rates of the 1970s encouraged LDC borrowing. As Sjaastad (1983) notes, when the real rate is negative, it is hard to borrow too much.

THE STRATEGY OF THE IMF
AND THE WORLD BANK

The IMF gives funds to the central banks of LDCs with external balance problems, but on the condition that the LDC impose draconian economic policies to restore fiscal balance and monetary order. A positive effect of this has been more responsible macroeconomic policies in the LDC in which it is intervening just after the crisis. However, one unintended effect has been greater borrowing because of its encouragement of greater LDC government risk sharing with LDC borrowers who are political insiders. When adverse states of nature materialize, LDC taxpayers help make international loan repayments, the LDC borrowers keep their international credit ratings intact and the IMF can be blamed by the LDC government for the situation. Thus, the IMF unwittingly promotes redistributive free rides and adverse political selection in LDC borrowing by its encouragement of macroeconomic crises. If powerful political insiders are going to profit from economic crises, we should not be surprised at their frequency in the LDCs.

Vaubel (1983a) argues that the ease with which the Third World countries can borrow from the IMF encourages them to engage in irresponsible behavior and borrow too much. Others argue that the IMF is politically procreditor, because of its imperialistic austerity programs. It is difficult to determine the political motives of the IMF because of the differing interests of its membership. A policeman such as the IMF might be a public good in enforcing repayment of debt contracts: the absence of one would limit DC bank lending in the Third World.

The goal of the World Bank is to foster economic development by "completing markets"—that is, by making loans to LDCs that would not qualify for commercial loans, even though these loans would foster economic development and eventually be repaid. Nonetheless, empirical work indicates that many of their loans follow the same criteria as private loans. Frey and Schneider (1984) estimated economic and political cross-sectional determinants of International Bank for Reconstruction and Development loans and International Development Association credits to approximately fifty developing countries in the period 1972–81. The coefficients on 7 of 9 of their independent variables predict that loans would be made by the IBRD and IDA to the same countries that might be funded by private markets. In other words, more of the loans go to countries with balance-of-payments surpluses, with government surpluses, with lower inflation, with faster growth of gross national product, with greater political stability, with a more capitalist investment climate, and to former colonies of the United States, the United Kingdom, and France. Only two of the independent variables suggest that these institutions are completing markets by lending to down-and-out LDCs: their loans were greater to lower income-per-capita LDCs and they were greater to countries with higher debts (the latter result is problematic because the latter are the higher income LDCs). Since IBRD loans are at concessionary rates, these loans increase Third World debt/equity ratios to the extent that IBRD debt substitutes for external equity.

THE STRATEGY OF THE LDC BORROWERS

Borrowers who are political insiders in the LDCs encourage government coverage of their debt since this increases the expected value of their wealth. In addition, because of the primitive state of equity markets and greater political separation from world markets in LDCs, borrowers there have a greater economic demand for political risk sharing (investors in LDCs are less able to share unsystematic risks with equityholders). In contrast to government sharing of primarily *systematic* risks with lenders in the DCs, LDC governments will be sought to share in the *total* risks with LDC borrowers (in primitive equity markets, even unsystematic risks are poorly diversified).

Another strategic consideration by LDC countries is that, like individuals, they go through financial life cycles. Initially, countries are borrowers but as they mature economically, they change into lenders. Just before the changeover point, strategic default on their international debt may be redistributively rational. Thus, at some point in this century, we expect the high-income LDCs may band together and repudiate their debts to the DCs. One consequence of this action is that they will have to form their own financial markets. If the repudiation is fully anticipated by the lenders, it should have inconsequential redistributive effects. LDCs who schemed to do this can be anticipated to borrow excessively in advance, a result consistent with the current situation.

Finally, a word is in order regarding the theory of a redistributive political equilibrium. Consider the large U.S. banks and the policies they obtain in the United States. The banks lobby for macroeconomic and microeconomic policies that have favorable economic consequences for their shareholders. In some cases, these interests coincide with those of the median voter (avoidance of financial panics and the like). In other cases (such as regulation Q), bank interests conflict with the interests of voters and other borrowers. In an endogenous political equilibrium, parties will adopt special interest policies that balance the marginal benefits of special interest support from the large banks (usually, though not always, economic resources) against their marginal electoral costs (voter disaffection with non-Pareto redistributive policy distortions, large borrower disaffection with high real interest rates). The big bank lobby will devote resources to a favored party to maximize the wealth of lobby members: in equilibrium, the marginal amount of wealth devoted to re-distributive political lobbying earns the same return as it would have in economic production. While neither the voters nor the special interests end up being completely happy, they are insufficiently unhappy to alter their behavior. This defines a political equilibrium (see Magee, Brock, and Young 1983).

ARE EQUITY HOLDERS IN THE LARGEST U.S. BANKS HEDGED POLITICALLY?

Press stories notwithstanding, were equity holders in the largest U.S. banks insulated (politically or otherwise) against their Third World debt exposure? If not, their equity prices should have revealed it in or before 1982. While the timing is problematic, we expected to find declines in the adjusted values of many of the big banks' equity values in the late 1970s or early 1980s. We examine here the equity movements for eight of the largest U.S. banks, after making two adjustments. First, we examine the stock market value of the equities of the banks relative to their book equity value (only in 1984 did these banks start writing some LDC loans off their books). Second, we adjust for overall U.S. stock market movements.

Our data comes from a study by Upadhyaya (1984) and the results are shown in Figure 10-4. The line shown for each of the largest U.S. banks is the ratio of the bank's market to book ratio divided by the market to book ratio for the Standard and Poors 400 industrials. The data are annual, end-of-year observations for the period 1963-83. The interesting feature of these plots is that since the mid-1970s, the Third World debt problem is not detectable in these series (except for the case of Continental Illinois). The Bank of America and Manufacturers Hanover experienced only modest declines from the mid-1970s through the end of 1983 but Citicorp, Morgan Guaranty, Chemical, First Interstate, and Chase are virtually unchanged since 1977. Continental shows a decline in 1982 and 1983, as well it should. This result is consistent with our hypothesis that most of these banks were politically and economically hedged or that whatever losses are anticipated on their LDC debt and deregulation are being offset by the real wealth transfer to them of the Federal Reserve policy of high real interest rates and other political and regulatory benefits.

Figure 10–4. Market to Book Ratios for the Banks Relative to the M/B Ratio for the Standard and Poors 400.

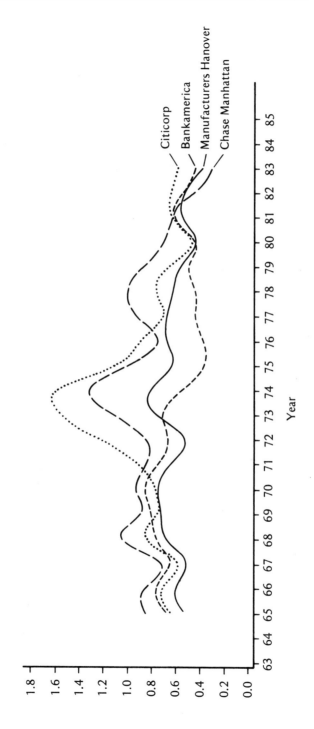

Figure 10–4. continued

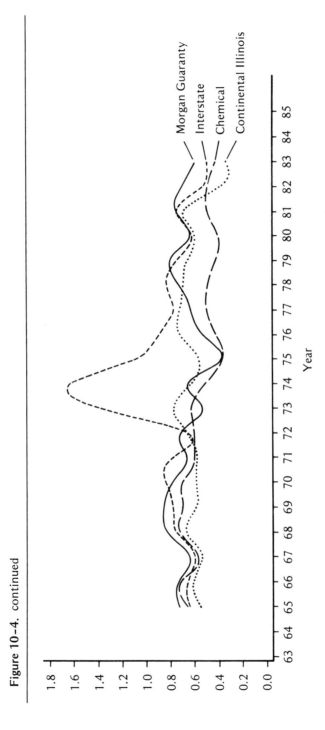

CONCLUSION

Redistributive political activity by both borrowers and lenders stimulated the substitution of international debt for equity in the Third World. Our arguments can be summarized as follows. The LDC investor will discourage the international competition which he faces by harassing multinational corporations through his government; he will fund high-return projects with debt to acquire the entire surplus; he faces primarily large banks trying to intermediate billions of petrodollars rapidly through large projects. The latter implies that the lenders will be primarily interested in large borrowers in the LDCs. This encourages loans to political insiders in charge of large public projects rather than entrepreneurs in charge of smaller private projects. Unfortunately, the former are more likely to be wealth redistributors than wealth creators. Banks inadvertently encourage the latter because redistributors take their wealth out of the LDCs, and this provides safer collateral for a DC bank loan than assets located in the LDC itself. The perverse (negative-sum) effects of the redistributive behavior contribute to the LDC debt crisis being an issue of insolvency rather than illiquidity. The large banks face low risk of runs, have diversified loan portfolios, and lend at low risk premiums because their systematic risks are partially covered by lenders of last resort and other redistributive policies obtained from their home governments. The banks realize that adverse selection is at work for their high-risk LDC borrowers; however, they do not ration funds (à la Stiglitz and Weiss) because of the volume of funds which they must recycle. Rather, they encourage LDC political risk sharing by first, insisting on LDC government guarantees of the debt and second, lending to LDCs with diversified tax revenue sources. (The theory of Ramsey taxation with diversified tax sources and empirical support from Third World data is contained in another paper.) Thus, if a high-risk LDC borrower cannot make repayments, the LDC government or an IMF stringency program will transfer part or all of the repayments to LDC taxpayers. If this does not work, the U.S. banks have the U.S. Federal Reserve and the American political system as a second line of defense.

We presented evidence showing that the negative effects of LDC lending by the eight largest U.S. banks are not apparent in the values of their common stock. The result does not establish our hypothesis, but it is consistent with their risks being covered politically. We conclude that the moral hazard problem in Third World lending is an economically serious one (see Arrow 1965). If the equity holders in large banks do not lose when they make bad loans and large LDC borrowers do not lose when they fail to repay, then international capital markets will not work efficiently.

11 DID THE COMMERCIAL BANKS PUSH LOANS ON THE LDC'S?

William Darity Jr.

Long-term lending to non-OPEC LDCs began to grow rapidly, albeit from a small base, in the late 1960s. The growth accelerated in the 1971–73 period, as banks began aggressively to seek new lending outlets by offering narrow spreads on syndicated credits and attractive terms on other types of loans. . . . [T]he volume of lending mushroomed after the quadrupling of oil prices in 1973–74.

Goodman (1981: 15)

The present signs suggest that the bankers of the world are bent on suicide.

Keynes (1963 [1938] : 178)

Debt woes on a global scale compel attention simultaneously to a host of unresolved theoretical problems for economists, including the appropriate theory of the firm, the appropriate theory of banking behavior, the proper analysis of the formation of contracts, the correct treatment of the formation of individual and market expec-

The author has benefited from comments, criticisms, and suggestions from James Galbraith, Michael Claudon, Ed Green, Bobbie Horn, Charles Kindleberger, Jeffrey Marquardt, Rodney Mills, Hyman Minsky, Steve Steib, and Guy Stevens. The author also is grateful to the Board of Governors of the Federal Reserve for providing him with support as a visiting scholar to extend this research effort. This chapter represents the views of the author and should not be interpreted as reflecting the views of the Board of Governors of the Federal Reserve System or other members of its staff.

tations, and the nature of trade cycles and financial crises. Along the fragile precipice of international credit arrangements, these problems surface flushed red with high drama—a world of big banks, smaller banks, multinational guardian institutions, allegations of neoimperialist conspiracies, borrowing governments of questionable competence and incorruptibility, and persistent poverty among the masses of the populations of many of the borrowing nations.

This chapter focuses on a particular controversy that has arisen amid the international debt crisis, the controversy over the extent to which multinational banks are responsible for the current situation. The claim that the commercial banks in some sense "pushed" loans on the less developed countries constitutes the indictment. Proponents of the loan-pushing notion suggest that the banks have engaged in self-victimization by advancing credit to foreign borrowers who have less than a prayer of making repayment.

The doctrine of loan pushing is the antithesis of Irving Friedman's picture of banks as waiting for applications for loans from around the world and evaluating each loan individually on its merits regardless of its country of origin.[1] Bankers as loan pushers become door-to-door salesmen, albeit in pinstripe suits. They persuade borrowers to agree to credits although the borrowers had no thought of borrowing at all or, at least, not such large amounts. Moreover from this perspective in euphoric times banks will sell loans to borrowers in regions they customarily leave alone.

Here are two contrasting views of banking practice. Irving Friedman treats the banks as passive agents; loan-pushing bankers, by contrast, are viewed as the active agents, covering the globe to find new borrowers.

THE CONCEPT OF "PUSHING" LOANS

The specific act of "pushing" loans requires elaboration. Obviously, it does not mean that bankers force LDC officials to accept loan contracts at gunpoint. For Andrew Brimmer, a former member of the Federal Reserve Board of Governors, pushing loans involves a drastic softening of terms relative to the expectations of the potential borrowers. Brimmer argues that the commercial banks, in an effort to dispose of their surplus funds, reduced the spread between their cost of funds (the London Inter Bank Offered Rate, LIBOR) and the loan rate that they offered LDC borrowers. They also lengthened the maturities on the loans and substantially raised the amounts they were willing to lend (Brimmer 1973: 17). This pattern is evident between the final quarter of 1975 and the final quarter of 1979 for both OPEC and non-OPEC LDCs (see Tables 11-1 and 11-2). Signs of reversal became visible in 1980 and 1981 as repayment difficulties accelerated and as reschedulings were negotiated on harsher terms than the initial loans.[2]

The key point in Brimmer's conceptualization of loan pushing is the implied segmentation of the global financial market between borrowers in the developed and developing worlds. The commercial banks turn in a comprehensive fashion toward the LDCs only when loan demand from sources in the developed world weakens sufficiently for the terms required to bring forth additional demand to be perceived as unprofitable. To make the new loans in the countries of the periphery may have necessitated comparatively soft terms for borrowers there, but those terms were still perceived as adequate to produce a desired degree of profitability by the lenders.

Charles Kindleberger's rhetoric conveys a dramatic picture:

> contemplate the enormous external debt of the developing countries, built up not only since the rise of oil prices but importantly—a widely ignored fact—in the several years before that time, as multinational banks swollen with dollars tumbled over one another in trying to uncover new foreign borrowers and practically *forced* money on the less-developed countries (Kindleberger 1978: 23–24, emphasis added).

While acknowledging that his observation "is a bit hyperbolic," Kindleberger has attempted to give precision to the idea of loan pushing.[3] He argues that sharp differences exist in opportunities to contract for interest rates across borrowers with varying risk characteristics. Kindleberger constructs a position that resembles the implications of the ancient mercantilist doctrine of the utility of poverty for the labor supply function; instead, Kindleberger is concerned with the shape of the supply curve for loanable funds. Kindleberger comments: "when interest rates decline sharply *for any reason*, lenders look around to make loans at high interest rates and take greater risks, in a sort of backward-bending supply curve, to preserve their old incomes."[4] According to Kindleberger the recent buildup of LDC indebtedness was triggered by former Federal Reserve chairman Arthur Burns's "cheap money efforts . . . in the early part of

Table 11–1. Interest Rate Spreads (over LIBOR) and Maturities on Eurocurrency Credits to Non-OPEC LDCs, OPEC Nations, and All Nations, 1975–81.

	1975 Q4	1976 Q4	1977 Q4	1978 Q4	1979 Q4	1980 Q4	1981 Q4
Non-OPEC LDCs							
Weighted mean spreads	1.65	1.87	1.77	1.06	.76	1.10	1.16
Unweighted mean spreads	1.82	1.90	1.76	1.04	.90	.93	.95
Weighted mean maturities	5.44	5.14	7.32	9.79	10.11	8.06	7.31
OPEC							
Weighted mean spreads	1.67	1.34	1.59	1.11	.75	.81	.69
Unweighted mean spreads	1.65	1.56	1.52	1.14	.82	1.16	.79
Weighted mean maturities	5.66	6.95	5.48	8.59	8.42	4.80	9.60
Total Sample							
Weighted mean spreads	1.63	1.58	1.48	.83	.68	.83	.88
Unweighted mean spreads	1.67	1.56	1.41	.88	.77	.81	.75
Weighted mean maturities	5.63	5.61	6.79	8.88	9.64	7.79	8.11

Note: Interest rate spreads are calculated as percent per annum. Maturities are calculated as numbers of years. Weights were based on the volume of credits for each country in the current quarter.

Source: Memorandum prepared by Rodney H. Mills, Jr. (1982).

Table 11–2. Interest Rate Spreads (over LIBOR) and Maturities on Eurocurrency Credits to Selected Major Debtor Nations, 1975–81.

	1975 Q4	1976 Q4	1977 Q4	1978 Q4	1979 Q4	1980 Q4	1981 Q4
Argentina							
Spread	—	1.88	1.58	.88	.76	.63	1.09
Maturity	—	4.00	9.14	11.05	10.43	7.65	7.33
Brazil							
Spread	1.72	1.95	2.20	1.26	.72	1.79	2.14
Maturity	6.80	5.71	7.76	11.52	12.03	8.87	8.00
Chile							
Spread	—	—	1.93	1.10	.92	.93	1.01
Maturity	—	—	4.33	9.57	9.80	7.30	5.06
Mexico							
Spread	2.00	2.05	1.88	.91	.69	.90	.60
Maturity	4.76	5.97	7.00	7.93	8.84	6.96	5.41
Korea							
Spread	1.47	1.63	1.75	.95	.69	.52	.63
Maturity	3.50	5.32	7.00	9.34	9.61	7.52	7.46
Poland							
Spread	1.50	1.50	—	—	.83	1.13	—
Maturity	6.00	7.00	—	—	3.00	3.00	—
Venezuela							
Spread	—	1.63	1.63	1.35	—	.68	—
Maturity	—	5.90	6.00	5.70	—	5.00	—

Note: Interest rate spreads are calculated as percent per annum. Maturities are calculated as numbers of years.
Source: Memorandum prepared by Rodney H. Mills, Jr. (1982).

1971." This depressed interest rates in the Eurodollar market and led the participating banks to chase down potential borrowers in the LDCs, particularly in Latin America.[5]

Thus, the commercial banks are portrayed as attempting to avert reductions in their profitability or earnings by shifting toward LDC borrowers.[6] The banks were unwilling to accept a decline in terms great enough to achieve full absorption of their loanable funds at the center. On the other hand, softening the terms for borrowers on the periphery to a sufficient degree to stimulate their consent to contract for large sums of indebtedness would still leave the banks with what they considered to be adequate margins for profitability.

"Pushing," then, amounts to design of loan packages that attract borrowers who formerly were denied access to international credit markets altogether or who were, at least, denied such large amounts of funds. The LDC borrowers' risk characteristics, which presumably were responsible for their previous exclusion from easy credit terms, remain unchanged. But suddenly instead of being pariahs to the major international lending institutions they find creditors clamoring for their attention. The one-time wallflowers become the belles of the dollar ball. Furthermore, the spreads offered to these new borrowers appear to bear no correspondence to the risks associated with the loan.

THEORIES OF THE DEBT CRISIS AND THE LOAN-PUSH PHENOMENON

The concept of loan pushing fits with varying degrees of ease within the folds of various theories of the current international debt crisis. Four theories are to be given critical consideration here; they rely upon (1) the rational expectations hypothesis, (2) institutional weaknesses in the commercial banking system, (3) overborrowing, and (4) the financial instability hypothesis.

The Rational Expectations Hypothesis

Explanations of the massive buildup of indebtedness in less developed countries compatible with the belief that bankers possess rational expectatifons (or stochastic perfect foresight) thus far have treated the growth in peripheral debt as no object for alarm or as due to unforeseeable shocks. The first view, in effect, says that the debt crisis is not really a crisis after all. The second view says that the bankers were surprised and the surprises could not have been prevented since they were purely random events. There is a third view, which has not been given an explicit airing in the literature thus far, that also will be presented here.

Michael Beenstock is perhaps the premier exponent of the first view. Beenstock's (1983) "transition theory" says that the LDCs are now becoming the major global industrial sites. Deindustrialization in the center and industrialization in the periphery, particularly in the so-called newly industrializing countries (NICs), has meant (autonomous?) shifts in the marginal product of capital schedules in each region. The downward shift in the center nations and the upward shift in the periphery nations raised the rate of return on capital in the developing countries relative to the developed countries. Short-term effects from the oil price hikes have contributed to the increased indebtedness of the non-OPEC LDCs, but the structural change in the world economy that has shifted industrial growth toward some of those nations becomes the fundamental cause of the increase in debt.

Beenstock points to the fact that growth in LDC manufactures has accompanied growth in their debt as evidence that the situation is analogous to the indebtedness incurred by United States borrowers during its nineteenth-century phase of industrialization. For Beenstock, growth in LDC debt today is merely an equilibrium adjustment reflecting the necessary flows in finance from low-return regions to high-return regions; there is no reason for panic. The NICs will become industrial centers within twenty to thirty years, and the current disarray is only a temporary period of pain that goes hand in hand with the international structural rearrangements.

From this standpoint, the bankers' loans were perfectly reasonable. If bankers did set terms that would lure LDC borrowers into their clutches, those terms reflected a reasonable calculation of prospects for efficacious use of their loans and subsequent repayment. After all, the greatest volume of loans were going to those LDCs that displayed the best prospects for industrial development. The biggest borrowers were members of what Lawrence Franko (1979: 292) has called the "charmed circle of ten."[7] Oil price shocks and export commodity price declines are all events that can make debt service problems for some of these borrowers, but they are transitory difficulties. The underlying trend is toward solvency. The bankers' loans were made wisely—that is, rationally—and there is no enduring international debt crisis.

Beenstock's secular explanation for the buildup of LDC debt is intriguing, but it poses its own set of puzzles. Is it believable that differentials in the interest rates that could be contracted on loans in the center and the periphery were grounded in differences in the real return on capital? Even if Brazil is destined to be where the United States is today by the year 2010, does it mean that the typical loan received will be utilized to generate earnings sufficient to pay the lender the prospective real return?

Kindleberger (1978b: 6), for one, has a far less felicitous view of the uses of borrowed funds by developing countries, contending that the historical record reveals that "productive loans in the developing countries are not very productive and do not stay long out of default. . . . " Indeed, one wonders why the grounds for optimism about the relative potential for economic development in Argentina in the 1970s ought to be any greater than it was in the 1920s. "Development" loans do not have an impressive history of success. They rarely have produced anything that resembles economic development, and they often have produced defaults.[8] Even where economic development has taken place—such as industrialization in the United States in the latter part of the nineteenth century—it has not ensured that loans have been paid off. Witness the colorful pattern of default on debts by various state governments in the United States between the 1860s and 1880s (Scott 1893).

Still the past need not provide a guide to the future. Calculation of the real returns on investments—which includes loans involving risk of repayment difficulties—is a dubious proposition (see especially ch. 12 of the *General Theory*, Keynes 1936). Consequently, Beenstock's view notwithstanding, the bankers cannot tell what real return will be earned on their loans to LDC borrowers, even on average. They cannot see the future. There are no facts that can tell them which region of the world genuinely offers the highest prospective yield.

It is true that losses on bank loans to LDC borrowers remain low relative to losses on loans to domestic borrowers for U.S. banks in particular. This fact may provide comfort to those who share the Beenstockian view that the crisis is not a crisis after all. But the figures on loan losses on foreign debts are deceptive. The large money-center banks are able to avoid listing their nonperforming foreign loans as officially "nonperforming" in their regulatory reports. They can roll the loans over through automatic or near automatic refinancing or rescheduling arrangements to avoid having to deduct them from their assets (Hill 1984: 1).[9]

The standard alternative to Beenstock's analysis of the debt crisis within the context of the rational expectations approach is the position that the debt crisis is the outcome of a random shock. This position is developed most fully by Sachs and Bruno (see Sachs 1981 and Bruno and Sachs 1982). They place special emphasis on the oil price shock and its repercussions as the key random event that sent the borrowing nations into arrears on their debt payments.

Sachs and Bruno have not selected the most satisfactory surprise, however, since (1) the buildup of LDC indebtedness *preceded* the first major price rise in the early 1970s, (2) it would be difficult to support the view that the second major oil price boost of 1978 and 1979 was a "shock" in light of the reaction to the first, and (3) the pattern of bank loan diversification was intended to cope with just such an eventuality.[10]

A superior candidate may be the Federal Reserve's maintenance of a stringent disinflationary policy. A case can be made that no one, not even the bankers, expected Chairman Volcker to stick to his hard money guns so intently. Economists attached to the Fisherian theory of interest rates were baffled as the real rate of interest on the dollar went from low and even negative rates to historically unprecedented levels over the course of the past several years. John Makin, for one, places the onus of the international debt crisis at the doorstep of the Federal Reserve's great success in bringing down the U.S. inflation rate; he depicts Walter Wriston as one money-center banker who was "shocked" by the vigilance of the Federal Reserve.

What remains is to determine what force on earth could bring to so sudden a stop the music that both borrowers and lenders had been so pleased to hear and dance to with such abandon from 1974 to 1981. In two words, it was Paul Volcker. Again Wriston is the spokesman who characterizes a transition from the banker's perspective. Asked in a 1978 interview whether he would welcome any restrictions on any U.S. lenders or borrowers, Wriston replied: "I just want the opposite. Let us have their freedoms." "Which ones?" asked the interviewer. Wriston replied: "I believe the most important thing the bank will have to deal with over the next 10 years is not money policy, because the options are limited and there isn't much elbow room. [Rather] it's the revolution in the financial business of America."

Five years later, asked the inevitable "what's gone wrong now" question in another interview just before the September annual meetings of the IMF and World Bank, Wriston replied: "We're beat upon the fact that we have imprudent moments. But I don't know anyone that knew Volcker was going to lock the wheels of the world." (Makin 1984: 152) [11]

From this perspective the banks and their borrowers got caught in the left-hand tail of the rate of return frequency distribution due to the random shock created by a surprising commitment to disinflation by the U.S. central bank. The bankers' lending terms were reasonable, conditional on their reasonable forecasts of the world economy's direction. Floating rates on loan contracts tied to reference nominal rates designed to protect the lenders from high inflation punished the carriers of dollar-denominated debt as inflation was wrung out of the U.S. economy. [12]

There is, however, a third somewhat unconventional, even cynical perspective compatible with the rational expectations approach that appeals neither to a claim that the debt crisis really is illusory nor to a claim that it is the product of unforeseen and unforeseeable events that made loans arranged by sensible-minded bankers go badly. According to this third perspective, bankers made the loans at worst fully expecting the overwhelming majority of them to go bad or at best being indifferent to whether or not the loans went bad.

This argument is the one variant among those utilizing the rational expectations hypothesis that feeds directly into an overlending or loan-pushing doctrine. But why would bankers rationally make bad loans? There is the possibility that a loan that is bad from a performance standpoint need not be bad from the standpoint of bank profitability.

The larger banks have a quite reasonable pecuniary motive for setting up the foreign loan syndication. They typically receive loan fees for assembling the consortium of lenders, and they receive this money at the outset regardless of the eventual disposition of the loan. The larger the loan, the greater the winnings due to economies of scale in banking:

Fees for arranging the loans averaged about 1 percent of their value. The difference between the bank's cost of funds and the lending rate are expressed as "spreads," percentages of the value of the loan—which, while typically lower for large borrowers, vary a good deal less than the size of the loan. One percent of a $200 million loan is $2 million, while 2 percent of a $100,000 loan is only $2,000. It does not require anywhere near one thousand times the effort expended on a $100,000 loan to arrange a $200 million loan, and even if syndication costs should be large, they can be covered by additional fees assessed "up front" (before the loan is granted). (Makin 1984: 139)

In general, the existing regulatory apparatus also makes it easier to avoid reporting foreign loans as nonperforming when payment difficulties emerge. Moreover, regulations governing lending overseas by U.S. banks are not preemptive. Foreign lending limits set ceilings relative to a particular bank's capital on the sum that can be lent to individual borrowing units overseas, but there is no legal ceiling on the total sum that can be lent to all the borrowing units in a given country. The U.S. bankers themselves contend, as well, that they were urged to lend to the LDCs in the early 1970s by U.S. Treasury and Federal Reserve officials for political reasons (Alexander 1984: 59). If such encouragement did occur, out of officialdom's perception of U.S. national interest, then the bankers may have legitimately believed there was a governmental obligation to bail them out in time of crisis.

Certain public institutions in the United States undoubtedly can perform as lenders of last resort. For bankers forming rational expectations, the existence of such authorities would enter into their calculations. The bankers may have assigned a high probability to the likelihood that the authorities would act on their behalf in the event that difficulties arose with loans. After all, what good is the knowledge that a lender of last resort exists, if its response in time of crisis is not tested?

U.S. based banks do have an insurance scheme embodied in the Federal Deposit Insurance Corporation and the capabilities of the Federal Reserve. To the extent that lenders perceive that there are institutions able to insure their operations they may become more willing to pursue loan options they might otherwise avoid.[13] This poses the classic moral hazard problem: "the existence of the insurance may have the particularly perverse effect of increasing the incidence of the contingency being insured against—bank failures in one case and burglaries in the other" (Solow 1982: 238).[14] Insurance against the consequences of bad loans may increase the incidence of bad loans.

But whom does the insurance protect? Do the bank managers gain security from the FDIC or Federal Reserve? When the senior management of Continental Illinois finally gave up on the effort to find a private institution to inject funds into their bank, they turned as a last resort solution to the FDIC. Part of the bail-out plan designed to keep the institution afloat involved the removal of Continental's chairman, David Taylor, as well as other senior managers, and their replacement by officials selected by the FDIC (Knapp 1984: 88).

However, it is not obvious that the FDIC's actions have been tragic for the dismissed officers. Unconfirmed reports indicate that the three top Continental Illinois officers who were fired draw $250,000 cash for three years and the head of Financial Services of America, who was fired, received a remarkably lucrative golden handshake. Plainly the FDIC is not responsible for these personal contracts, but if it had chosen to put the banks through one-day bankruptcy then the contracts would have been void aside from general claims.[15]

Continental's stockholders also are suffering. In addition to the plunge Continental stock already has weathered, they "could lose the largest share of some $2.2 billion in equity [when] the government takes over" (Knapp 1984). The FDIC also has removed ten members of Continental's board of directors (Gruber 1984).

Although individual bank managers, shareholders, and directors are not free from jeopardy when loans sour, banks as going enterprises are protected from failure, especially those with intricate interbank deposit arrangements. The large money-center banks have such arrangements; their major depositors often are other banks. The Continental rescue was outright unlike the still unsettled demise of Penn Square Bank. The rescue seems to provide a clear signal to the larger banks—and their depositors, inclusive of other large banks—that they will continue to exist regardless of the decisions of their present array of senior managers.[16] The FDIC's rescue of Continental Illinois shows that big banks can expect a degree of help not available to smaller banks, giving them a further advantage in attracting depositors over smaller banks.

The Federal Reserve's stance as lender of last resort carries no similar repercussions for senior bank officials. Perhaps this was the true reason for the bankers' "surprise" (if, they were surprised by the Federal Reserve's actions after October 1979). The adamant disinflationary stance undercut "insurance" the bankers had counted on when loans were contracted initially. The Federal Reserve would not "validate" the debts as long as monetary policy steered a course away from inflation.

Foreign loans possess a unique advantage given the potential insurance provided by the International Monetary Fund (and more recently by the World Bank as well). For although the banks cannot control how funds are used by sovereign borrowers when loans are contracted initially, the IMF can perform the task for them when the borrower runs into a balance-of-payments difficulties and is turned toward the fund for "relief" (Lipson 1979). The IMF already has become the monitor of Mexican finances and appears to be moving toward a general role as the loan broker between banks and debtors (Witcher 1984b).

Reliance upon the IMF as an insurance agent on foreign loans involves a high degree of brinksmanship on the part of the commercial banks. Not only must the banks believe that the IMF's conditions for new lending are the correct ones, but they also must believe that LDC regimes can contain the political reaction of their citizens to national debt peonage that often is aggravated when the Fund comes on the scene.[17] Or, at least, they must believe that regimes that fail will be replaced by those better able to restore order and to stay on a course of cooperation with the multinational banks and the IMF.

The rational basis for loans to LDCs, regardless of the likelihood of repayment, is reinforced by the needs of their domestic customers seeking to export abroad. S. G. Gwynne's (1983) revelations on the foreign loan business as a one-time employee of a medium-sized Ohio bank provides such a case. A loan Gwynne himself arranged in the Philippines was prompted by the insistence of one of his bank's key customers: an "earth-moving equipment company, a subsidiary of a major auto company and an old client of the bank." The earth-moving company anticipated, correctly, that the loan would finance shipments of its product to the Philippine construction company receiving the loan. Borrowed funds fueled imports from U.S. producers by Mexican state-owned enterprises (Frazier 1984). In recent agreements with the Mexican government European banks have begun to link their loans to purchases of exports from their home countries (Witcher 1984b).

When nervousness about LDC loans sets in, smaller banks tend to be first to pull back (Johnson 1983, 1984).[18] The larger banks have an incentive to keep the second or third-line banks involved in new lending efforts, even if it simply means rollover of existing debt: to extract the loan fees (D'Arista 1979: 69–70). But if they cannot keep them involved they still can take over some of the smaller banks' claims when the latter withdraw from funding a country having difficulties meeting payments (Johnson 1983, 1984). One can speculate that the larger banks absorb these claims from lower tier banks at a reduced price, while the second- and third-line banks must correspondingly write down their asset position.

The upshot is bankers knowingly can make bad foreign loans. Smaller banks, it can be argued, were pressed into the foreign loan business to support the foreign export initiatives of their major customers. Larger banks, presumably facing similar pressures, could exert further leverage through correspondent relations to pull lower tier banks into foreign loan syndications. In sum, there are a variety of reasons why foreign loans are beneficial to the large money-center banks, regardless of loan quality: (1) there are loan fees up front for arranging the syndication, (2) foreign loans can be kept on the books as performing far longer than domestic loans when borrowers are in arrears, (3) there might even be a net gain for the bank's equity position from foreign loan commitments, and (4) loans by large money-center banks have potential public sector insurance in the forms of their respective nations' lenders of last resort. But foreign loans to LDCs have potential international insurance agents as well, especially the IMF.

Institutional Weaknesses

Virtually at the opposite pole from debt crisis explanations based on rational expectations are explanations that identify flaws in banking practice—either outright poor judgment by the bankers or problems with the incentive arrangements governing the activities of different levels of actors in commercial banks. Each of these arguments is considered in turn.

Unlike the rational expectations view that the bankers were as well informed as possible in making their loans, the poor-judgment view holds that bankers lacked the best possible information and frequently operated out of avoidable ignorance. Bad loans were made because of carelessness and inadequate investigation of the circumstances of the borrowers. Poor knowledge coupled with incautiousness led to the present debt crisis.

The explanation can be given a generational cast. The current wave of bank managers either have forgotten or never were familiar with the troubled history of loans to the developing world. Fifty-year waves of LDC loans occur precisely because it takes that much time for the older group of captains of finance to be replaced with a younger group unaware of the lessons to be learned from the past.

Gwynne's (1983) revelations, mentioned earlier, provide some support for this explanation. Gwynne describes his own rise in the trenches as a twenty-five-year-old front-line loan officer in the Philippines in 1978 after "one and a half years of banking experience [after joining] the bank as a 'credit analyst' on the strength of an MA in English [and after promotion] eleven months later to loan officer and [assignment] to the French-speaking Arab nations [because of his fluency in French]." Gwynne adds further that he was not unique:

> I am far from alone in my youth and inexperience. The world of international banking is now full of aggressive, bright, but hopelessly inexperienced lenders in their mid-twenties. They travel the world like itinerant brushmen, filling loan quotas, peddling financial wares, and living high on the hog. Their bosses are often bright but hopelessly inexperienced twenty-nine-year-old vice presidents with wardrobes from Brooks Brothers, MBAs from Wharton or Stanford, and so little credit training they would have trouble with a simple retail installment loan. (1983: 23)

As for bosses above the young, Whartonized vice-presidents, the senior loan officers, Gwynne describes them as "pragmatic, nuts-and-bolts bankers whose grasp of local banking is often profound, the product of twenty or thirty years of experience [; however, they] are fish out of water when it comes to international lending" (1983: 23).

On the face of it, Gwynne's story is one of ignorance at all levels of the decisionmaking apparatus, at least among the second tier of banks, if not the money-center banks as well. But his story also involves the market-making function of the loans on behalf of the banks' domestic corporate depositors. The loan Gwynne himself arranged in the Philippines was prompted by the insistence of one of his bank's key customers. According to Gwynne, generally speaking the senior bankers had no desire to move into the foreign loan market "but were forced into it by the internationalization of American commerce; as their local clientele expanded into foreign trade, they had no choice but to follow them or lose the business to the money-center banks" (1983: 23).[19] Were senior loan officers who approved foreign loans that subsequently went bad acting out of ignorance or sheer self-preservation?

Keynes explained the manic lending of 1920s by the failure of the bankers to attempt to sensibly forecast the future. The bankers, in Keynes's (1960: 176–77) view, were partially the victims of bad advice from his fellow economists, who, he continued to argue throughout the 1930s, were misleading practical men with policy recommendations rooted in unsound theory. The bankers also were, Keynes argued, victims of their own penchant for convention—convention that paved a path to ruin: "A sound banker, alas! is not one who foresees danger and avoids it, but one who, when he is ruined is ruined in a conventional and orthodox way along with his fellows, so that no one can really blame him" (1960: 176). Better to go down doing what everyone believes a banker should be doing, than to stay afloat by being a maverick in the world of high finance. For Keynes the bankers were prisoners of custom and habit that propelled them onto unwarranted lending sprees from which they eventually recoiled only to deepen their peril. They "pushed" loans—low-quality loans—because that was the conventional thing to be doing at the time.

Like virtually all of Keynes's hypotheses this one fascinates, but it, too, leaves several important questions unanswered. Who sets the convention of the moment? How is it recognized as such, so that the herd follows? If, in fact, there are profit advantages in not following the convention, why does it remain so attractive to follow it to assure that, if failure comes, it comes only "in a conventional and orthodox way"? Or, if the profit advantages from unconventional and unorthodox behavior are supremely uncertain, then why *not* follow the convention, since to do otherwise holds no assurance of success? In the latter case the bankers are not "blind" to the future and mere victims of their own habitual behavior. They may have rationally adopted such habitual behavior to cope in a world that is arational in providing guidance about the future. Indeed, the latter perspective is consistent with much of Keynes's later argument about subjective uncertainty in the *General Theory* (see especially his ch. 12).

A second type of institutional weakness in banking explanation arises from an application of the problems confronted in the analysis of the relationship between a "principal" and an "agent" in pure contract theory. The principal in this case could be either the senior loan officer or vice-president in the commercial bank's home office; the agent would be the junior loan officer working overseas who makes firsthand arrangements for the loan.

The junior loan officers are rewarded by their success in meeting and surpassing assigned loan quotas. They gain by arranging as many loans as possible, loans that must meet with the approval of their superiors. It is to the junior loan officers' advantage to doctor the loan package sufficiently to sell it successfully to those higher up. This may include setting up all manner of "guarantees" from sources in the borrowers' country. But perhaps more important, before the results of any particular junior loan officer's loans are realized, he or she is likely to have moved on to new employment. Bankers at this level are highly mobile participants in the lending industry.[20] The junior loan officers receive high points for bringing the loan package to fruition and few demerits when the loan proves to be of poor quality.

The principals, in this case senior loan officers or bank vice-presidents, have not managed to construct an incentive scheme for the junior loan officers abroad that will extract greater prudence in their efforts to arrange loans. The debt mess, then, is due to a breakdown in the hierarchical operations of the lending institutions.

This is a clever explanation for an international liquidity crisis but probably not a substantive one. It leaves unanswered why the failure to rein in the junior loan officers would be so widespread and persistent as to produce a decade-long accumulation of low-caliber loans. Sooner or later, one presumes, a new scheme of rewards would be designed for the strata of bankers who do the legwork in foreign countries. Sooner or later the results of their lending records even should follow them to new employers.

Presumably, their supervisors, the "principals," have strong incentives to get the junior loan officers to stop pushing loans, unless the loans are of a reliable quality. The penalties for the results of the actions taken by inferiors fall on superiors in the corporate world. For example, the Drysdale and Penn Square Bank incidents led to the removal of two high-level Chase Manhatten Bank officials and five middle-level executives there. In addition, two more vice-presidents resigned after news reports identified them as accepting loans generated by Penn Square ("Chase Reports . . . " 1982). Citibank is a bit more benign in its treatment of executives who make decisions that later prove to be bad. Instead of firing those "who show potential" they are removed from decisionmaking authority (put in the "penalty box") for twelve to eighteen months. Obviously this slows an executive's advancement (Hertzberg 1984: 1). In either case, those penalties should have a chilling effect on overexuberant upper level bank personnel and make them look far more carefully at loan packages brought to them for approval and support (unless, of course, their own sweetheart contracts are so sweet that being fired is not terribly painful).

One can speculate that with such penalty systems in operation for upper level bank managers, if junior loan officers have had a relatively free hand in arranging foreign loans it must be because those loans do not go as blatantly bad as domestic loans. There has been no publicized major housecleaning of bank personnel over LDC loans as of this time. The aforementioned capacity to roll over foreign loans means indefinite postponement of the day of reckoning. For example, Thomas Theobald, vice-chairman of Citicorp, whose Citibank has the largest exposure in the Third World, continues to maintain that his bank still makes a profit on its Latin loans. Skeptics suggest that this is due to various steps that have been taken to delay a precipitous markdown of earnings (Hertzberg 1984: 16). All this suggests it is less likely that it was the actions of the junior loan officers that were as critical as the permissiveness toward those actions by senior bank management.

Regardless, either argument invoking institutional weaknesses in banking, however implausible, can yield loan-pushing outcomes. If senior loan officers are simply foolish or are fooled by their subordinates in the field loan pushing will come about.

Overborrowing

A third approach to the international debt crisis shifts responsibility exclusively onto decisionmakers in developing countries. Borrowers simply absorbed an unreasonable amount of debt. This could have been due to lack of good sense about policymaking to achieve growth via borrowing on the part of LDC finance ministers. Or it could be due to entirely sensible judgments by national leaders, given their personal political objectives and the tenuousness of their tenure of leadership. Nations may continue to exist, as Citicorp's executives always point out, but regimes can change, sometimes quite rapidly. A large debt burden can be passed on to the successor regime as a problem for them to solve, while the accumulation of debt may have resolved a variety of other problems faced by the regime incurring the debt.

This approach is the most fiercely incompatible with loan pushing by the banks. If anything, it amounts to a thesis of "loan pulling." But overreaching for credit by borrowing nations actually throws the ball back into the lenders' court. If the world really follows Irving Friedman's description, where banks are passive agents waiting patiently for potential borrowers to appear on their doorstep, the banks still have the option of denying applications for loans from borrowers whose prospects for repayment are dubious. It is possible that the potential borrower will provide individual banks with false information, especially about the number of other banks from whom it has already obtained funds. But this presses the argument back to the position that bankers acted out of ignorance. Moreover, ignorance about the other banks who have made loans to an overextended borrower is less likely when commercial bank loans have been made through wide-ranging syndications.

Alternatively, in a game-theoretic context one could argue that the borrowers were able to exert extraordinary leverage—that the borrowers had the bargaining edge. But what leverage the borrowers held prior to the initial loan commitments is unclear. After substantial lending already has begun, large borrowers could threaten default to pressure the banks into renewed lending. But in the absence of a collective warning of imminent default by a cartel of large debtor nations, such a threat is not likely to be credible. According to Dornbusch (1984a: 5),

> An outright default or repudiation appears quite remote. The advances made since the 1930s in private and public survival techniques assure that a debtor can be kept "on the machine" almost indefinitely. Creditors are well organized to avoid accidental default, and international institutions and governments take an active interest in keeping the debts in a semireforming status. In the meantime they have made clear the consequences of default.

Dornbusch quotes remarks of Robert T. McNamara:

> A second obligation of the LDC debtors is to work with their creditors within the international financial system to bring about orderly rescheduling of their debt-service burdens. . . . A repudiation takes place when a borrower unilaterally renounces responsibility for some or all of his debt obligations. Under such circumstances the foreign assets of a country would be attached by

creditors throughout the world; its exports would be seized by creditors at each dock where they landed; its national airline would be unable to operate; and its sources of desperately needed capital goods and spare parts virtually eliminated. In many countries, even food imports would be curtailed. Hardly a pleasant scenario.

Of course, the officials of the nine U.S. money-center banks whose foreign loans represent more than 150 percent of their capital assets rest easier at night with the belief that neither Mexico, Argentina, Venezuela, nor Brazil are willing to suffer the consequences outlined by McNamara.

The Financial Instability Hypotheses

Hyman Minsky (1979) has begun the extension of his financial instability hypothesis to the foreign loan push of the 1970s. Minsky's theory directly addresses the empirical details of frequency and clustering of LDC lending.

The financial instability hypothesis mandates that the credit mechanism of capitalistic economies is *inherently* prone to breakdown, contributing directly to recurrent cyclical downturns.[21] Cast in the context of a long-wave analysis, Minsky contends that long periods of prosperity lead lending institutions to extend credits to borrowers with increasingly weaker financial positions. Profit-seeking enterprises that receive new credits are more leveraged than their predecessors in the borrowing game and more vulnerable to being unable to repay their debts when a decline occurs in after-tax profits. Older borrowers taking on additional credit, at least in part to refinance previous debt obligations, acquire less sturdy financial postures. Eventually a dropoff in after-tax profits occurs, and businesses fail to meet their payment commitments. The lenders subsequently retreat from extending additional credit. The credit crunch that supplants the prior credit boom propagates a generalized fall in investment, income, and employment.

It is convenient to graft a new set of borrowers onto the Minsky model, specifically foreign borrowers in developing countries. They become the object of attention of lenders to a greater degree as the long upswing advances. This group of borrowers may, from the time their loans first are contracted, possess speculative or Ponzi finance positions. These positions are the most dangerous to sustain in a Minsky world.[22] The longer the duration of a cyclical upturn, the larger the proportion of businesses and, now, foreign governments, who come to hold these more dangerous positions.

Minsky seems to view these long waves culminating in near manic lending booms as occurring cyclically.[23] The upswings in chronologic time appear to be relatively long from the perspective of a business cycle, perhaps forty to fifty years. But if Minsky has detected the periodicity in these events, why have the bankers failed to do so? Why do they repeat the overlending practices that have contributed to major downturns in the past? Why have they not learned from the mistakes of the 1920s, for instance?

This is virtually the same as asking, why do the bankers fail to display behavior rooted in rational expectations if the Minsky model provides an accurate picture of the structural features of the U.S. economy? Of course, if holding rational expectations means that they adopt more conservative lending practices during a long upswing, then the process Minsky depicts would not happen. To maintain the Minsky position, it is more satisfying to establish that the credit cycles could occur even if bankers could foresee the adverse consequences of their collective actions.

Minsky tends to argue that the bankers believe their loans would perform, but individually they cannot manage the performance of the world economy. Policymakers like the Federal Reserve could avert the credit crunch, but to do so would require reflation of the economy. Furthermore, the bankers and the Federal Reserve officials alike are prisoners of the false doctrine of monetarism, which purports to argue that, if the Federal Reserve maintains steady money growth, the economy will be self-adjusting or self-correcting.[24]

The first part of his argument can take on the flavor of the version of the rational expectations approach that says the bank loans went bad due to the random shock of the Federal Reserve's disinflation policy. Otherwise, if the Federal Reserve had continued an easy money policy, the debt crisis might never have materialized. For Minsky, the cyclical fluctuations are characteristic of the unregulated capitalistic economy; *appropriate* regulation will eliminate the cyclical swings.

Without regulation, *competitive* pressure among the banks leads them to extend loans to less and less well secured borrowers. Even if there are lessons to be learned from past lending booms, the profit wars of today place an insuperable impetus on the commercial banks to increase their assets through new lending. If it fails to "keep up," a bank must accept a lower rate of return than its competitors during the long upswing as the price paid for greater stability in its performance.[25]

Finally, it is worth noting, that certain regulatory policies might aggravate overlending. If the Federal Reserve, for example, performs as lender of last resort without any major quid pro quo from the rescued financial institution, its action would only serve to encourage others to continue making injudicious loans:

> If lender-of-last-resort interactions are not accompanied by regulations and reforms that restrict financial market practices, then the intervention sets the stage for the financing of an inflationary expansion, once the "animal spirits" of businesspeople and bankers have recovered from the transitory shock of the crisis that forced the lender-of-the-last resort activities in the first place. (Minsky 1979: 35)

CONCLUSION

The concept of loan pushing embodies the idea that commercial bankers produce financial crises by their own actions. It has gained renewed interest in the present context and appears to be compatible with a variety of explanations of the current international debt crisis.

The unavoidable ignorance version of the rational expectations hypothesis can yield loan pushing, although it is only valid to conceive of overlending as having occurred in that view in a strictly ex post sense. More provocative is the version of the rational expectations hypothesis that has the bankers consciously making loans to LDCs that they know are of dubious quality. The latter argument has loan pushing emerge because the quality of the loans is not directly relevant to their profitability to the banks.

Loan pushing also is consistent with the somewhat less satisfying arguments alleging institutional weaknesses in the banking system. Either senior loan officers made loan decisions despite available information that would have muted their boldness or they made loan decisions as captives of ambitious subordinates. In each case, the underlying irrationality of bankers' behavior predisposes them toward overlending.

Thus, loan pushing can be a product of theories that are premised either on extreme rationality or irrationality. The Minsky theory is ambiguous about its premise on that score, but an assumption of competitive pressures can reconcile it with bankers' rationality. It is a particularly rich approach in explaining the debt crisis via loan pushing because it explicitly tackles the observed periodic bunching of credit flows to the developing regions.

On the other hand, the rational expectations hypothesis in Beenstock's hands and the overborrowing hypothesis both amount to denials that loan pushing took place. The Beenstock view even seeks to annihilate the conviction that there is a debt crisis, while the overborrowing hypothesis indicts the debtors (or loan pullers) rather than the creditors (or loan pushers). In the latter argument, then, the onus shifts exclusively to the demand side of the foreign credit market.

Neither of the latter two perspectives is convincing. LDC loans have advantages, regardless of quality, especially to the larger banks. It may be the case that they typically gain at the expense of smaller banks in times of crisis, even if their own actions fomented the trauma. Historically, overlending occurs with regularity. There are numerous episodes where banks have seen large portions of their loan portfolios go into default. But, among U.S. banks at least, only the large consistently have survived the shakeout.

If this proves to be true again, at least for those larger commercial banks with substantial exposure in Latin America and throughout the developing world, their loan-pushing activities may compel a redefinition of the notion of a "bad" loan. But if the international debt crisis persists and deepens, a "bad" loan will still be "bad" for those whose deposits will be extinguished and those whose jobs will be lost as the financial system goes into revulsion from lending. After all, ultimately the creditors themselves can make the loans "good" by continuing to lend. But to guarantee that is to create their own moral hazard problem. Eventually they will retreat, leaving the outcome in the hands of the putative lender of last resort, their collective insurance agent. How the lender behaves will determine the magnitude of the shakeout. Regardless, the larger loan pushers probably will survive to push again as long as the provision of credit remains largely a private activity, sanctified by public authorities. Keep in mind that Continental Illinois still exists, albeit with a sign in the window saying, "Under new management."

NOTES TO CHAPTER 11

1. Irving Friedman (1978: 20) writes: "the response of the banks is the response to a demand. Bankers do not make loans to countries, or entities within countries, that do not ask for a loan. The fact is that someone comes to a bank and asks for a loan. Then the banker judges whether to do it. Banks compete for attractive loans, but the borrower is essentially the genesis of the loan." And also, "it is sometimes said that banks are 'reaching' for loans. This is a concept that is often found, even in periodicals which are considered friendly to the private banks. I do not think it is right."

2. Henry S. Terrell (1984: 756) reports that by 1983 the lending spreads and fees charged to the four major Latin American borrowing nations "were substantially higher than the terms on the credits they had arranged in the base period of 1981 through the summer of 1982." However, Terrell also reports that in 1984 terms have softened somewhat, although they have not been restored to the conditions that existed on loans in 1981 and 1982.

3. Personal correspondence with Charles P. Kindleberger, dated July 6, 1984.

4. Ibid.

5. In further correspondence, dated October 2, 1984, Kindleberger has added that the 1971 monetary expansion occurred while "Germany was trying to tighten . . . which speeded up the outflow and accentuated the 'currency substitution.'"

6. A simple explanation for the commercial banks' movement toward LDC borrowers could be the claim that the elasticity of loan demand by borrowers at the center is much greater than the elasticity of demand by borrowers from the periphery with respect to the terms. Therefore, a point is reached on a phase of loan expansion when the commercial banks perceive that they will have to make unacceptably large reductions in the terms to continue lending at the center. But the Kindleberger view has the banks having to accept softer terms at the center for *any* reason, including central bank monetary policy.

7. The "charmed circle" as of September 1983 consisted of Brazil, Mexico, Argentina, Venezuela, Poland, Yugoslavia, Chile, Nigeria, Peru, and Romania. The first four Latin borrowers had an estimated indebtedness totaling more than $250 billion at that time. See "The International Debt Crisis" (1983: H1).

8. Metais (1982: 222) contends that 1970s constitutes the fifth wave of lending to the "backward" regions. He (p. 234 n. 2) identifies the periods 1817–25, 1860–76, 1900–14, and the 1920s as the four previous waves. "Unfortunately," he concludes, "they all ended in widespread defaults."

Some of the same countries were involved in the lending booms in the latter three waves—1900–1914, the 1920s, and the 1970s: Argentina, Brazil, Egypt, Mexico, Spain, and Turkey.

9.   Makin (1984: 135) provides details on how the major U.S. money-center banks "handled" their nonperforming loans to Brazil in 1983:

> Citicorp was not alone in facing heavy write-downs on Brazilian loans, where arrearages had mounted by the fall of 1983 to over $4 billion. Among Citicorp's fellow New York Banks, Manufacturers Hanover had $2.0 billion in Brazilian loans, and development-loan-oriented Chase, $2.6 billion—both exposures comparable to Citibank's in view of their smaller net worth. It is likely that some judicious rolling over of loans had been required to avoid triggering the "nonperforming" alarm bell on Brazilian loans. We have already seen that loans that had a sixty-day nonpermanence clause had in September 1983 been relaxed to a ninety-day clause to avoid the costly nonperformance designation. With respect to their LDC clients, the mighty banks were in the position of a bomb squad disarming a time bomb. Top priority at the moment was to disarm the nonperforming fuse—or worse yet, the default fuse—before it ignited the debt bomb. At such a critical moment capturing the bomber—like reflection on fundamental causes of, and long-run solutions to, the massive overhang of developing country debt—was a secondary consideration.

It is interesting to note that the initial loan contracts included a contingency clause, the sixty-day nonperformance clause, but that the banks effectively *recontracted* with the Brazilian borrowers by extending the nonperformance clause to ninety days. At first blush, recontracting may appear to be incompatible with the behavior associated with invocation of rational expectations on the part of the bankers. But in the context of strategic gamesmanship where both partners to the contract—lender and borrower—must form expectations about the other's reactions, the possibility of renegotiation and recontracting can mute the moral-hazard problem, to be discussed in greater detail below. See Crawford (1984: 19–42).

10.   The recycling of OPEC surpluses in the aftermath of the first major oil price increase aggravated the surplus funds condition of the commercial banks but was not fundamental to its beginnings. In his Westerfield address delivered at Atlanta University on October 25, 1973, prior to the bite of the first oil "shock," Brimmer (1973: 15) said that the seeds already had been sown for an international debt crisis: "there was a growing awareness in the late 1960s and early 1970s that the developing countries, as a group, had incurred very large foreign debts and were faced with heavy debt service requirements in the years ahead." As early as 1969, Brimmer noted (p. 16) that a Commission on International Development headed by Lester Pearson warned about difficulties posed for short and long-term debt management problems for LDCs. The World Bank (1974: xvii) reported that by the late 1960s and the early 1970s several countries already were "unable to continue meeting their debt servicing obligations." These included Chile, Ghana, India, Indonesia, Pakistan, Peru, and Turkey seek-

ing debt relief on a multilateral basis, and Afghanistan, Egypt, and Yugoslavia seeking relief on a bilateral basis.

11. Not everyone accepts Wriston at his word. See Chapter 10 of this book, by Brock and Magee, for the case that the money-center bankers advocate the Federal Reserve's disinflationary policy.

12. Rudiger Dornbusch (1984a: 7) provides a revealing example of the impact of a rise in U.S. interest rates on the debtor nations: "Consider Brazil, with exports of $23 billion; an extra 3 percent in export growth would yield $690 million in revenue. But an extra point on the prime, it is estimated, would raise debt service by $750 million."

13. Whether or not bankers tend toward more conservatism in the absence of a lender of last resort is an open question. In the era before public sector authorities with the capacity to insure private sector foreign lending, U.S. banks engaged heavily in promotion of bond finance with Latin America. As underwriters of the bond issues it was possible for the banks in the 1920s to transfer the risks of lending onto the shoulders of the bondholders. It could be argued that the resort to bond finance rather than direct lending was due to the lack of a lender of last resort. But this does not explain the eagerness of the commercial banks to make direct loans to Germany in the late 1920s after investment bankers stopped issuing German bonds.

14. Jack Guttentag and Richard Herring (1982) advocate public sector insurers "explicitly assum[ing] full liability for deposit insurance commitments" to deter completely runs on the banks. But the moral hazard problem justifies the maintenance of ambiguity over its response by an insuring agency. See Crawford, op. cit.

15. I am grateful to Charles Kindleberger for pointing out this latter effect of the FDIC's actions as the commercial banks' insurer.

16. At least such security exists up to the limits of the FDIC's insurance fund. The Treasury must make additional funds available to the insured institutions, so that the taxpayers are the ultimate backstop.

17. For example, Richard Alm (1984: 3C) reports,

IMF aid rarely comes without strings. In most cases, the IMF imposes rigid austerity, a formula that usually includes sharp cutbacks in budget deficits, an end to consumer subsidies, currency devaluations, and ceilings on wage rates.

"They all hit very hard at poor people," says Richard Feinberg of the Overseas Development Council.

Poor people made poorer often take to the streets, and that's what frightens Latin America's political leaders. The Dominican Republic, a Caribbean island nation with a debt of $2.5 billion erupted in riots that killed 60 people and injured 200 others in April after the government raised prices on basic foods to help quality for renewal of a $450 million IMF loan.

Also see Witcher (1984a: 33).

18. Johnson (1983) suggests that the smaller banks can pull back more easily because they hold a larger proportion of short-term claims on LDCs. Her

work is most detailed on differences in lending to Latin borrowers by banks of different sizes.

19. There is a wonderful balance sheet puzzle here as well. To the extent that bank customers are able to make sales to enterprises borrowing funds from the bank, some of the funds lent abroad may return to the bank's; balance sheet through the customers' own deposits.

20. For example, the ubiquitous S. G. Gwynne (1983: 26) was long gone from his midwestern bank when his Philippine loan went bad.

21. The financial instability hypothesis has been elaborated by Minsky in a variety of places: Minsky 1964, 1978, and 1982.

22. Minsky (1978) indicates that enterprises can take up "three types of financial postures—hedge finance, speculative finance, and Ponzi finance positions. In the first case the inflow of cash is expected to exceed the outflow of ʻcash in every period, so that financial units in such a position expect to cover their immediate debt obligations with current gross receipts. Speculative finance units can be expected to run shortfalls in the near term but "in the longer term are expected to [have cash inflows that] exceed cash payments commitments that are outstanding." In the short term the speculative finance unit will have "to roll over or refinance debt." Finally, the Ponzi finance unit only can cover its debt obligations by reaping "a 'bonanza' in the future which makes the present value positive for low enough interest rates." In the meantime, it must continually raise "its outstanding debt to meet financial obligations."

23. In the late 1970s, Charles Kindleberger (1978: passim) adopted a Minsky interpretation of lending bursts leading to borrower default and a repulsion on the part of the lenders. He seems to have moved somewhat away from this interpretation lately.

24. See Minsky (1980). In personal correspondence dated July 11, 1984, Minsky wrote the following to me:

> No banker and businessman—not even Continental Illinois and its clients—entered upon contracts with the expectation that loans would not perform. But the individual decision makers—even at the scale of Citicorp—do not have command over system performance. Furthermore, the prevailing conventional wisdom is that the economy is capable of sustained expansion at stable prices and of course the Captains of industry (and Finance) believe in the virtues of Capitalism and consider anyone pointing out the flaws of capitalism as such as being subversive or worse. Past crises and depressions are imputed to institutional weaknesses or policy errors—not any inherent characteristics of our economy. The "alibis" for preceding performance shortfalls are believable: for example, if you read Friedman and Schwartz's Great Contraction would you believe that the contraction reflected deep flaws in our economy or that it was due to avoidable policy errors by the Federal Reserve in managing *The Money Supply?* (Emphasis in original)

25. My colleague Bobbie Horn suggested this interpretation of the repetition of overlending in the Minsky model.

12 DEBT CRISIS
North-South, North-North, and in Between

Lance Taylor

In the mid-1980s there are two debt crises that may tip the scales of international economics. The old, familiar one is the debt owed by developing countries. Most is denominated in dollars, and its volume is in the upper hundreds of billions. The new problem is the external debt of the United States, soon to become positive for the first time in decades. Payment of interest *in dollars* on both the United States' own debt and the dollar-denominated debt owed by others represents a continual flow demand on exchange markets; the United States is forced into a current-account deficit position to meet this demand. This fact can lead to dollar market instability, as will be shown presently.

The enormous accumulation of developing country debt took place in the ten years before 1982, when the War of the Malvinas (or Falkland Islands) and collapse of the scaffolding under the Mexico peso led bankers to flee the tropics for safer climes. Aside from a predominance of commercial bank as opposed to bond lending the events in the 1970s did not differ markedly from those in preceding debt booms. Darity (1985) identifies the following key features of the episode in the 1920s:

1. An early perceived surplus of lendable resources, which set off promotion of loans (or "loan pushing") by banks and other

agents. (The parallel in the 1970s would be recycling of surpluses amassed by members of the Organization of Petroleum Exporting Countries.)

2. The loans were often aimed at creating markets for producers in industrialized countries. On the receiving end, nepotism and corruption were apparent.

3. When borrowers began to be troubled by their obligations, lenders tried to save the situation by pumping in more money. Again, this happened just before the crisis of 1982 (see Brau and Williams 1983).

4. Finally, the lenders withdrew in a financial revulsion that took decades to overcome.

On a broader canvas, Kindleberger (1983) sketches the same denouement:

> the bond market experienced spurts of lending—for Latin America in the 1820's, the United States in the 1830's, for Latin America again in the 1850's, Egypt in the 1860's and 1870's, Latin America and Australia in the 1880's, Canada from 1900 to 1913, Latin America and Australia (plus Germany) in the 1920's—but . . . foreign lending to a particular area died away between spurts . . . it is perhaps fair to say that after a boom in lending to LDCs followed by default, *European capital markets lost interest for roughly 30 years before lending again.*

The emphasis is added, but the point is clear. When revulsion from a lending boom occurs, it takes years to overcome. Ambitious loan officers in banks must give way for a time to cautious risk analysts before their kind can flourish again; rentiers must change their generations and forget their fears of tropical finance.

In international markets, revulsion followed not only political and economic spasms in the Third World, but also the monetary squeeze administered by Paul Volcker and colleagues at the Federal Reserve in late 1979. Tight money led to slow growth in the Organization for Economic Cooperation and Development from high interest rates and dollar appreciation. The latter, as Sjaastad argues in the next chapter, helped shift the terms of trade against the southern hemisphere. Hence, the developing countries' difficulties with earning from their exports and meeting their floating rate interest payments were to a large extent caused by policy changes in the northern hemisphere, especially the United States. It is argued in this chapter that those moves were a natural consequence of the U.S. foreign payments position, especially the need for the United States to send dollars abroad to meet interest payments on dollar-denominated debt.

A NORTH–SOUTH DEBT CRISIS

To an extent the two crises—loan pushing and revulsion—and the dilemmas of the dollar can be modeled formally. Separate exercises are undertaken here, beginning with the debt of less developed countries. The starting point is a model of North–South interactions proposed in various forms by Kaldor (1976) and by Vines (1984), Darity (1984), and Taylor (1983: ch. 10). If only on grounds of familiarity, I stick with my own version of the model (from Taylor 1983).

There are two countries: "North" and "South." The former is modeled along Kalecki's (1971) lines, with mark-up pricing and persistent excess capacity. With a constant mark-up rate, the North's profit rate r_n (firms' cash flow divided by their value of capital stock) is a convenient measure of the region's economic activity. Following Kalecki, assume that Northern saving comes only from profits (at rate s_n).

Let g_n stand for investment demand (divided by capital stock) in the North. If we take current profits as an indicator of expected future earnings, g_n should be an increasing function of r_n. Investment will also depend negatively on the interest rate i. Finally, we introduce a variable ρ to measure investors' and bankers' confidence. Confidence will rise when profit rates are high and interest rates low. Its fluctuations can underlie long swings in economic activity, as will be shown below.

Let investment demand in the North be given by a linear equation for simplicity,

$$g_n = g_0 + b(r_n + \rho - i) \ . \tag{1}$$

With this equation, we have specified one component of the North's aggregate demand. From the functional form, ρ can be interpreted as expected future profits over the current rate r_n.

The second component is the level of the North's real net trade surplus with (or real capital exports to) the South. During the loan-pushing period of the 1970s, it is reasonable to assume that capital exports as mediated by the banks responded to Southern profits (at rate r_s), confidence, and the interest rate. If the surplus divided by the capital stock is z, we have

$$z = z_0 + j(r_s + \rho - i) \ . \tag{2}$$

The North's investment-saving balance is

$$g_n = s_n r_n - z \ . \tag{3}$$

Putting (3) together with (1) and (2) lets us write the aggregate equilibrium for the North as

$$(b - s_n)r_n + jr_s - (b + j)i + (b + j)\rho + z_0 + g_0 = 0 \ . \tag{4}$$

Note that the higher activity r_s in the South stimulates Northern activity r_n so long as $s_n > b$ (the Keynesian stability condition). The South can be an engine of growth for the North along the global Keynesian lines of the Brandt Commission (1980).

I follow Taylor (1983) in treating the South as a surplus labor economy. That is, the following conditions pertain.

1. The region's real wage is fixed, and its output is determined by available capital.
2. The capital stock must be imported from the North, under modern technical conditions of production.
3. The South exports primary commodities, with a price that varies to clear world markets in the classical manner described by Adam Smith. (This assumption ignores manufactured exports by major borrowers in the South, but could be relaxed without changing the main conclusions of the model.)
4. From the assumptions 1–3, the South's profit rate will depend on the export price level or terms of trade; in turn, the price depends on economic activity in the North (ignoring Sjaastad's effect of the dollar exchange rate on the terms of trade).
5. Saving from Southern profits together with capital inflows from the North determine the region's investment and growth rate. There is no room in the model for an independent investment demand function in the South.
6. Finally, Southern profit recipients consume only Northern goods, while Southern wage earners consume only Southern goods.

Under these assumptions, modest manipulation gives the following expression for the South's profit rate.

$$\beta \lambda r_n - r_s = 0 \ , \tag{5}$$

where λ is the ratio of the North's capital stock to the South's and β is a demand parameter. Demand for Southern goods will be higher when the North is large relative to the South (a high value of λ) or the Northern economy is booming (a high r_n). Growth of capital in the South is given by

$$g_s = z \lambda + s_s r_s \ , \tag{6}$$

where s_s is the South's saving rate from profits.

From Eqs. (4) and (5) the two regions' economies stimulate each other. The overall system will be stable if the South's effect on the North is weak (a big increase in r_s leads to only a modest increment in r_n). Such is the case in Figure 12-1, where Eqs. (4) and (5), representing North and South market equilibrium relationships, cross. More confidence, ρ, or a higher capital stock ratio, λ, will cause profits and growth in both regions to rise. An increase in the former shifts the North's equilibrium locus up, while a rise in the latter does the same for the South.

Now we turn to financial markets. The stylized story about the 1970s is that "depositors" or rentiers from the North (and OPEC) put money in the banks, which in turn lent to the South. At any moment, the ratio of the Southern debt to Northern capital stock (say σ) will be fixed. The supply of loans to meet this debt requirement (say m) will depend on the interest rate, confidence, and profit rates. Since, as shown in Figure 12-1, r_s and r_n move together, we concentrate on the latter.

What will be the impact of an increase in r_n on loans to the South? Substitution from Southern loans toward Northern plants would suggest a negative effect. However, higher profits and confidence in the North bid up the region's net worth and also drive up Southern profits. During the debt boom, banks' loan supply to the North was stagnant as compared to supply to the South, so that higher Northern profits in effect were associated with more loans to the poorer region.

Figure 12-1. Joint Determination of the Profit Rates r_n and r_s in Commodity Markets. (The rightward shift in the North's market locus is due to an increase in the expected profit rate ρ, and the upward shift in the South's locus is due to a higher value of the capital stock ratio λ.)

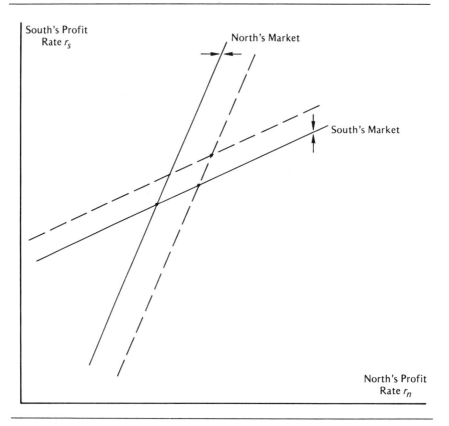

In formal terms, the loan market equilibrium is $\sigma - m = 0$, or in differential form

$$d\sigma - \eta_i \, di - \eta_r (dr_n + d\rho) - dm = 0 \ . \tag{7}$$

The usual assumption is the profit rate derivative η_r is negative; the 1970s story makes $\eta_r > 0$. A higher interest rate will increase loans, so $\eta_i > 0$. Equations (4), (5), and (7) are a worldwide short-run macroeconomic system in the variables r_n, r_s, and i. The simplest way to think about the three variables is pairwise. We have already discussed how r_s and r_n affect each other in Figure 12–1. Next we turn to r_n and i. Their interactions are illustrated in Figure 12–2.

The upper diagram corresponds to the case where $\eta_r < 0$. When the expected profit rate differential ρ increases in this case, pressure is placed on financial markets and the interest rate i tends to rise; there is an upward shift in the asset market equilibrium schedule from Eq. (7). The increase in ρ also stimulates investment demand, and as shown the interest rate increases and the profit rate r_n may either rise or fall. There is a degree of financial crowding-out of the higher investment demand and also (from Figure 12–1) the South's capital inflow and profit rate.

The case where $\eta_r > 0$ is shown in the lower diagram. Now the asset market schedule (essentially an LM curve) slopes downward. The story is that if realized profits increase, then Northern asset holders enjoy an increase in wealth due to the higher valuation of their capital stock. Part of the gain is channeled toward higher deposits with international banks, and the interest rate i falls to accommodate the increased demand. An increase in expected profits ρ has a similar effect, so the asset market schedule shifts downward. The outcome is financial crowding-in, so profit rates go up and the interest rate falls. Of course, a fall in confidence or a decrease in ρ in this case will lead to lower profits and higher interest. If these changes reduce confidence further still, the lower diagram of Figure 12–2 contains the germ of a financial crisis along the lines discussed by Minsky (1975) and Taylor and O'Connell (1985).

The remaining pairwise interaction is between r_s and i. Here the only linkage is that an increase in the interest rate i raises income in the North from holding deposits, and thus may stimulate demand for Southern products and bid up r_s. This effect is weak, and we ignore it in what follows.

Figures 12–1 and 12–2 illustrate comparative statics in the model. The next step is to take up dynamics. The discussion goes in terms of "state variables," which evolve in steady fashion over time. One is λ, the ratio of the North's capital stock to the South's. If we use a "hat" over a variable to denote growth rate, then

$$\hat{\lambda} = g_n - g_s \ . \tag{8}$$

Figure 12-2. Short-Run Adjustment in Response to an Increase in the Expected Profit Rate ρ. (The upper diagram shows the case where $\eta_r < 0$ and there is financial crowding-out of increased investment demand. The lower diagram has $\eta_r > 0$, and there is financial crowding-in.)

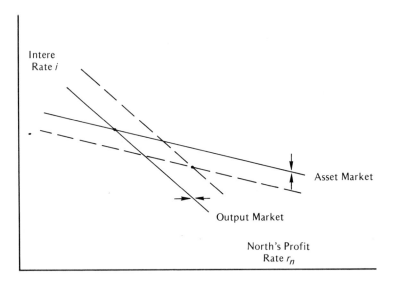

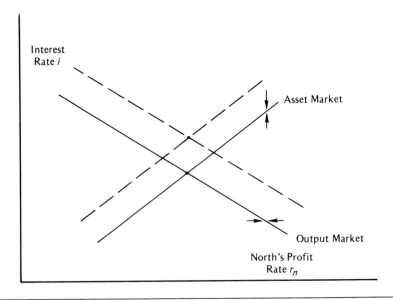

Figure 12-3. Comparative Dynamics across Steady States of λ and σ. (An increase in Northern deposits *m* leads the South to grow faster than the North and to build up debt so that λ falls and σ rises.)

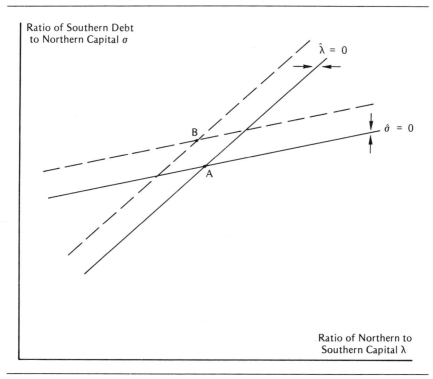

The second state variable is σ, or the ratio of the South's debt to the North's capital. The South can only owe more by borrowing through its trade deficit or the North's surplus, so that

$$\hat{\sigma} = (z/\sigma) - g_n \quad , \tag{9}$$

where the g_n term captures the effect on σ of growth in the North's capital.

The world economy will come to a steady state when capital stocks in North and South grow at equal rates (so that $\hat{\lambda} = 0$) and the ratio of South's trade deficit to its debt is equal to the world growth rate (or $\hat{\sigma} = 0$). Let us examine the dynamic adjustment around this long-run equilibrium. Figure 12-3 illustrates the details, using loci along which $\hat{\lambda}$ and $\hat{\sigma}$ equal zero. The tradeoff between the two state variables explains the positive slopes. An increase in λ would make $\hat{\lambda}$

negative, and would be offset by a higher σ; the same argument goes in reverse for $\hat{\sigma}$.[1] The stable case in steady state is shown in Figure 12-3. In this framework we want to look at the effects of an event favorable to the South, the case where looser Northern monetary policy leads to more international bank lending; that is, $dm > 0$ in (7). The asset market schedule in Figure 12-2 will shift downward, so that the interest rate will fall and stimulate capital flows southward from (2). For a given λ, $\hat{\sigma}$ tends to rise. The increase can be countered by higher investment in Southern debt σ, so that the $\hat{\sigma} = 0$ locus shifts upward. For a given value of σ, $\hat{\lambda}$ will decrease as m goes up. A reduction in λ itself will offset this tendency, so the locus for $\hat{\lambda} = 0$ shifts to the left. The outcome can be shown to be an overall reduction in λ as the South grows more rapidly than the North for a time, and an increase in σ as the South builds up debt; the adjustment is from A to B.

A contractionary monetary policy in the North would have the opposite effect. The South would be forced to grow more slowly than the North (as its terms of trade deteriorate and profit rate falls). It would also have to reduce its debt burden relative to the Northern capital stock, by smaller or perhaps even negative capital inflows. One explanation of the post-1982 debt crisis is simply that it represents a situation similar to a movement from B to A in Figure 12-3— the South is suffering pneumonia transmitted by a heavy Northern monetary sneeze. However, deeper underlying forces of a crisis in investor confidence may be at work in creating secular as opposed to conjunctural depression for the South.

Apprehension about commiting resources to the developing world can be modeled by fluctuations in the variable ρ over time. Suppose ρ declines for some reason—say the Volcker interest rate shock. Is there some way this reduction in confidence can affect the global macroeconomic system to increase investors' worries still more? If so, the positive feedback of lowered confidence into itself can lead to a long period of global retrenchment and reduced finance for the South.

The most plausible theory about the expected profit rate differential is that it should depend on the overall state of the world economy: ρ might increase, for example, when current profit rates r_n and r_s are high or the interest rate i is low. In light of the lower diagram of Figure 12-2 (the case in which we are interested) both hypotheses will give the same general results since profit and interest rates move in opposite directions in response to ρ. We use the interest rate linkage here, since it involves easier algebra. The dynamic story about ρ is that it responds to the interest rate in an equation such as

$$\hat{\rho} = \theta(i^* - i) \ . \tag{10}$$

When the rate of interest exceeds its normal long-run level i^*, expected profits begin to fall.

An increase in ρ has an ambiguous effect on its time-derivative. In the crowding-in case i falls as ρ rises, so that $\partial\hat{\rho}/\partial\rho > 0$. This positive derivative can cause international financial instability, as discussed shortly. With crowding-out, $\partial\hat{\rho}/\partial\rho < 0$, and world macroeconomic stability is more likely.

Once again, we have a three-variable dynamic system, this time for the medium-term evolution of the world economy. The relevant equations are (8) for $\hat{\lambda}$, (9) for $\hat{\sigma}$, and (10) for $\hat{\rho}$. As before, we consider the interactions pairwise. Figure 12–3 has already been used to illustrate relationships between λ and σ. Figure 12–4 does the same for ρ and λ, with the crowding-out case in the upper diagram and crowding-in in the lower one.[2]

We take as a reference point an initially low value of ρ—say from "bad news" or monetary contraction. With ρ reduced below its steady state level under crowding-out, interest rates will be low and recovery will commence. It will be led by the North in the stable case shown in the figure—g_n will exceed g_s and λ will rise. The South will eventually catch up, but bears the initial burden of worldwide adjustment.

In the lower diagram the situation is worse. The interest rate stays high for a time and leads ρ to fall from its initially low level. Both regions grow slowly, but the South lags and λ rises. Recovery, if it comes, will be long delayed as the world economy stalls in what amounts to an international liquidity trap, in which even very high interest rates will not induce asset holders to shift their portfolio preferences toward the South. If the system is stable, the trajectory will finally turn the corner in the diagram and return toward steady state. As argued previously, the time span involved may be long. It is easy to see from (9) and (10) that adjustment also involves a contraction of the South's debt relative to Northern capital, from small trade deficits or even surpluses. With crowding-in, the adjustment is prolonged and may not be stable.

Figure 12-4. Evolution of ρ and λ When There Is Financial Crowding-out (upper diagram) or Crowding-in (lower diagram). (In both cases, recovery involves an initial period of faster growth in the North than in the South (λ rises), but with crowding-in the episode may be prolonged and the world macro economic system is potentially unstable with wider and wider swings of ρ and λ.)

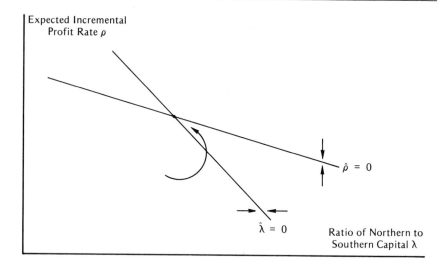

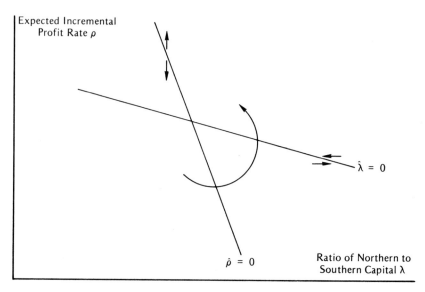

A NORTH–NORTH DEBT CRISIS

A major driving force in the foregoing story is the interest rate shock that leads to a low initial level of confidence ρ in Figure 12–4. In this section, we take up a model that may help explain that event.

The action in the short run centers around effects of changes in the money supply and foreign holdings of dollar-denominated assets on the American exchange and interest rates. Increases in both variables lead to lower interest and dollar depreciation. Suppose that *appreciation* leads foreigners to hold more dollar-denominated assets. The interest rate will fall and the Federal Reserve will respond with tighter money, which will cause the dollar to appreciate further. There will be positive feedback into still higher foreign holdings — a flight to the dollar. Such a mechanism may well have precipitated events in the world economy before and after 1979. In the earlier period, there was a potential flight from the dollar, accompanied by fairly loose monetary policy. The Volcker shock reversed the process, leading to flight toward the dollar in the early 1980s. The financial crises of 198?—if it occurs—will mark another reversal of this unstable dynamics.

The best way to understand the details is through the standard Mundell-Fleming open economy model, of which Williamson (1983) gives a clear exposition. Let e be the U.S. exchange rate expressed as units of foreign currency per dollar, so an increase in e represents appreciation. Using the profit rate r to measure activity again, we can write the trade balance t as $t = t(e, r)$, with negative partial derivatives since appreciation harms trade performance and more economic activity draws in imports. Taking into account the multiplier process, a reduced form expression for the profit rate is

$$r = r_0 - \alpha e - \gamma i + \epsilon f \qquad (11)$$

where the negative coefficient on i captures investment demand effects, and f is net fiscal spending. As the exchange rate rises, the trade surplus diminishes and domestic profits decline.

Let q stand for holdings by foreigners of dollar-denominated assets within the United States, for example Treasury bills. An increase in foreign holdings will have the same effect on interest rates as an open market purchase by the Federal Reserve; the bill price will rise and short-term rates will fall. Hence the demand–supply balance for money can be written as

$$\xi r - \phi i - \phi h - q = 0 \ , \tag{12}$$

where money demand rises with r for transaction purposes, and declines with i. Money creation by the Federal Reserve's open market purchases is represented by h, while an increase in q drives down the interest rate i for the reasons just discussed.

Total holdings of dollar-denominated debt by foreigners will be a substantial multiple of q; as Minsky (1983) points out, foreign portfolios contain not just Treasury bills, but also the Eurodollar deposits that are the banks' liability counterpart of developing country debt. To provide interest payments on a flow basis for these deposits, the United States must run a trade deficit, which will become larger as the economy shifts toward an overall net debtor position. The U.S. balance of payments can be written as

$$t(e, r) + \delta iq = 0 \ , \tag{13}$$

where δ blows up Treasury bill holdings to dollar-denominated deposits plus other claims outstanding.

From (13), as q rises the trade balance $t(e, r)$ becomes increasingly negative. The deficit will be a drag on economic activity, which from (11) must be countered by higher fiscal expenditures f. On Minsky's interpretation, the trade deficit causes recent American deficits, not the other way round.

It is easy to substitute (11) into (12) and (13) to get a two-variable system in the exchange rate e and interest rate i. In the domestic money market, a higher e reduces transactions demand, by cutting back the trade surplus and thereby economic activity. Hence, i will decrease. In the foreign exchange market, a higher i drives up the interest payment obligation and improves the trade balance by reducing activity. To compensate, e must rise to wipe out the incipient payments surplus. We get the crossed solid lines of the diagrams in Figure 12–5.

The upper diagram illustrates a standard result. With a given e, monetary expansion will reduce the interest rate, shifting the money market locus downward. The outcome is that easier money leads to lower interest rates and exchange depreciation.

Figure 12-5. Effects of an Increase in the Money Supply (upper diagram) and of Foreign Holdings of Dollar-Denominated Assets (lower diagram) on the Interest Rate and the Foreign Currency/Dollar Exchange Rate. (The interest rate reduction is greater and dollar depreciation is less when foreign asset holdings rise instead of the money supply.)

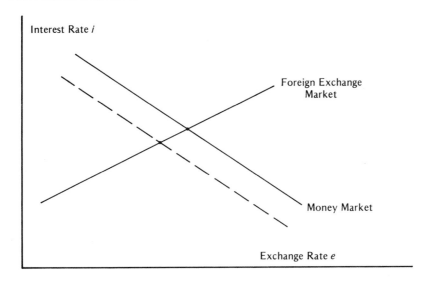

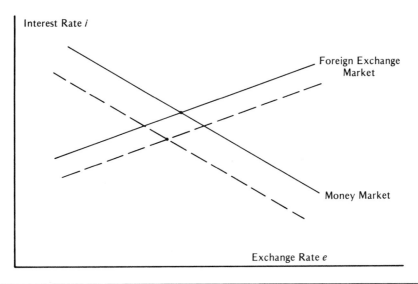

Now consider increased foreign holdings of dollar-denominated assets (lower diagram). In the money market, the effect is like an open market purchase: the curve shifts downward. But there is also an effect in the exchange market. As q goes up, dollar interest rate obligations rise, and there must be appreciation to worsen the trade deficit; the curve shifts to the right. The interest rate decrease is proportionately greater and depreciation less when q rises instead of b. The next step is to show how these different short-run responses can underlie dynamic instability of the dollar.

If they wish, foreign asset holders can increase q instantaneously, by switching into interest-bearing paper from money or other forms of wealth within the United States, and from non-dollar-denominated Eurocurrency deposits. However, it is reasonable to postulate gradual adjustment, for the usual reasons. Assume that q increases according to a rule such as

$$\hat{q} = A_1 (e - \bar{e}_1) + B_1 (i - \bar{i}_1) , \tag{14}$$

so that there is a steady portfolio switch toward dollar assets when the dollar is strong and American interest rates are high.

The Federal Reserve will follow a similar rule, increasing the money supply when there is overvaluation and tight credit markets:

$$\hat{b} = A_2 (e - \bar{e}_2) + B_2 (i - \bar{i}_2) . \tag{15}$$

In most of what follows, we will assume that $(A_1/B_1) > (A_2/B_2)$; that is, foreigners target their bond purchases more strongly on the exchange rate or the Federal Reserve targets its open market interventions more strongly on the interest rate. It is simplest to go to the extreme with these assumptions and write

$$\hat{q} = e - \bar{e} \tag{16}$$

and

$$\hat{b} = i - \bar{i} \tag{17}$$

as the basic dynamic relation.

Let e_q stand for the partial derivative $\partial e/\partial q$, and so on. The slope of the $\hat{q} = 0$ locus in the (b, q) plane is $-e_b/e_q$ and the slope of the $\hat{b} = 0$ locus is $-i_b/i_q$. Figure 12–5 shows that $(e_q/i_q) < (e_b/i_b)$. It is easy to transform this condition to show that the $b = 0$ locus is *less* negatively sloped than the $q = 0$ schedule at the central point C

Figure 12-6. Point C Is an Unstable Saddlepoint Equilibrium between the U.S. Money Supply and Foreigners' Dollar Asset Holdings. (Extreme easy and tight money stable equilibriums, E and T respectively, may possibly exist.)

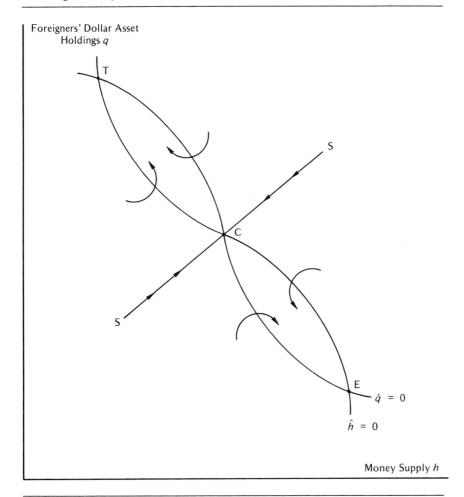

in Figure 12-6. Moreover, this equilibrium is a saddlepoint, with the only stable adjustment path represented by the separatrix SCS.

In the jargon of the model, SCS is a bifurcation in the (h, q) plane.[3] A trajectory starting to its right will ultimately tend toward decreasing q and increasing h. An "easy money" stable equilibrium may exist at point E if the reduction in q makes the interest burden parameter δ in (13) small or even negative, so that the drag of dollar-

Figure 12-7. An Increase in the Federal Reserve's Interest Rate Target Shifts the Money Equilibrium Locus to the Left and the Separatrix Downward. (A flight from the dollar toward A is reversed and becomes a run to the dollar in the direction of B.)

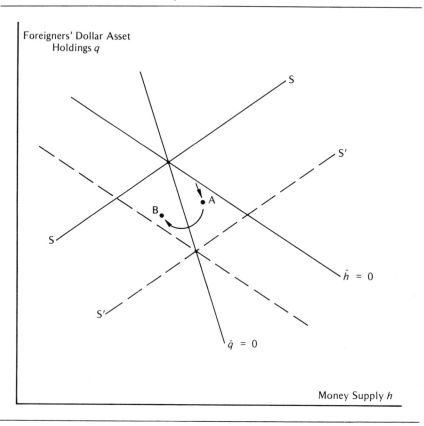

denominated debt on the U.S. balance of payments disappears. Point E would feature a weak dollar and low interest rates, as in the 1970s.

A trajectory starting to the left of SCS will ultimately involve a falling h and a rising q. A "tight money" equilibrium may exist at T if extreme appreciation of the dollar leads the Federal Reserve to shift targeting from the interest rate to the exchange rate by increasing B_2 in (15). The situation above the separatrix will resemble the 1980s—a run toward the dollar under high interest rates with steady exchange appreciation.

What could change the world from one regime to the other? One possibility is a revision of the Federal Reserve's interest rate target. In Figure 12-7 the initial trajectory is one from the 1970s, running toward A. Now suppose that the Federal Reserve suddenly increases its interest rate target $\bar{\imath}$ in (17). The $\hat{b} = 0$ locus will shift to the left, and the separatrix downward from SS to S'S'. The money supply will begin to be restricted, and interest and exchange rates to rise. The latter will after a time lead foreign asset holdings to increase, and a run to the dollar in the direction of point B will commence.

There are limits even to what the United States can borrow abroad, so the run to the dollar cannot last forever. In this model, there are two ways for it to end. One is simply for the Federal Reserve to lower its interest rate target, shift the separatrix back toward SS, and set off a capital flight. Alternatively, foreign investors may respond to the worsening American trade position by demanding more security in the form of a higher target exchange rate. Their equilibrium locus will shift downward, again causing a flight from the dollar—perhaps rapid and beyond the Federal Reserve's control. The first possibility is an orderly policy retreat; the second is a capital market rout reminiscent of Latin American borrowers' experience after 1982. Those countries combined overvaluation with extremely open capital markets during the debt boom; they suffered immense capital flight thereafter. A run on the dollar would show the same policy combination to be risky for industrialized countries as well as their tropical neighbors. If the risks are to be avoided the Federal Reserve must steer an adroit policy course, in effect hopscotching across bifurcations in Figures 12-6 and 12-7. Such agility may prove difficult to sustain in the long run.

DEBT CRISIS BETWEEN THE REGIONS

The world is more complicated than simple models, but the foregoing results may help us somewhat to understand what is going on with international debt. Borrowing countries do seem to suffer from a lack of confidence, which may take a long time to overcome. There is a run to the dollar, which either the Federal Reserve or panic among foreign investors will reverse. When that happens, interest rates will fall and the dollar will depreciate, aiding the South's terms of trade. Whether those events will restore lenders' confidence remains to be seen; adjustments in Figure 12-4 *are* long run. What is clear is that current debt payment problems of the South would be much less severe with a weaker dollar. The North–South crisis will be easier to deal with once there is relaxation of the international macroeconomic tension in the North.

NOTES TO CHAPTER 12

1. The reasoning justifying the slopes of the locuses in Figure 12-3 is straightforward, but tedious. First consider changes in λ. An increase in this capital stock ratio directly raises the Southern profit rate r_s from Eq. (5); there is a derived increase in the Northern rate r_n as illustrated in Figure 12-1. Capital stock growth rates respond to profit rates from Eqs. (3) and (6). With plausible parameters, the initial increase in the South's profit rate will dominate the responses, so that g_s rise more than g_n, or $\partial\hat{\lambda}/\partial\lambda < 0$ from (8).

   Changes in profit rates also affect the financial market. When r_n goes up in response to a higher λ, we see from Figure 12-2 that the interest rate will fall if there is crowding-in ($\eta_r > 0$), and rise otherwise. In the crowding-in case, it is clear from (2) that capital flows z will rise; an increase of lesser magnitude is also likely when there is crowding-out. From (9) the main determinant of $\hat{\sigma}$ is z since it is divided by σ (a fraction) and the effect of λ on g_n is weaker than on z. The conclusion is that $\partial\hat{\sigma}/\partial\lambda$ will be positive.

   Next we take up variations in σ. An increase in this ratio of Southern debt to Northern capital leads the interest rate i to rise. Investment demand and capital flows decline, so that the profit rates r_n and r_s fall. The effect on both regions' growth is negative, so that from (8) the change in $\hat{\lambda}$ is ambiguous. However, as I have argued more fully elsewhere (Taylor 1983), the South bears a double adjustment burden to most international shocks: activity falls in the North plus its demand shifts from the South. Under such circumstances, it is likely that g_s will fall by more than g_n when financial markets tighten, or $\partial\hat{\lambda}/\partial\sigma > 0$. Finally, an increase in σ reduces capital flows z and has a direct negative effect on $\hat{\sigma}$ from (9): $\partial\hat{\sigma}/\partial\sigma < 0$.

2. The slopes of the schedules in Figure 12-4 are based on reasoning similar to that set out for Figure 12-3. It is safe to assume that an increase in the expected profit rate increases actual Northern profits in the short run, so that $\partial r_n/\partial\rho > 0$. Since higher activity in the North stimulates demand for the South, $\partial r_s/\partial\rho > 0$ as well. It was argued in the text that the effect of ρ on Southern growth would exceed that on growth in the North, or $\partial\hat{\lambda}/\partial\rho < 0$. An increase in the capital stock ratio λ will bid up interest rates when

there is crowding-out and reduce them when there is crowding-in. Hence $\partial\hat{\rho}/\partial\lambda$ is negative under crowding-out and positive under crowding-in. The effect of an increase in ρ on the interest rate i is seen in Figure 12–2 to be ambiguous: $\partial i/\partial\rho$ is negative when there is financial crowding-in ($\eta_r < 0$ in the lower diagram) and positive otherwise. In the former case, (10) shows that $\partial\hat{\rho}/\partial\rho$ is positive; it is the destabilizing positive feedback of confidence into itself discussed in the text. Since $\hat{\lambda}$ decreases with both λ and ρ, the two variables must trade off inversely to hold $\hat{\lambda} = 0$ as in Figure 12–4. Both variables also affect $\hat{\rho}$ the same way, leading to the negative slope for the $\hat{\rho} = 0$ locus.

3. The variables q and b follow predator-prey dynamics. For a clear discussion, see ch. 12 in Hirsch and Smale (1974).

13 CAUSES OF AND REMEDIES FOR THE DEBT CRISIS IN LATIN AMERICA

Larry A. Sjaastad

The world's external debt problem is concentrated in Latin America. By the end of 1984 five major Latin borrowers had amassed external debt that in the aggregate amounts to approximately $300 billion. Of this amount, Brazil and Mexico account for nearly $100 billion each, Venezuela $35 billion, Argentina $45 billion, and Chile nearly $20 billion. Numerous smaller countries also have significant external debt, most commonly in relation to gross domestic product and export receipts.

This debt was accumulated in large part since the mid-1970s, particularly from 1978 to 1980, when dollar interest rates were negative in real terms and the liquidity of the international commercial banks was ever renewed by the current-account surpluses of members of the Organization of Petroleum Exporting Countries. Since 1980, all of that has reversed; annual OPEC revenues have fallen by a full $200 billion, fiscal deficits of the Organization for Economic Cooperation and Development countries (not just the United States) have increased by another $200 billion, and dollar interest rates in real terms are the highest since the deflation of the Great Depression.

Whereas the Latin American countries, their public sectors in particular, were major borrowers from the international capital market during the 1970s and 1980, they are now significant exporters of

The author is grateful for earlier comments by Robert Zevin.

249

capital. Although the private sectors of several Latin American countries were net capital exporters throughout much of that period, the public sectors were exhibiting ever larger foreign-financed fiscal deficits. Much of the pain of adjustment in Latin America has come about precisely from the contraction required to eliminate deficits and develop fiscal surpluses. As most of the external debt is owned by the public sectors, the requisite fiscal surpluses are enormous indeed.

The remainder of this chapter consists of three sections, the first of which deals with the determinants of the magnitude of debt service and various scenarios for servicing the external debts. The section following that examines the real interest rate issue, concluding that little relief is in sight for the debtor countries insofar as that portion of their debt service is concerned. The final section looks at means by which the debt issue might be resolved, given that, for some countries at least, the magnitude of debt service exceeds their capacity to pay on a sustained basis. It is this section that will surely be the most controversial.

THE DEBT SERVICE ISSUE

The difficulty of the external debt service problem in Latin America varies widely from country to country. In a number of smaller countries—Costa Rica, Chile, and Panama most remarkedly—the magnitude of external debt relative to GDP is simply so large that, without a major decline in interest rates, one seriously doubts that that debt can be serviced even under very favorable rescheduling terms. In other and larger countries—Argentina, Brazil, Mexico, and Venezuela—the problem is onerous but manageable even in the face of current interest rates *if* economic growth can be reestablished despite the fiscal austerity dictated by the debt service itself.

In the former countries, the ratio of external debt to GDP is close to 100 percent, whereas in the latter group it runs approximately 40 percent. With an average interest rate on outstanding external debt of about 10 percent in most countries (but rising with rescheduling), interest alone amounts to 10 percent of GDP in the heavily indebted countries, but "only" about 4 percent in the others.

The amount of actual debt service, of course, depends upon a number of factors. During the 1970s and early 1980s, none of the major debtor countries had any positive debt service from a balance-of-payments point of view; new borrowing more than paid the interest *and* amortization. Since mid-1982 availability of new funds has declined dramatically, forcing major internal adjustments on those countries.

To examine the determinants of debt service, we develop a small model in which the following notation will be used:

D = nominal external debt, in dollars

Y = nominal gross domestic product (GDP), in dollars

GB = gross new borrowing, in dollars

i = ratio of interest payments to external debt

d = D/Y (debt to GDP ratio)

δ = amortization rate

γ = GB/D

g = $\dot{Y}/Y$ (growth rate of GDP)

DS = $(i + \delta)D$ = debt service, in dollars

NDS = $(i + \delta - \gamma)D$ = net debt service (i.e., requisite trade account surplus), in dollars

The growth of external debt, $\dot{D}$, is the surplus in the capital account of the balance of payments, and is given by

$$\dot{D} = GB - \gamma D$$
$$= (\gamma - \delta)D \ . \tag{1}$$

The contribution of interest payments to the deficit in the service account of the balance of payments is obviously (iD); hence the needed surplus, NDS, in the commercial (trade) account of the balance of payments is clearly

$$NDS = iD - \dot{D}$$
$$= (i - \gamma + \delta)D \ .$$

Since the growth of external debt relative to GDP is

$$\dot{d} = (\gamma - \delta - g)d \ ,$$

we obtain

$$NDS/Y = d\,[i - g - (\dot{d}/d)] \ , \tag{2}$$

as the necessary commercial account surplus as a fraction of gross domestic product.

Let us consider various scenarios. First, there was the situation of the 1970s, when external debt for all non-OPEC developing countries was increasing at a rate of nearly 20 percent per annum. Obviously, with $\dot{d}/d = 0.20$, NDS was substantially negative, permitting countries to service their debts while enjoying large trade account deficits. That situation is, of course, not sustainable as the ratio d will become arbitrarily large, with default ultimately a virtual certainty.

A second scenario, still favorable, is when $\dot{d} = 0$, which implies that $\gamma = \delta + g$; the debt not only is rolled over, but also net new borrowings occur at the rate gD. In this case:

$$NDS/Y = (i - g)d \quad ,$$

which, under current circumstances with a growth rate of dollar-denominated GNP in the neighborhood of 5 percent, would require a current account surplus of about 2 percent of GNP for countries such as Argentina and Brazil, but about 5 percent for Chile and Panama. In fact, however, growth rates in all major debtor countries, measured in dollars, have been negative or, at best, zero. Anything that will improve growth rates, either real growth or U.S. inflation, will also improve the debt service burden. It goes without saying, of course, that an increase in the U.S. rate of inflation is likely to be quickly reflected in nominal interest rates and with a relative short lag in i, so the relief from that source would be short-lived.

A less favorable scenario, but one closer to the current circumstances, is when $\gamma = \delta$; that is, amortization is rescheduled, but no new net borrowing is allowed. In this case, $\dot{d}/d = -g$ and:

$$NDS/Y = id \quad .$$

For countries such as Panama and Chile, this implies a current account surplus of the order of 10 percent of GNP, which is difficult to imagine on a sustained basis.

The worst scenario occurs when no gross borrowing whatsoever is permitted, which implies $\gamma = 0$, $\dot{d}/d = -(\delta + g)d$, and:

$$NDS/Y = (r + \delta)d \quad .$$

While amortization rates vary widely over time and across countries, the average on all external debt is currently about 10 percent per year, which implies a current account surplus of 20 percent of GNP in countries such as Chile and Panama, and nearly 10 percent for larger debtor countries of Latin America. Debt service on such a scale, even for a limited amount of time, would almost surely result in massive default.

THE OUTLOOK FOR REAL INTEREST RATES

As I have argued elsewhere, the acute debt service problem in several Latin American countries arises not so much from size of the external debt as from high real interest rates (Sjaastad 1983). According to W. Arthur Lewis, ratios of external debt to exports in even the most heavily indebted countries are lower than in 1913.[1] Consider the case of Panama, one of the most heavily indebted countries, relative to GNP, in the world. Total public-sector debt in Panama is nearly three times current exports, and interest is approximately one-third of those exports.[2] However, were the rate of interest to be 4 percent on that debt, Panama's public-sector interest bill would be only slightly more than 10 percent of export revenues, and easily managed even in the absence of any increase in external debt. A similar conclusion applies to the other debtor countries of Latin America.

One must, of course, distinguish between real and nominal interest rates. In the late 1970s and until 1981, the relevant measure of the real rate of interest on foreign debt was negative for most Latin American countries. Table 13-1 provides the data for Chile, in which the real rate of interest is defined as LIBOR adjusted for the rate of change of dollar prices of Chilean tradeables. As debt is always serviced with either fewer imports or more exports and as the external debt of most debtor nations is denominated primarily in dollars, it is the rate of dollar inflation of prices of tradeables that is relevant. We see from Table 13-1 that, in the case of Chile, the real interest on newly incurred external debt rose from -12.3 percent in 1979 to 22.4 percent in 1982—a rise of over 36 points! Given that a large part of the external debt is "capital market" debt indexed to either LIBOR or U.S. prime, can it be surprising that debt service has become such a source of difficulty for Chile? And similar data can be found for other Latin American debtor nations as well.

The dramatic increase in the real rate of interest on Latin American external debt came about mainly because of an equally dramatic

Table 13-1. External Prices of Chilean Tradeables and Interest Rates.

Period	Annual Rate of Change of Prices[a]	U.S. $ Interest Rate[b]	U.S. $ Real Interest Rate[c]
1977	5.1	7.0	1.8
1978	6.1	6.4	0.3
1979	26.8	11.2	-12.3
1980	16.6	13.9	-2.3
1981	-5.5	15.7	22.4
1982	-8.6	13.3	24.0

a. Rate of change of a simple average of unit values of Chilean imports and exports as calculated by the United Nations Economic Commission for Latin America.

b. Annual averages of six-month LIBOR rates.

c. Defined against the prices of Chilean tradeables.

Source: José Gil-Diaz, "Del Ajuste a la Deflación: La Política Económica Entre 1977 y 1981 (Chile)," November 1983 (Mimeo).

collapse in the rate of dollar inflation of tradable goods prices; as is evident from Table 13-1, the increase in nominal interest rates played a very small role. How did this increase in real rates of interest come about?

A plausible answer lies in the behavior of the U.S. dollar vis-à-vis other major currencies. During the period of very low real rates of interest (1978–80), the dollar was declining sharply against virtually all other major currencies, with the result that dollar prices of many traded goods were rising rapidly, indeed, at a rate much higher than the U.S. price level. With the recovery of the U.S. dollar, a recovery that began in late 1980 reversed that tendency; indeed, deflation rather than inflation of dollar prices of tradable goods became quite evident.[3] We now turn to a formal analysis of the manner in which changes in the exchange rates between the dollar and other major currencies affect the dollar prices of tradable goods.[4]

Exchange Rate Fluctuations and Relative Prices

Appreciation of a major currency, say the U.S. dollar, with respect to other major currencies (represented by the deutsche mark) clearly will cause the dollar prices of (homogeneous) traded goods to be depressed (assuming underlying demand and supply factors for that commodity to remain unchanged), and the deutsche mark prices to rise. If the law of one price holds exactly, the decline in the dollar price plus the increase in the deutsche mark price, both in percentage terms, must sum to the percentage appreciation of the dollar. For certain highly homogeneous goods, such as metals and certain agricultural products, there is ample casual evidence that the law of one price holds quite well, and that the phenomenon described does indeed occur.

For a small country pegging its currency to the dollar and engaging heavily in the international commodity trade, appreciation (depreciation) of the dollar vis-à-vis other major currencies will immediately result in deflationary (inflationary) pressures transmitted by changes in the dollar prices of its tradables. This is in fact what appears to have happened in the cases of Chile and Uruguay (and in the opposite direction in Europe and Japan) as well, but presumably with less speed and intensity. The asymmetry comes about because the commodity trade—for which the law of one price holds well even in the short run—is much less important for the large, developed economies. If changes in the prices of tradables have a more rapid impact on small economies than on large ones, as appears to be the case, then appreciation of the dollar will impose stronger deflationary pressures on countries such as Chile and Uruguay and on the United States, and consequently real interest rates in the former countries will rise relative to those in the United States.

A Formal Model

To develop the behavior of the price of traded goods for a small country, consider the case of a homogeneous commodity, the price of which obeys the "law of one price." We will assume a four-country world, three of the countries having large economies and major currencies, and the fourth being a small country in the sense that it is a price taker in both the goods and asset markets. All variables expressed in capital letters will be natural logarithms: $X = \ln x$.

Without loss of generality, we assume that country A is an exporter of the good in question, and countries B and C are importers. Country D, the small country, can be either an importer or exporter

but is assumed to be sufficiently small that it does not influence the
world price.[5] This permits us the following approximation:

$$q_A^s \, (P_A - \bar{P}_A) \simeq q_B^d \, (P_B - \bar{P}_B) + q_C^d \, (P_C - \bar{P}_C) \; , \qquad (3)$$

as the equilibrium condition for the world market for a particular
traded good. q_A^s is the excess supply of the good in country A, and
the q^d's are the excess demands. P_j is the logarithm of the nominal
price (in domestic currency) in country j, and $\bar{P}_j$ is the logarithm of
the prime level in that country. For simplicity, all other variables
affecting excess demands and supplies are suppressed; these would,
of course, have to be taken into account in empirical implementation
of the model.

Prices are linked through exchange rates:

$$P_A \; = \; P_B \; + \; E_B \; = \; P_C \; + \; E_C \; , \qquad (4)$$

where E_j is the logarithm of price of the jth currency in terms of A's
currency. As usual, import duties, transport costs, and other expenses
of trade are ignored as we will focus on *movements in* rather than the
level of the price of the good in question.

Substituting (4) into (3) and using the time derivative operator for
variable x denoted by dx, we have

$$dP_A \; = \; \rho_B \, (dE_B) + \rho_C \, (dE_C) + \rho_A \, \pi_A + \rho_B \, \pi_B + \rho_C \, \pi_C \; , \qquad (5)$$

where

$$\rho_A \; = \; q_A^{s\prime}/(q_A^{s\prime} - q_B^{d\prime} - q_C^{d\prime}) > 0 \; ,$$
$$\rho_B \; = \; -q_B^{d\prime}/(q_A^{s\prime} - q_B^{d\prime} - q_C^{d\prime}) > 0 \; ,$$
$$\rho_C \; = \; 1 - \rho_A - \rho_B > 0 \; ,$$
$$\pi_j \; = \; d\bar{P}_j \; (\text{rate of inflation in country } j) \; ,$$

and the prime (') indicates the first derivative of the excess supply
and demand functions. Clearly the ρ_j's sum to unity, and their magnitudes reflect the degree of market power a country possesses in the
world market for the good in question. In this context, the small
country has a ρ of zero; since it is a price taker, changes in its exchange rate will not affect the major currency prices of the good in

question. At the other extreme, a "price-making" country will have a ρ of unity; it alone determines the world price of the good.

Equation (5) indicates that the rate of change of the dollar price of a homogeneous traded good is a weighted average of the rates of inflation in the large countries that trade the good internationally *plus* the sum of two positive fractions of the changes in the major currency exchanges rates.[6]

If purchasing power parity held across all countries at all points in time:

$$\pi_A = \pi_B + dE_B = \pi_C + dE_C \ ,$$

then obviously $dP_A = \pi_A$. The point, however, is that purchasing power parity does *not* hold between the major currency countries in the short run, so that exchange rate changes alone are sufficient to introduce large variations in the relative prices of traded goods. In terms of Eq. (5), it is clear that a depreciation of the dollar (currency A) against, say the deutsche mark (currency B), will generate a step-wise change in the dollar price of the good in question quite independent of underlying inflation rates. To the extent that the good is somewhat heterogeneous (e.g., motor cars), the law of one price would hold only over time, and the change will be gradual rather than stepwise. In either case, the change in the dollar price of the good would be a positive fraction of the amount of dollar depreciation.

Let us now generalize the preceding results to all goods traded internationally by country D. Define

$$dP_t = \sum_i \omega_i \, dP_{D_i} \ , \tag{6}$$

where P_t is an appropriate index of the logarithms of *dollar* prices of traded goods in country D, and P_{D_i} is the logarithm of the dollar price of the ith traded good. The ω_i's are the relevant weights, and sum to unity. Inserting i subscripts into Eq. (3) and combining it with Eq. (6), we obtain

$$dP_t = \sum_i (\omega_i \rho_{Bi}) dE_B + \sum_i (\omega_i \rho_{Ci}) dE_C + \sum_i (\omega_i \rho_{Ai}) \pi_A$$
$$+ \sum_i (\omega_i \rho_{Bi}) \pi_B + \sum_i (\omega_i \rho_{Ci}) \pi_C \ , \tag{7}$$

where dE_D is the rate of *re*valuation of D's currency against the dollar. Note that the magnitude of ρ_{ji}'s depends upon the structure of the world market for good i, and that of the ω_i's depends upon the nature of the internal market in country D.[7] Given that $\sum_j \rho_{ji} = \sum_i \omega_i = 1$, we can rewrite (7) as

$$dP_t = K_B(dE_B) + K_C(dE_C) + \pi_w \;, \qquad (8)$$

where

$$K_j = \sum_i (\omega_i \rho_{ji}) > 0, \quad j = A, B, C,$$

$$\sum_j K_j = 1, \text{ and}$$

$$\pi_w = \sum_j K_j \pi_j \;.$$

The term π_w will be referred to as the rate of "world" inflation (from the point of view of country D), and is a weighted average of individual country rates.

Equation (8) is the centerpiece of the analysis. Note that, in the face of external exchange rate instability, the dollar prices of trade goods can move quite differently from what would be indicated by the inflation rate in the United States. During 1978–80, the terms $K_B(dE_B) + K_C(dE_C)$ were strongly positive, and reinforced the rate of world inflation. Thereafter, those terms became highly negative, sufficiently so to dominate world inflation. Eventually, of course, the world inflation declined, reflecting the same phenomenon as affected dP_t.

The Real Rate of Interest on External Debt

The ex post real U.S. prime rate of interest was 8.5 percent in 1982, but the deflation of dollar prices of traded goods was sufficient to propel the real interest rate on new Chilean borrowing to 24 percent during that same year. That effect can be analyzed in terms of Eq. (8). From that equation, we obtain (as an approximation) the real interest rate, R, on newly incurred and indexed external dollar debt as

$$R \equiv i_A - dP_t$$
$$= i_A - K_B(dE_B) - K_C(dE_C) - \pi_w \;,$$

where i_A is a measure of nominal U.S. dollar interest rates (either the London Interbank Offered Rate or U.S. prime). By using the earilier definition of π_w, the preceding expression is transformed into

$$R = R_A + K_B(\pi_A - \pi_B - dE_B) + K_C(\pi_A - \pi_C - dE_C) \ , \quad (9)$$

where R_A is the U.S. real rate of interest (i.e., $R_A \equiv i_A - \pi_A$).

Equation (9) indicates that the real rate of interest on tradables (and hence on newly incurred as well as indexed debt) is the real rate in the U.S. plus a linear combination of deviations from purchasing power parity among the major currency countries. As is well known, those deviations have been very large since floating rates were introduced in 1973. During the late 1970s in particular, the depreciation of the dollar against other major currencies was far in excess of that predicted by purchasing power parity (i.e., $dE_B \gg \pi_A - \pi_B$). Since late 1980, just the opposite has been true, causing real interest rates on newly incurred and indexed external debt to be extraordinarily high.

The real interest rate on that debt can also be written in terms of deviations from strong interest rate parity. Combining the following definition:

$$R_w \equiv K_A R_A + K_B R_B + K_C R_C \ ,$$

with Eq. (9), we obtain

$$R = R_w + K_B(i_A - i_B - dE_B) + K_C(i_A - i_C - dE_C) \ . \quad (10)$$

Thus the real rate of interest on newly incurred and indexed debt is the "world" real rate plus a linear combination of deviations from strong interest rate parity among the major currency countries. As those deviations have been notorious since 1973, especially since 1978, real interest rates have also gyrated.

The implication of the foregoing analysis is that the extraordinarily weak Carter dollar had a lot to do with the incentive for Latin American countries to incur debt (and for the bankers to lend to them!) during the late 1970s and 1980. And it is precisely the much appreciated Volcker dollar that is at the root of their current debt service problems. In 1984 and 1985 the dollar remained extraordinarily strong. Even without additional appreciation, further dollar deflation is clearly indicated for the next few months (and perhaps even deflation in the United States). Thus even if nominal dollar interest rates were to fall, it is doubtful that the debtor countries would experience any relief insofar as real interest rates are concerned. The only development that would bring instant alleviation of debt service would be a major depreciation of the dollar.

POSITIVE STEPS TOWARD A SOLUTION

The debt problem is unlikely to fortuitously disappear; real interest rates are likely to remain high in the immediate future, and as long as the debtor countries continue having difficulty making interest payments, new money from the capital market will remain scarce. This presumably is the rationale for seeking other, more positive solutions.

The first thing to be recognized is that the severity of the debt burden varies enormously across countries. Those countries whose external debt is less than 50 percent of their annual GDP are clearly capable of paying the interest on that debt even at current dollar interest rates; even if their debt is not increased over time, the requisite trade surplus will not exceed 5 percent of their GDPs and any additional borrowing they might be able to undertake will reduce that balance. This means, of course, that these countries must generate fiscal surpluses of the same order of magnitude, and therein lies the rub. Several of the major debtors—Argentina, Brazil and Mexico—have experienced extremely large fiscal deficits in the recent past, and the transformation of the deficits into surpluses requires substantial tax increases or reductions in expenditure.

As noted earlier, a number of Latin American countries have accumulated external debt that far exceeds 50 percent of their respective GDPs, and these are the countries for which some form of debt relief is likely to be required, particularly if dollar interest rates do not decline substantially. Countries such as Chile, Panama, Bolivia, and Costa Rica, whose debts range from 80 to 100 percent of GDP, are unlikely to service those debts on an extended basis (at current interest rates) without further borrowing, and that borrowing will only postpone the day of reckoning. For such countries, some solution involving the functions of a bankruptcy court must be found.

One will be forgiven for failing to remember all such solutions that have been put forward since the crisis arose, and they will not be reviewed in detail here. These proposals, however, tend to fall into two broad sets: those that emphasize the international institutional aspects, and those that emphasize debtor-credit relationships. Into the former category come those proposals that would expand the role of the World Bank, the International Monetary Fund, and perhaps the Bank for International Settlements; an example is the World Bank Structural Adjustment Loan program (SAL) and the proposal for a substantially broadened IMF compensatory financing facility (CFF). Into the latter set comes proposals such as the well-known Brunner-Meltzer suggestion that a portion at least of the debt in the more heavily indebted countries be retired by assets transfers (Meltzer 1984: 63–69). The fundamental difference between these two approaches is that the first would provide at least temporary relief for the debtor countries by extending them additional credits through international financial institutions (with varying degrees of "conditionality") whereas the authors of the latter set of proposals view the problem as essentially one of a "private" nature to be resolved by negotiations between debtor and creditor.

The major problem with resolving the debt issue by further transfers from the international financial institutions is the inescapable moral hazard that would result. "Bailing out" the debtor governments (and indirectly the creditor banks) would cause the discipline that ordinarily governs financial transactions to be eroded; to avoid that undesirable development, an elaborate set of guidelines and controls would have to be developed, which would conflict with perceptions of national sovereignty much as does the widely detested IMF conditionality.

Indeed, in the face of the debt problem the World Bank has revived a form of lending that it abandoned with good cause two decades ago. The World Bank SAL program is an only thinly disguised resumption of its earlier "program lending," which in turn was a mere euphemism for balance-of-payments assistance. Countries were directed to draw up development plans and estimate the amount of investment that would be required to achieve the target growth rate; from that they would subtract the amount of domestic saving that would be associated with that growth rate, the difference being the external saving required to realize the target growth rate, external saving to be provided by both private and public sources, but with the public sources responsible for the residual. The developing countries quickly learned how to manipulate their "savings gaps" so as to justify large amounts of foreign aid, which was frequently used to reduce public sector saving—that is, to increase the size of the public sector with no increase in investment. Thus, if past behavior is a good guide, one would anticipate that the SAL program will impede rather than promote structural adjustment.

The CFF would operate in much the same way.

> The [CFF] facility should cover all exports, whether manufactured goods, services or primary commodities. Expected medium-term real export trends would be jointly estimated by the CFF staff and the authorities of each country, refining present practice while relying on the accumulated expertise. Faulty expectations could be fully, automatically and speedily covered by SDR credits, which would also be quickly repaid when real export earnings surpass expectations. (Diaz-Alejandro 1984: 18)

While the idea of smoothing the effect of the international business cycle has considerable merit of its own, the argument for the CFF just cited neglects the fact that exports are endogenous, declining when domestic expenditure increases (as for example, when fiscal deficits rise). Since governments can readily devise policies that directly affect their supply of exportables (and demand for importables), experience suggests that "faulty expectations" might well be the rule rather than the exception.[8]

When applied to the debt problem, this type of proposal essentially seeks to solve the problem by direct or indirect transfers to the debtor countries, transfers that would be financed in the final analysis by either higher taxes in the creditor countries, or world inflation. What these proposals systematically ignore is the simple fact that the current debt problem is primarily one between the debtor countries and a small number of self-selected banks. It is not, as is frequently argued, a "global problem that requires a global solution" (Schumacher 1984: 1093). To be sure, some of the more ambitious transfer proposals would indeed transform the existing problem into a "global" one.

The major motivation for the transfer solution is the argument that the debt problem constitutes a financial time bomb, given that the external debt of the developing countries—particularly those in Latin America—is held in large part by a relatively small number of (mainly U.S.) commercial banks. Were one or more of those banks to become insolvent in the event of a major default, a bank run of international proportions might ensue, with catastrophic effects. Clearly the price of a certain degree of moral hazard would be cheap indeed if it were to insure us against such a disaster.

It is becoming increasingly clear, however, that the possibility of a major run on the international banking system is quite remote. In the first place, only a tiny number of banks are heavily exposed, and those are confined to the United States and England. No continental European or Japanese banks face significant write-offs because of loans to developing countries. Second, there are the lessons of the recent Continental Illinois episode. One lesson from that experience is an old one: bankrupt banks do experience runs, but the funds quickly reappear in other banks. Indeed, a run on a bankrupt bank is an act of mercy. Nor has the fear of a generalized run on the U.S., or possibly the world, banking system, been borne out even during a recent period when Argentine default appeared imminent. While there is no proof that a run will *never* develop as a consequence of insolvency on the part of one or more major banks, neither can there be any assurance that implementation of any of the transfer schemes would significantly reduce the threat of insolvency.

A second lesson from the Continental Illinois episode is that even managers of major banks are quite capable of making a sufficiently large number of bad *domestic* loans to bring on insolvency. Thus there can be no assurance that, even if sufficient transfers are effected to protect the stockholders of, say, Chase Manhattan and Manufacturers Hanover from loss of their risk capital, the managers of those banks will reinvest their recuperated losses in a manner more intelligent than in the past.

A further difficulty with the transfer schemes is that the ultimate recipients of the transfers will be the stockholders of the major banks, not the debtor countries. While transfers to Chile, Ecuador, Peru, and perhaps even Argentina might be justified on grounds of equity, no such case exists for the stockholders and managers of the major creditor banks.

The solutions emphasizing the debtor-creditor relationships, which we shall designate "market" solutions, are not without their own difficulties. The Brunner-Meltzer proposal to reduce external debt by transferring existing public sector real assets to creditor banks has considerable merit but may not be feasible. Even if, say, PEMEX were formally owned by U.S. banks, it would remain in Mexico and be subject to control by the Mexican government which could, by regulation, extract the assets from PEMEX and reduce its value to virtually zero.

Table 13-2. Foreign Debt and Asset Positions of Four Major Debtor Countries (*$ Billions*).

Country	Gross External Debt	Privately Held Foreign Investments[a]	Cumulated Interest on Foreign Assets[b]	Total Foreign Assets	Net External Debt
Argentina	$44	$20.2	$11.3	31.5	$12.5
Brazil	98	11.4	9.9	21.3	76.7
Mexico	95	36.3	21.9	58.2	36.8
Venezuela	35	25.5	9.6	35.1	-0.1
Total	$272	$93.4	$52.7	$146.1	$125.9

a. The source for this column is Dooley et al. (1983). These data refer to the increase in foreign investments during the 1974–82 period.

b. Author's calculations assuming an annual average rate of return of 10 percent.

There are, of course, other assets. One of the ironic aspects of the debt problem is that, even in some of the most debt-ridden countries, the private sector owns large amounts of foreign assets, whereas nearly all of the debt is owed by the public sector. As is shown in Table 13-2, it is estimated that Argentine private sector claims on nonresidents *grew* by over $30 billion, for Mexico the figure is nearly $60 billion, and for Venezuela, $35 billion during the 1974–82 period. These funds have been placed abroad simply because the residents of those countries do not trust their own governments enough to invest in domestic assets.

If the governments of debtor countries were to pursue policies that would induce their own citizens to repatriate at least the interest earned on their foreign financial investments, the problem of debt service would be somewhat alleviated in a number of countries. Repatriation of capital is hardly a panacea, however, as debt service is first and foremost a *fiscal* issue, and only secondarily a balance-of-payments problem. With approximately 80 percent of the external debt either owned by or guaranteed by governments, debt service requires either that they generate fiscal surpluses or borrow domestically. Repatriation of capital would somewhat augment the tax base and facilitate domestic borrowing, but it would not in itself solve the problem.

The most direct and viable market solution to the international debt problem is to let the banks renegotiate the debt with the borrowing countries. Banks will resist that as long as they have confidence in the political feasibility of the transfer solution; meanwhile, they are trading that debt among themselves at prices well below par values. This activity underscores the essence of the debt issue: *the losses have already been incurred*, and the only remaining question is how they are to be distributed. It is in this sense that any solution involves transfers.

Critics of the market solutions to the debt issue are concerned with the stability of the international financial system and worry that, if left to themselves, the banks would precipitate default. In my own view, default is the most unlikely of all outcomes, as virtually any other outcome is preferable to both borrowers and lenders. A sovereign default is quite different from a domestic bankruptcy in that a sovereign default will undoubtedly result in a 100 percent loss to the lender, whereas in domestic bankruptcy, the lender has legal access to whatever assets may remain. In the case of default, the banks lose everything; with a renegotiation they "lose" only what they have acknowledged to have already been lost—the difference between par value and the actual prices at which they have traded these assets among themselves. Thus virtually any renegotiation is preferable to default from the point of view of the banks.

Default is also unattractive for the debtor countries for the simple reason that in most cases the actual external debt is simply not large enough to merit the costs of default. As was argued earlier, the ratio of debt to GNP in the major debtor nations is not excessive by historical standards; it is the high level of real interest rates that is the main source of the problem. In the case of the Argentine government, for example, the gain from default is, relative to GDP, about the same as the gain to the U.S. taxpayer were the U.S. government to default on its debt. A rational government will not willingly contemplate the enormous costs of default to gain a mere 40 percent of a single year's GDP.

The only genuine obstacle to debt renegotiation between the banks and the governments of debtor countries is the prospect that there may be an even better deal to be struck by waiting—namely, the transfer solution. Both sides see advantages in exaggerating fears of international financial chaos to increase the probability of the transfer solution, which would permit the debtors to keep their credit rating seemingly intact and bank equity holders to escape the loss of their risk capital. Thus the debt problem has become a waiting game with periodic crises.

To date, the transfer solution has not been accepted, and a number of the major debtor countries are in fact making internal adjustments essential to their debt service. Brazil, for example, has turned around from a $3 billion commercial account deficit to a surplus that is expected to total $12.5 billion in calendar year 1984. Similar adjustments have been made in Mexico, and to a lesser extent in Argentina. If this tendency continues, the acute debt service problems will be confined to those countries with very high ratios of debt to GDP; fortunately, those countries account for a relatively small portion of the total debt and none of them are large enough to seriously threaten the stability of the international financial community. There is, then, reason for cautious optimism.

NOTES TO CHAPTER 13

1. The ratio of debt to exports for all of Latin America is estimated to have been 5.2 in 1913; see Lewis (1979).
2. Nasser Saidi (1984) estimates total public sector debt of Panama to have been $4.467 billion in 1983, almost identical to Panama's gross internal product. In the same year, exports were about 38 percent of gross internal product.
3. From mid-1980 to early September, 1984, the deutsche mark price of the U.S. dollar rose by over 60 percent.
4. The immediately following two subsections are taken from Sjaastad (1985).
5. This assumption is made for expositional simplicity only; the qualitative nature of the results are preserved even if country D has monopoly or monopsony power in the world market.
6. The preceding analysis is intended to convey the flavor of a world in which the major currencies are the dollar, the deutsche mark (representing the EMS countries), and the yen. Clearly it generalizes to any number of countries and currencies.
7. The ω_i's would be defined arbitrarily, of course, so as to make P_t reflect whatever might be desired by policymakers.
8. Ronald Vaubel (1983b: 65–79) has compiled a statistical history of IMF lending, which provides incontestable evidence of moral hazard.

BIBLIOGRAPHY

Aliber, Robert Z. 1985. "The Future of International Commercial Banking." In Paolo Savona and George Sutija, eds., *Strategic Planning in International Banking*. London: Macmillan.

Aliber, Robert Z. 1980. *A Conceptual Approach to the Analysis of External Debt of Developing Countries*. World Bank Staff Working Paper 421. Washington, D.C.: World Bank.

American Express Bank. 1984. AMEX Bank Review Special Paper 10 (March).

Arrow, Kenneth. 1970. "Insurance, Risk and Resource Allocation." *Essays in the Theory of Risk-Bearing*. Amsterdam: North Holland.

Avramovic, D. et al. 1964. *Economic Growth and External Debt*. Baltimore: Johns Hopkins University Press.

Balassa, Bela. 1983. "The Adjustment Experience of Developing Economies After 1973." In John Williams ed., *IMF Conditionality*. Washington, D.C.: Institute for International Economics.

Balassa, Bella. 1981. "The Newly-Industrializing Developing Countries after the Oil Crisis." *Weltwirtschaftliches Archive* 117: 142–194.

Bank for International Settlements. 1978–84. *Maturity Distribution of International Bank Lending*. Basel, Switzerland: BIS.

Barth, James R., and Joseph Pelzman. 1984. "International Debt: Conflict and Resolution." Fairfax, Virg.: Department of Economics, George Mason University.

Beck, Nathaniel. 1984. "The Political Economy of Monetary Policy: A Rational Actor Perspective." Presented at the Conference on the Political Economy of Public Policy, Stanford University, Stanford, Calif. (March 17).

Beenstock, Michael. 1983. *The World Economy in Transition.* London: George Allan and Unwin.

Bennett, Paul. 1984. "Applying Portfolio Theory to Global Bank Lending." *Journal of Banking and Finance* 8: 153–169.

Blanchard, Oliver. 1983. "Debt and the Current Account Deficit in Brazil." P. Aspe Armella et al., eds. *Financial Policies and the World Capital Market: The Problem of Latin American Countries.* Chicago: University of Chicago, pp. 187–197.

Borchard, Edwin. 1951. *State Insolvency and Foreign Bondholders,* Vol. I: *General Principles.* New Haven, Conn.: Yale Univ. Press.

Bradley, Michael; Gregg Jarrell; and E. Han Kim. 1984. "On the Existence of an Optimal Capital Structure." *Journal of Finance* 39 (July).

Brandt Commission (International Commission on International Development Issues). 1980. *North-South: A Program for Survival.* Cambridge, Mass.: MIT Press.

Brau, Edward, and Richard C. Williams. 1983. "Recent Multilateral Debt Reschedulings with Official and Bank Creditors." Occasional Paper 25. Washington, D.C.: IMF.

Brimmer, Andrew. 1973. "International Capital Markets and the Financing of Economic Development." In *Addresses, Essays, Lectures of Andrew Felton Brimmer,* vol. 13. Washington, D.C.: Federal Reserve Library.

Brock, William A. 1984. "Trade and Debt: The Vital Linkage." *Foreign Affairs* 62 (no. 5).

Brock, William A., and Stephen P. Magee. 1978. "The Economics of Special-Interest Politics: The Case of the Tariff." *American Economic Review* 68 (May): 246–50.

Bruno, Michael, and Jeffrey Sachs. 1982. "Adjustment and Structural Change in the World Economy." National Bureau for Economic Research Working Paper 852.

Carli, C. F. Guido, and Paolo Savona. 1985. "International Trade and International Finance." In Paolo Savona and George Sutija, eds., *Strategic Planning in International Banking.* London: Macmillan.

Chase Economic Observer. 1984. 4: 3.

"Chase Reports Operating Loss for Second Quarter." 1982. *The Wall Street Journal.* (July 21).

Cline, William R. 1982. "External Debt: System Vulnerability and Development." *Columbia Journal of World Development* (Spring): 4–14.

Cline, William R. 1983. *International Debt and the Stability of the World Economy.* Cambridge, Mass.: MIT Press.

Cline, William R. 1984a. *International Debt: Systematic Risk and Policy Response.* Washington, D.C.: Institute for International Economics.

Cline, William R. 1984b. "The Issue Is Illiquidity, Not Insolvency." *Challenge* (July/August).

Congressional Record. 1983. S16698.

Cooper, Richard N. 1984. *Is There Need for Reform?* Federal Reserve Bank of Boston.

Crawford, Vincent. 1984. "International Lending, Long-Term Credit Relationships, and Dynamic Contract Theory." Discussion Paper 84–14. University of California, San Diego, pp. 19–24.

Dale, Richard S. 1983. "Country Risk and Bank Regulation." *The Banker* 133, no. 685 (March).

Dale, Richard S, and Richard P. Mattione. 1983. *Managing Global Debt.* Washington, D.C.: Brookings Institution.

D'Arista, Jane. 1979. "Private Overseas Lending: Too Far, Too Fast?" In Jonathan D. Aronson, ed., *Debt and the Less Developed Countries.* Boulder, Colo.: Westview Press.

Darity, William Jr. 1984. "Debt, Production and Trade in a North-South Model: The Surplus Approach." Mimeo. University of North Carolina, Chapel Hill.

Darity, William Jr. 1985. "Loan-Pushing: Doctrine and Theory." International Finance Discussion Paper. Board of Governors of the Federal Reserve.

Davis, Stephen I. 1979. *The Management Function in International Banking.* New York: John Wiley and Sons.

"Debate Likely to Continue over Proposal to Cap Interest Rates for Debtor Nations." 1984. *Wall Street Journal* (May 18).

Dean, James W., and Ian H. Giddy. 1981. "Averting International Banking Crises." *Monograph Series in Finance and Economics.* New York University Graduate School of Business Administration, no. 1981-1.

"Democracy in Peru Threatened by Terrorism and Debt." 1984. *Wall Street Journal* (August 24).

de Vries, Barend A. 1984. "Restructuring Debtor Economies: Long-term Finance." *Journal of International Affairs* (Summer).

de Vries, Margaret. 1969. *The International Monetary Fund, 1945–1965: Twenty Years of International Monetary Cooperation.* Washington, D.C.: IMF.

de Vries, Margaret. 1985. *The International Monetary Fund, 1966–1971: The System under Stress.* Washington, D.C.: IMF.

de Vries, Dr. Margaret. 1985. *The International Monetary Fund, 1972–1978: International Monetary Cooperation on Trial.* Washington, D.C.: IMF.

Diaz-Alejandro, Carlos F. 1984. "International Markets in the 1980s." *Journal of International Affairs* (Summer).

Diaz-Alejandro, Carlos F. 1984. "Latin American Debt: I Don't Think We Are in Kansas Anymore." *Brookings Papers on Economic Activity*, no. 2, 335–405.

Diaz-Alejandro, Carlos F., and Edmar Lisboa Bacha. 1982. "International Financial Intermediation: A Long and Tropical View." *Essays in International Finance.* Princeton University 147 (May).

Dooley, Michael; William Helkie; Ralph Tyron; and John Underwood. 1983. "An Analysis of External Debt Positions of Eight Developing Countries through 1990." International Finance Discussion Paper No. 227. Board of Governors of the Federal Reserve System (August).

Dornbusch, Rudiger. 1984a. "The International Debt Problem." Testimony before the Subcommittee on Economic Goals and Intergovernmental Policy, Joint Economic Committee, U.S. Congress (March 28).

Dornbusch, Rudiger. 1984b. *External Debt, Budget Deficits and Disequilibrium Exchange Rates.* National Bureau of Economic Research Working Paper No. 1336. Cambridge, Mass.: NBER (April).

Dornbusch, Rudiger. 1984c. "On the Consequences of Muddling Through the Debt Crisis." *The World Economy* (June): 133–144.

Dornbusch, Rudiger. 1984d. "The Latin American Dimension." *Challenge* (July/August).

Dornbusch, Rudiger, and Stanley Fischer. 1984. "The World Debt Problem." Report prepared for the United National Center for Transnational Corporations.

"Dresdner Bank Tops Up Its Reserves." 1982. *Financial Times* (December 30).

Eaton, Jonathan, and Mark Gersovitz. 1981a. "Debt With Potential Repudiation: Theoretical and Empirical Analysis." *Review of Economic Studies* 48 289–309.

Eaton, Jonathan, and Mark Gersovitz. 1981b. "Poor-Country Borrowing in Private Financial Markets and the Repudiation Issue." *Princeton Essays in International Finance* 47 (June).

Emminger, Otmar. 1984. *Adjustments in World Payments: An Evaluation.* Paper presented to the Conference on the Problems of the International Monetary System: Forty Years after Bretton Woods, Federal Reserve Bank of Boston.

Enders, Thomas P., and Richard P. Mattione. 1984. *Latin America: The Crisis of Debt and Growth.* Washington, D.C.: Brookings Institution.

Evans, David, ed. 1983. *Breaking Up Bell.* New York: North Holland.

Feldstein, Martin. 1984. "From Crisis to Renewed Growth." *Challenge* (July/August).

Ferguson, Thomas, and Joel Rogers. 1981. *The Hidden Election: Politics and Economics in the 1980 Presidential Campaign.* New York: Pantheon.

Fieleke, Norman S. 1982. "International Lending in Historical Perspective." *New England Economic Review* (November/December).

Fieleke, Norman S. 1983. "International Lending in Historical Perspective." *New England Economic Review* (May/June).

Fishlow, Albert. 1984. "The Debt Crisis: Round Two Ahead?" *Adjustment Crisis in the Third World.* Richard E. Feinberg and Valeriana Kallub, eds. Washington, D.C.: Overseas Development Council, pp. 1–38.

Franko, Lawrence G. 1979. "Debt, Trade, and the Prospects for World Economic Growth." In L. G. Franko and Marilyn Seiber, eds., *Developing Country Debt*. New York: Pergamon Press.

Frazier, Steve. 1984. "Oils Lure Led Mexico and Banks into Payment Woes." *Wall Street Journal* (May 15).

Friedman, Irving. 1978. "Emerging Role of Private Banks." In Stephen S. Goodman, ed., *Financing and Risk in Developing Countries*. New York: Praeger, pp. 19–24.

Frey, Bruno S., and Friedrich Schneider. 1984. "Competing Models of International Lending Activity." Working Paper, University of Zurich.

Gold, Joseph. 1982. Order in International Finance: The Promotion of IMF Stand-By Arrangements and the Drafting of Private Loan Agreements, IMF Pamphlet Series No. 39 (June).

Goodman, Laurie. 1981. "Bank Lending to Non-OPEC LDCs: Are Risks Diversifiable?" *Federal Reserve Bank of New York Quarterly Review* 6, no. 2 (Summer).

Goreux, Louis M. 1980. *Compensatory Financing Facility*. IMF Pamphlet Series, Washington, D.C.: IMF.

Gruber, William. 1984. "Many Question FDIC's Purge of Continental." *The Chicago Tribune* (December 9).

Guttentag, Jack M., and Richard Herring. 1982. "The Insolvency of Financial Institutions: Assessment and Regulatory Disposition." In Paul Wachtel, ed., *Crisis in the Economic and Financial Structure*. Lexington, Mass.: D.C. Heath, pp. 99–126.

Guttentag, Jack M., and Richard Herring. 1983a. "Uncertainty and Insolvency Exposure by International Banks." The Wharton Program in International Banking and Finance, University of Pennsylvania (November).

Guttentag, Jack M., and Richard Herring. 1983b. "What Happens When Countries Cannot Pay Back Their Loans? The Renegotiation Process." *Journal of Comparative Business and Capital Market Law* 5: 209.

Guttentag, Jack M., and Richard Herring. 1984. "Commercial Bank Lending to Less Developed Countries: From Overlending to Underlending to Structural Reform." Presented at World Bank Seminar on Debt and the Developing Countries, Washington, D.C.

Guttentag, Jack M., and Richard Herring. 1985. "Strategic Planning by International Banks to Cope with Uncertainty." In Paolo Savona and George Sutija, eds., *Strategic Planning in International Banking*. London: Macmillan.

Gwynne, S. C. 1983. "Adventures in the Loan Trade." *Harper's* 267, no. 1600 (September).

Hanley, Thomas H., and Lynne M. Christian. 1983. "Comparative Market Valuation Statistics." Bank Securities Department, Salomon Brothers Inc., New York, August 19.

Harberger, C. F. Arnold. 1983. *Welfare Consequences of Capital Inflows.* Washington, D.C.: World Bank.

Heller, H. Robert. 1983. "The Debt Crisis and Commercial Lending to Developing Countries." Paper presented at American Economics Association annual meeting, December.

Hertzberg, Daniel. 1984. "Banking Behemoth: Citicorp Leads Field in Its Size and Power—and Its Arrogance." *Wall Street Journal* (May 11): 1, 16.

Hertzberg, Daniel, and S. Karene Witcher. 1984. "New U.S. Rules on Latin Debt to Affect Banks." *Wall Street Journal* (June 19): 3.

Hill, G. Christian. 1984. "Lender Beware: List of Troubled Banks Shows Realty, Energy Lead Bad-Loan Areas." *Wall Street Journal* (March 19): 1.

Hirsch, Morris W., and Stephen Smale. 1974. *Differential Equations, Dynamic Systems and Linear Algebra.* New York: Academic Press.

Horowitz, Morris. 1965. "The Horowitz Proposal." Staff Report, International Bank for Reconstruction and Development. Washington, D.C.: IBRD.

"How Peru's President Views the IMF and the Banks." 1978. *Euromoney* (March).

Institutional Investor. 1976. (October).

"[The] International Debt Crisis: The Major Third World Trouble Spots." 1983. *The Washington Post,* (September 25): H1.

International Monetary Fund. 1979. *IMF Survey* 8 (October 15).

International Monetary Fund. 1981. *External Indebtedness of Developing Countries.* Occasional Paper 23. Washington, D.C.: IMF.

International Monetary Fund. 1982a. *IMF Survey* 11 (May 24): 146–47.

International Monetary Fund. 1982b. *Summary Proceedings of the Thirty-Seventh Annual Meeting of the Board of Governors.* Washington, D.C.: IMF.

International Monetary Fund. 1983a. *Annual Report: 1983.* Washington, D.C.: IMF.

International Monetary Fund. 1983b. *Balance of Payments Statistics, 1983 Yearbook,* part 1. Washington, D.C.: IMF.

International Monetary Fund. 1983c. *International Capital Markets: Developments and Prospects, 1983.* Occasional Paper 23. Washington, D.C.: IMF (July).

International Monetary Fund. 1983d. *Recent Multilateral Debt Restructuring with Official and Bank Creditors.* Occasional Paper 25. Washington, D.C.: IMF (December).

International Monetary Fund. 1984a. *International Financial Statistics 1984 Yearbook.* Washington, D.C.: IMF.

International Monetary Fund. 1984b. *IMF Survey* (June 18): 178–82.

International Monetary Fund. 1984c. *World Economic Outlook, September 1984: Revised Projections by the Staff of the International Monetary Fund.* Occasional Paper 32, Washington, D.C.: IMF.

International Monetary Fund. 1984d. *World Economic Outlook.* Washington, D.C.: IMF.

Jensen, Michael C., and William H. Meckling. 1976. "Theory of the Firm: Managerial Behavior, Agency Costs and Ownership Structure." *Journal of Financial Economics* 3: 305–360.

Johnson, Willene A. 1983. "Bank Size and U.S. Bank Lending to Latin America." *Federal Reserve Bank of New York Quarterly Review* 8, no. 3 (Autumn).

Kaldor, Nicholas. 1976. "Inflation and Recession in the World Economy." *Economic Journal* 86: 703–14.

Kalecki, Michael. 1971. *Selected Essays on the Dynamics of the Capitalist Economy.* Cambridge, England: Cambridge University Press.

Kane, E. 1980. "Politics and the FED Policy-Making: The More Things Change, the More Things Stay the Same." *Journal of Monetary Economics* 6 (April): 199–211.

Keynes, John Maynard. 1936. *The General Theory of Employment, Interest, and Money.* London: Macmillan.

Keynes, John Maynard. 1963. "The Consequences to the Banks of the Collapse of Money Values." *Essays in Persuasion.* New York. W. W. Norton.

Khan, Mohsin S., and Malcolm Knight. 1983. "Sources of Payment Problems in LDCs." *Finance and Development* (December).

Kindleberger, Charles P. 1978a. *Manias, Panics, and Crashes: A History of Financial Crises.* New York: Basic Books.

Kindleberger, Charles P. 1978b. "Debt Situation of the Developing Countries in Historical Perspective." In Stephen H. Goodman, ed., *Financing and Risk in Developing Countries.* New York: Praeger.

Kindleberger, Charles P. 1983. "Historical Perspectives on Today's Third World Debt Crisis." Mimeo. Cambridge, Mass.: Massachusetts Institute of Technology.

Knapp, Stephen. 1984. "Rescuer of Last Resort." *Time* (July 30): 88.

Kraft, Joseph. 1984. *The Mexican Rescue.* New York: Group of Thirty.

Kuczynski, Pedro-Pablo. 1983a. "International Lending Facilities: Are They Adequate?" Paper presented at the Bretton Woods Conference organized by the Federal Reserve Bank of Boston, May 18–20.

Kucsynski, Pedro-Pablo. 1983b. "Latin American Debt: Act Two." *Foreign Affairs* 62, no. 1 (Fall): 17.

Kyle, Steven C., and Jeffrey D. Sachs. 1984. "Developing Country Debt and the Market Value of Large Commercial Banks." Working Paper 1470, National Bureau of Economic Research, Inc., Boston, Mass. (September).

Lessard, Donald. 1983. "North-South: The Implications for Multinational Banking." *Journal of Banking and Finance* 7: 521–536.

Leven, Ronald, and David L. Roberts. 1983. "Latin America's Prospects for Recovery." *Federal Reserve Bank of New York Quarterly Review* (Autumn).

Lever, Harold. 1984. "The Road to Solvency." *Wall Street Journal* (June 7).

Lewis, Arthur W. 1979. *Growth and Fluctuations, 1870-1913.* London: Allen Unwin.

Lipson, Charles. 1979. "The IMF, Commercial Banks, and Third World Debts." In Jonathan D. Aronson, ed., *Debt in the Less Developed Countries.* Boulder, Colo.: Westview Press, pp. 317-333.

Lipson, Charles. 1981. "The International Organization of Third World Debt." *International Organization* 35, no. 4: 603.

Macedo, Robert. 1983. *The Economic Crisis and the Welfare of Brazilian Children: A Case Study of the State of Sao Paulo.* New York: UNICEF.

Madden, John T.; Marcus Nadler; and Harry C. Sauvain. 1937. *America's Experience as a Creditor Nation.* Englewood Cliffs, N.J.: Prentice-Hall.

Magee, Stephen P.; William A. Brock; and Leslie Young. 1983. "Endogenous Redistribution Theory and Endogenous Tariffs in General Equilibrium: Regulation, Black Hole Politics, Lobbying, and Trade." Unpublished manuscript, University of Texas at Austin (November).

Makin, John. H. 1984. *The Global Debt Crisis: America's Growing Involvement.* New York: Basic Books.

Martin, Sarah. 1981. "Western Bankers Agree to Delay Payments on $3 Billion of Poland's Commercial Debt." *Wall Street Journal* (October 2): 31.

Martin, Sarah. 1981. "The Secrets of the Polish Memorandum." *Euromoney* (August): 9.

McMullen, Neil J. 1979. "Historical Perspectives on Developing Nation's Debt." In Lawrence G. Franko and Marilyn Seiber, eds., *Developing Country Debt.* New York: Pergamon Press, pp. 3-16.

Meltzer, Allan H. 1984. "The International Debt Problem." *The Cato Journal* 4, no. 1 (Spring/Summer): 63-69.

Mendelsohn, Lawrence A. 1984. "International Lending to the Developing Countries: Criteria and Practices." Professional Report, School of Business, University of Texas at Austin (August).

Mentre, Paul. 1984. *The Fund, Commercial Banks, and Member Countries.* IMF Occasional Paper 26. Washington, D.C.: IMF.

Metais, Joel. 1982. "Less Developed Countries' Indebtedness and the Lender of Last Resort in International Context." In C.P. Kindleberger and Jean-Pierre Laffargue, eds., *Financial Crisis: Theory, History, and Policy.* Cambridge, England: Cambridge Univ. Press.

Mills, Rodney H. Jr. 1982. "Spreads and Maturities on Eurocurrency Credits—Fourth Quarter 1981 and Two-Year Review." Board of Governors of the Federal Reserve System (March 3).

"Minimum Capital Guidelines Amendments." 1983. *Federal Reserve Bulletin* (July).

Minsky, Hyman P. 1964. "Longer Waves in Financial Relations: Financial Factors in the More Severe Depressions." *American Economic Review: AEA Papers and Proceedings* 54, no. 3 (May): 324-35.

Minsky, Hyman P. 1975. *John Maynard Keynes.* New York: Columbia Univ. Press.

Minsky, Hyman P. 1978. "The Financial Instability Hypothesis: A Restatement." Thames Papers in Political Economy (Autumn).

Minsky, Hyman P. 1979. "Financial Interrelations, the Balance of Payments, and the Dollar Crisis." In Jonathan D. Aronson, ed., *Debt and the Less Developed Countries.* Boulder, Colo.: Westview Press, pp. 103–22.

Minsky, Hyman P. 1980. "The Federal Reserve: Between a Rock and a Hard Place." *Challenge* (May/June): 30–36.

Minsky, Hyman P. 1982. *Can "It" Happen Again?: Essays on Instability and Finance.* Armonk, N.Y.: M. E. Sharpe, pp. 3–13.

Minsky, Hyman P. 1983. "Monetary Policies and the International Financial Environment." Working Paper 56, Department of Economics, Washington University, St. Louis, Mo.

Morgan Guaranty Trust Company. 1983. "Global Debt: Assessment and Long-Term Strategy." *World Financial Markets* (June).

Morgan Guaranty Trust Company. 1984a. "Mexico: Progress and Prospects." *World Financial Markets* (May).

Morgan Guaranty Trust Company. 1984b. "Stabilization Prospects in Brazil." *World Financial Markets* (July).

"The New Crisis for Latin Debt." 1984. *New York Times* (March 12).

Nowzad, Bahram. 1982. "Debt in Developing Countries: Some Issues for the 1980s." *Finance and Development* (March).

Olson, Mancur. 1965. *The Logic of Collective Action.* Cambridge, Mass.: Harvard Univ. Press.

Olson, Mancur. 1982. *The Rise and Decline of Nations.* New Haven, Conn.: Yale Univ. Press.

Organization for Economic Cooperation and Development. 1981. *External Debt of Developing Countries.* Paris: OECD.

Organization for Economic Cooperation and Development. 1982a. *External Debt of Developing Countries, 1982 Survey.* Paris: OECD.

Organization for Economic Cooperation and Development. 1982b. Annual Report of the Chairman of the DAC. Paris: OECD.

Organization for Economic Cooperation and Development. 1983a. Report of the Chairman of the Development Assistance Committee of the OECD. Paris: OECD.

Organization for Economic Cooperation and Development. 1983b. *Development Cooperation 1983.* Report of the Chairman of the Development Assistance Committee of the OECD. Paris: OECD.

Organization for Economic Cooperation and Development. 1984a. *External Debt of Developing Countries, 1983 Survey.* Paris: OECD.

Organization for Economic Cooperation and Development. 1984b. *Financial Market Trends.* Paris: OECD.

Payer, Chery. 1977. "Will the Government Bail Out the Banks?" *The Bankers Magazine* 160, no. 2 (Spring).

Polak, J. J. 1984. The International Monetary System: Forty Years After Bretton Woods. Federal Reserve Bank of Boston conference series No. 28. Boston: Federal Reserve Bank of Boston.

Ranis, Gustav. 1984. "Needed: Commitment to Structural Adjustment." *Challenge* (July/August).

Ritter, Lawrence S., and T. J. Urich. 1984. *The Role of Gold in Consumer Investment Portfolios.* Salomon Brothers Monograph, New York: New York University.

Sacchetti, U. 1983. "Conditionality in International Finance and the Crisis of the International Monetary System." In *Economic Notes*, Second Issue. Monte Dei Paschi Dei Siena, Siena, Italy.

Sachs, Jeffrey D. 1981. "The Current Account and Macroeconomic Adjustment in the 1970s." *Brookings Papers on Economic Activity* 9, no. 1: 189–253.

Sachs, Jeffrey D. 1982. "LDC Debt in the 1980s: Risks and Reforms." In Paul Wachtel, ed., *Crises in the Economic and Financial Structure.* Lexington, Mass.: Lexington Books.

Sachs, Jeffrey D. 1983. "Theoretical Issues in International Borrowings." *National Bureau of Economic Research.* Working Paper 1139. Boston, Mass. (August).

Saidi, Nesser. 1984. "Public Debt, Expenditure and Revenue, Panama 1956–83: Assessment and Policy Recommendations." Mimeo. Geneva.

Saini, Krishan G., and Philip S. Bates. 1984. "A Survey of the Quantitative Approaches to Country Risk Analysis." *Journal of Banking and Finance* 8: 341–56.

Schneider, Friedrich, and Bruno S. Frey. 1984. "Economic and Political Determinants of Foreign Direct Investment." Working Paper 25–83–84 Government Service Information Agency. Pittsburgh, Penn.: Carnegie–Mellon University (January).

Schumacher, Edward. 1984. "Argentina and Democracy." *Foreign Affairs* (Summer).

Shapiro, Alan C. 1982. "Risk in International Banking." *Journal of Financial and Quantitative Analysis* (December).

Scott, B.; J. Rosenblum; and A. Sproat. 1979. *Japan: 1965–1978.* Boston: Harvard Business School.

Scott, William A. 1893. *The Repudiation of State Debts: A Study in the Financial History of Mississippi, Florida, Alabama, North Carolina, South Carolina, Georgia, Louisiana, Arkansas, Tennessee, Minnesota, Michigan, and Virginia.* Boston: Thomas Y. Crowell.

Sjaastad, Larry A. 1983. "International Debt Quagmire—To Whom Do We Owe It?" *The World Economy* 6: 305–324.

Sjaastad, Larry A. 1985. "Exchange Rate Regimes and the Real Rate of Interest." In Michael Connolly and John McDermott, eds., *Economics of the Caribbean Basin.* New York: Praeger.

Solis, Leopoldo, and Ernesto Zedillo. 1984. "Considerations on the Foreign Debt of Mexico." Presented at World Bank Seminar on Debt and the Developing Countries, April.

Solow, Robert M. 1982. "On the Lender of Last Resort." In C. P. Kindleberger and Jean-Pierre Laffargue, eds., *Financial Crisis: Theory, History, and Policy.* Cambridge, England: Cambridge Univ. Press.

Stiglitz, Joseph B., and Andrew Weiss. 1981. "Credit Rationing in Markets with Imperfect Information." *American Economic Review* 71: 393–410.

Takahashi, Kamekichi. 1969. *The Rise and Development of Japan's Modern Economy.* Tokyo: Jiji.

Taylor, Lance. 1983. *Structuralist Macroeconomics.* New York: Basic Books.

Taylor, Lance, and Stephen A. O'Connell. In press. "A Minsky Crisis." *Quarterly Journal of Economics* 100, no. 1.

Teeters, Nancy H. 1983. "The Role of Banks in the International Monetary System." Paper presented to the International Conference on Multinational Banking and the World Economy, Tel Aviv, June.

Terrell, Henry S. 1984. "Bank Lending to Developing Countries: Recent Developments and Some Considerations for the Future." *Federal Reserve Bulletin* 70, no. 10 (October).

"Two Banks Drop Suits after Ex-Im Bank Alters Zaire Loan Pact." 1976. *Wall Street Journal* (October 14): 20.

United Nations. 1984. *Monthly Statistical Bulletin* 39 (September).

Upadhyaya, Prakash. 1984. "Banks and the International Debt Crisis." Professional Report, School of Business, University of Texas at Austin (August).

Vaubel, Roland. 1983a. "The Moral Hazard of IMF Lending." *The World Economy* 6: 291–304.

Vaubel, Roland. 1983b. "The Moral Hazard of IMF Lending." In Allan H. Meltzer, ed., *International Lending and the IMF.* Washington, D.C.: The Heritage Foundation, pp. 65–79.

Vines, David. 1984. "A North-South Model Along Kaldorian Lines." Discussion Paper 26. London: Center for Economic Policy Research.

Volcker, Paul A. 1983. "How Serious is U.S. Bank Exposure?" *Challenge* (May/June).

Volcker, Paul A. 1984. Statement before House Committee on Foreign Affairs, August 8, 1984. *Federal Reserve Bulletin* (August).

Wallich, Henry C. 1978. "How Much Private Bank Lending is Enough?" In Stephen Goodman, ed., *Financing and Risk in Developing Countries.* New York: Praeger.

Wallich, Henry C. 1984. *Insurance of Bank Lending to Developing Countries.* New York: Group of Thirty.

Waltz, Kenneth. 1965. *Man, the State, and War.* New York: Columbia Univ. Press.

"Western Bankers Agree to Delay Payments on $3 Billion of Poland's Commercial Debt." *Wall Street Journal* (October 2): 31.

Williamson, John. 1983. *The Open Economy and the World Economy.* New York: Basic Books.

Witcher, S. Karene. 1984a. "As Latin Debtor Nations Prepare to Meet, Political Unrest Becomes a Cancer." *Wall Street Journal* (June 19): 33.

Witcher, S. Karene. 1984b. "Developing Issue: Loans to the Third World to be More Politicized by Mexican Debt Pact." *Wall Street Journal* (October 10): 17.

Witteveem, H. Johannes. 1983. "Developing a New International Monetary System: A Long-term View." Lecture before the Per Jacobsson Foundation, Washington, D.C.

World Bank. 1984. *World Debt Tables 1983–84.* Washington, D.C.: World Bank.

Wriston, Walter B. 1984. "Global Recovery and World Debt." Address at the International Monetary Conference, June 4.

Wynne, William H. 1951. *State Insolvency and Foreign Bondholders,* vol. 2: *Case Histories.* New Haven, Conn.: Yale Univ. Press.

Young, Leslie, and Stephen P. Magee. 1984. "A Prisoners' Dilemma Theory of Endogenous Tariffs in General Equilibrium." Presented at the American Economic Association Meetings, December 1982 and at the Conference on the Political Economy of Public Policy, Stanford University, March.

Zajac, E. 1978. *Fairness or Efficiency: An Introduction To Public Utility Pricing.* Cambridge, Mass.: Ballinger.

INDEX

279

ABOUT THE CONTRIBUTORS

William A. Brock is currently the F.P. Ramsey Professor of Economics at the University of Wisconsin. He is a general economic theorist and has published over fifty articles and several books, and has given over 100 invited lectures around the world. He was a Sherman Fairchild Distinguished Scholar at California Institute of Technology in 1978 and was elected a Rumms Faculty Fellow at the University of Wisconsin at Madison in 1981.

William J. Darity, Jr. is Associate Professor of Economics at the University of North Carolina at Chapel Hill, and recently was a Visiting Scholar, Board of Governors of the Federal Reserve (1984 summer). Since receiving his Ph.D. from M.I.T. in 1978, Professor Darity has constructed a prodigious publication record. Among his more recent publications are "On the Long-Run Outcome of the Lewis-Nurske International Growth Process," *Journal of Development Economics*, 10 (1982): 271-8.

Barend A. de Vries is a Guest Scholar at the Brookings Institution. Until 1984 he worked in the World Bank as a Senior Advisor and Chief Economist. Earlier in his career he was an economist with the International Monetary Fund. He has a Ph.D. in Economics from M.I.T.

Margaret Garritsen de Vries has been Historian of the International Monetary Fund since May 1973. She was one of the Fund's first staff members, joining in 1946, and subsequently held various positions. She holds an A.B. in economics from the University of Michigan and a Ph.D. in economics from M.I.T.

Kristin Hallberg, Assistant Professor of Economics at Colby College, completed her University of Wisconsin Ph.D. in 1982. Her research combines her interests in international trade and finance and economic development. Among her publications is "Debt and Development in Latin America: The Role of Foreign Direct Investment," in *Conditions for Economic Growth in Latin America.*

Robert A. Jones is Chairman of the Board of The Institute of Economic and Monetary Affairs. After a distinguished career with the Bank of America, where he came to be known as Mr. Fed, Mr. Jones started his own Fed-watching and market forecasting firm, Money Market Services. That firm grew into its present multinational configuration under Mr. Jones' leadership.

Stephen P. Magee is the Fred H. Moore Professor, Department of Finance, at the University of Texas. He has authored many books and articles, including *International Trade Distortions in Factor Markets* (Marcel-Dekker, 1976), and *International Trade* (Addison Wesley, 1980). Professor Magee's recent work has been devoted to exploring the interface between international trade theory and public choice theory.

Richard P. Mattione is Associate Economist, International Economics Department, Morgan Guaranty Trust. He was most recently a Research Associate at the Brookings Institution Foreign Policy Studies program. While at Brookings, Dr. Mattione and Thomas O. Enders coauthored *Latin America: The Crisis of Debt and Growth*, the first in the Brookings Studies in International Economics series (1984), and with Richard S. Dale, he wrote *Managing Global Debt* (Brookings, 1983).

Robert N. McCauley is Chief of the Developing Economies Division at the Federal Reserve Bank in New York. He joined the International Financial Markets Division there and specialized in the Euro-Securities Markets after graduate study in Economics at Harvard University. He published a study, "A Compendium of IMF Troubles," in *Developing Country Debt* in 1979.

Frank E. Morris has been President of the Federal Reserve Bank of Boston since 1968. Under his leadership, the Boston Federal Reserve Bank has developed into a significant source of important research in the areas of monetary economic theory and policy. Dr. Morris is also Chairman of the Boston Private Industry Council and Chairman of the Advisory Committee, Tri-Lateral Council for Quality Education, Inc.

Leonard J. Santow is Managing Director of Griggs and Santow Incorporated which provides consulting and Telerate services to a select group of foreign and domestic clients. He is the co-author of the *Griggs & Santow Report*, a weekly letter analyzing developments in the money and capital markets. Prior to establishing his firm in 1982 with his colleague, William N. Griggs, Dr. Santow who took his Ph.D. at the University of Illinois, was the Financial Economist for the Federal Reserve Bank of Dallas, and was associated with both Aubrey G. Lanston & Co., Inc. and Lehman Brothers.

Larry A. Sjaastad is Professor of Economics, University of Chicago; Professor, Graduate Institute of International Studies (Geneva); and Consultant to the Central Bank of Uruguay. Professor Sjaastad has published widely, including "International Debt Quagmire—To Whom Do We Owe It?" *The World Economy* 6 (1983): 305-324, and "Exchange Rate Regimes and the Real Rate of Interest," in Michael Connolly and John McDermott, editors, *Economics of the Caribbean Basin* (Praeger, 1985).

Lance Taylor is Professor of Nutrition and Economics at the Massachusetts Institute of Technology, whose research has been devoted to theoretical examination of macroeconomic and food policy problems in developing nations. Professor Taylor has published numerous journal articles and books. Of particular note are his *Structuralist Macroeconomics: Applicable Models for the Third World* (Basic Books, 1983), and "Rising Economic Surplus, the Falling Rate of Profit and the Dynamic Equivalent," *Social and Economic Studies*, 31, no. 2 (June): 53-151.

Philip A. Wellons is Associate Professor at Harvard Graduate School of Business Administration. He is a consultant to the Organization for Economic Cooperation and Development and for the World Bank/International Finance Corporation. He has written about various aspects of doing business in developing countries, including "International Banking," *Handbook of Modern Finance* (Warren, Gorham & Lamont, 1984), *World Money and Credit: The Crisis and Its Causes* (The Harvard Business School, 1983), and *Transnational Banks: Operations, Strategies, and Their Effects in Developing Countries* (United Nations Centre on Transnational Corporations, 1981).

ABOUT THE EDITOR

Michael P. Claudon is Professor of Economics and Chairman of the Economics Department at Middlebury College. Since joining the Middlebury staff in 1970, he has devoted himself to building a productive, highly visible economics department at the College, and has been a driving force behind the development of the annual Middlebury Conference on Economic Issues, from which this volume eminates. Among his publications are *International Trade and Technology: Models of Dynamic Comparative Advantage* (U.P.A., 1978); *An Incomes Policy for the United States: New Approaches*, coedited with Richard Cornwall (Martinus Nijhoff Publishing, 1980); and *Eco Talk*, coauthored with Stuart Bogom (Academic Press, 1985), an interactive education software system.